SHORTLIST

Berlin

WHAT'S NEW | WHAT'S ON | WHAT'S BEST

www.timeout.com/berlin

Contents

Published by Time Out Guides Ltd
Universal House
251 Tottenham Court Road
London W1T 7AB
Tel: + 44 (0)20 7813 3000
Fax: + 44 (0)20 7813 6001
Email: guides@timeout.com
www.timeout.com

Managing Director Peter Fiennes
Editorial Director Ruth Jarvis
Deputy Series Editor Dominic Earle
Financial Director Gareth Garner
Editorial Manager Holly Pick
Accountant Kemi Olufuwa

Time Out Guides is a wholly owned subsidiary of Time Out Group Ltd.

© Time Out Group Ltd
Chairman Tony Elliott
Financial Director Richard Waterlow
Time Out Magazine Ltd MD David Pepper
Group General Manager/Director Nichola Coulthard
Managing Director, Time Out International Cathy Runciman
Time Out Communications Ltd MD David Pepper
Group Marketing Director John Luck
Group Art Director John Oakey
Group IT Director Simon Chappell

Time Out and the Time Out logo are trademarks of Time Out Group Ltd.

This edition first published in Great Britain in 2007 by Ebury Publishing

Ebury Publishing is a division of The Random House Group Ltd
Company information can be found on www.randomhouse.co.uk
10 9 8 7 6 5 4 3 2 1

Distributed in USA by Publishers Group West (www.pgw.com)
Distributed in Canada by Publishers Group Canada (www.pgcbooks.ca)
For further distribution details, see www.timeout.com

ISBN 10: 1-84670-037-X
ISBN 13: 978184670-0378

A CIP catalogue record for this book is available from the British Library

Colour reprographics by Wyndeham Icon, 3 & 4 Maverton Road, London E3 2JE

Printed and bound by Firmengruppe APPL, aprinta druck, Wemding, Germany

Papers used by Ebury Publishing are natural, recyclable products made from wood
grown in sustainable forests

Berlin Shortlist

The **Time Out Berlin Shortlist** is one of a new series of guides that draws on Time Out's background as a magazine publisher to keep you current with everything that's going on in town. As well as Berlin's classic sights and the best of its eating, drinking and entertainment, the guide picks out the most exciting venues to have recently opened, and gives a full calendar of annual events. It also includes features on the important news, trends and openings, all compiled by locally based editors and writers. Whether you're visiting for the first time in your life, or you're a frequent repeat visitor, you'll find the *Time Out Berlin Shortlist* guide contains everything you need to know, in a portable and easy-to-use format.

The guide divides central Berlin into seven areas, each of which contains listings for Sights & museums, Eating & drinking, Shopping, Nightlife and Arts & leisure, along with maps pinpointing all their locations. At the front of the book are chapters rounding up each of these scenes city-wide, and giving a Shortlist of our overall picks in a variety of categories. We also include itineraries for days out, as well as essentials including transport information and hotels.

Our listings use phone numbers as dialled from within Germany. From abroad, use your country's exit code followed by 49 (the country code for Germany) and the number given. We have noted price categories by using one to four euro signs (€-€€€€), representing budget, moderate, expensive and luxury. Major credit cards are accepted unless otherwise stated. We also indicate when a venue is NEW .

All our listings are double-checked but businesses do sometimes close or change their hours or prices, so it's a good idea to call a venue before visiting. While every effort has been made to ensure accuracy, the publishers cannot accept responsibility for any errors that this guide may contain.

Venues are marked on the maps using symbols numbered according to their order within the chapter and colour-coded according to the type of venue they represent:

- ❶ Sights & museums
- ❶ Eating & drinking
- ❶ Shopping
- ❶ Nightlife
- ❶ Arts & leisure

SHORTLIST
Online

The *Time Out Berlin Shortlist* is as up to date as it is possible for a printed guidebook to be. And to keep it completely current, it has a regularly updated online companion, at **www.timeout.com/berlin**. Here you'll find news of the latest openings and exhibitions, as well as picks from visitors and residents – ideal for planning a trip. Time Out is the city specialist, so you'll also find travel information for more than 100 cities worldwide on our site, at www.timeout.com/travel.

Time Out Berlin Shortlist

EDITORIAL
Editor Dave Rimmer
Deputy Editor Anna Norman
Copy Editing Cathy Limb
Researcher Mark Reeder
Proofreader Deborah Nash

STUDIO
Art Director Scott Moore
Art Editor Pinelope Kourmouzoglou
Senior Designer Josephine Spencer
Graphic Designer Henry Elphick
Digital Imaging Simon Foster
Ad Make-up Jenni Prichard
Picture Editor Jael Marschner
Deputy Picture Editor Tracey Kerrigan
Picture Researcher Helen McFarland

ADVERTISING
Sales Director/Sponsorship
  Mark Phillips
International Sales Manager
  Fred Durman
International Sales Executive
  Simon Davies
International Sales Consultant
  Ross Canadé
Advertising Sales (Berlin) In Your Pocket
Advertising Assistant Kate Staddon

MARKETING
Marketing Manager Yvonne Poon
Marketing & Publicity Manager, US
  Rosella Albanese
Marketing Designer Anthony Huggins

PRODUCTION
Production Manager Brendan McKeown
Production Co-ordinator Caroline Bradford

CONTRIBUTORS
All new content for this guide was researched and written by Dave Rimmer and
Nickolas Woods. Thanks also to the writers of *Time Out Berlin*.

PHOTOGRAPHY
All photography by Britta Jaschinski, except: pages 2 (bottom left), 3 (top right), 21, 87,
92, 101, 114, 129, 144 Elan Fleisher; page 31 Michèle Anne De Mey Charleroi, Sinfonia
Eroica, © Hermann Sorgeloos; page 32 Florian Bolk; page 37 Daniela Incoronato;
page 62 S Greuner & T Seidel; pages 106, 111, 115, 125, 136 Hadley Kincade.

The following images were provided by the featured establishments/artists: pages 2
(top left), 3 (bottom right), 11, 16, 17, 20, 25, 33, 34, 65, 162, 166, 173.
Cover photograph: The Reichstag. Credit: f1 online/Alamy.

MAPS
JS Graphics (john@jsgraphics.co.uk).

Thanks to Angelina Richter, Orhan Orhanovitch, Udo Victor.

About Time Out

Founded in 1968, Time Out has expanded from humble London beginnings into the
leading resource for those wanting to know what's happening in the world's greatest
cities. As well as our influential what's-on weeklies in London, New York and Chicago,
we publish more than a dozen other listings magazines in cities as varied as Beijing,
Beirut and Mumbai. The magazines established Time Out's trademark style: sharp
writing, informed reviewing and bang up-to-date inside knowledge of every scene.

Time Out made the natural leap into travel guides in the 1980s with the City Guide
series, which now extends to over 50 destinations around the world. Written and
researched by expert local writers and generously illustrated with original photography,
the full-size guides cover a larger area than our Shortlist guides and include many
more venue reviews, along with additional background features and a full set of maps.

Throughout this rapid growth, the company has remained proudly independent, still
owned by Tony Elliott nearly four decades after he started Time Out London as a
single fold-out sheet of A5 paper. This independence extends to the editorial content
of all our publications, this Shortlist included. No establishment has been featured
because it has advertised, and no payment has influenced any of our reviews. And,
for our critics, there's definitely no such thing as a free lunch: all restaurants and
bars are visited and reviewed anonymously, and Time Out always picks up the bill.
For more about the company, see www.timeout.com.

Don't Miss

Potsdamer Platz

Sights & Museums

No European city in recent times has changed as much as Berlin. In the process of transforming itself from divided geopolitical anomaly into modern mainstream capital, Berlin has undergone a major infrastructural overhaul at every level. Old landmarks have been renovated, new ones acquired and others wiped out altogether – including what was once the most famous Berlin landmark of them all, the Wall.

The Brandenburg Gate is Berlin's signature sight, its Tower Bridge or Eiffel Tower. To its north and south, various new central landmarks catch the eye: the postmodern towers of Potsdamer Platz; the Legoland of tilting concrete blocks that is the Denkmal für die ermordeten Jüden Europas (Memorial to the Murdered Jews of Europe); the new Bundeskanzleramt (Federal Chancellery) and government quarter. There's also Norman Foster's revamped Reichstag, complete with visitable glass cupola. A walk to the top is a must.

These new landmarks all lie along the line of the former Wall and, in one way or another, are intended to heal that wound of history and stitch the city back together. On what is now merely the border of Mitte and Tiergarten (the city's central park stretches away on the western side), the Brandenburg Gate was once the ceremonial entrance to Berlin as capital of Prussia. Unter den

Linden, the grand avenue leading east, is dotted with the major baroque and neo-classical landmarks of the Imperial era, and winds up at Museumsinsel, where the city was born. This is the biggest agglomeration of more traditional landmarks, such as the Pergamonmuseum (p56), the Altes Museum (p53), the Staatsoper (p60) and the Berliner Dom (p53). There are also more cathedrals and concert halls to the south, around the Gendarmenmarkt.

The slow demolition of the Palast der Republik on Museumsinsel, once home to the East German parliament, is a reminder that, although the big unifying projects are now mostly finished, there is still plenty of tidying up to do. Just east of Potsdamer Platz, the octagon of Leipziger Platz is still being filled in. And over on the far side of Museumsinsel, some huge new building projects are just beginning around Alexanderplatz.

Elsewhere around the city, other post-Wall additions to the landscape include the Jüdisches Museum (p138) in Kreuzberg, housed in a remarkable building by Daniel Libeskind; a whole slew of new embassies, mostly clustered south of the Tiergarten; the renovated Olympia-Stadion (p153) in the west of Charlottenburg, scene of Zidane's head-butt; and the huge new Berlin Hauptbahnhof (see box p101), Europe's biggest railway station.

Neighbourhoods

Our book is organised according to area. Mitte is the city's historic centre. In the days of division it lay on the eastern side, but today it is once again the centre in every respect – historically, culturally, politically, commercially. Its southern reaches are full of big

DON'T MISS

S H O R T L I S T

Best new
- Berlin Hauptbahnhof (p101)
- Denkmal für die ermordeten Jüden Europas (p56)
- Museum für Fotografie (p12)

Best revamped
- Deutsches Historisches Museum (p56)
- Olympia-Stadion (p153)
- Reichstag (p99)

Best modern museums
- Filmmuseum Berlin (p95)
- Jüdisches Museum (p138)

Best old-school
- Altes Museum (p53)
- Ethnologisches Museum (p152)
- Pergamonmuseum (p56)

Best World War II
- Gedänkstätte Haus der Wannsee-Konferenz (p153)
- Museum Berlin-Karlshorst (p153)

Best Cold War
- Alliierten Museum (p151)
- Forschungs- & Gedänkstätte Normannenstrasse (Stasi museum) (p152)
- Gedänkstätte Berliner Mauer (p152)

Best for kids
- Gruselkabinett (p138)
- Haus am Checkpoint Charlie (p138)
- Zoologischer Garten (p99)

Best art
- Bauhaus Archiv (p94)
- Brücke Museum (p151)
- Gemäldegalerie (p95)
- Hamburger Bahnhof (p64)
- Neue Nationalgalerie (p99)

Best views
- Fernsehturm (p79)
- Funkturm (p152)
- Siegessäule (p99)

sights and grand avenues, major hotels and new department stores. Things get more bohemian at the borough's northern end, particularly around the Scheunenviertel, Berlin's historic Jewish quarter, whose narrow streets are dotted with cafés and restaurants, venues and galleries. In recent years, nightlife has been migrating even further north, and today the area around Zionskirchplatz and the Mitte end of Kastanienallee is probably the city's most happening neighbourhood.

Kastanienallee leads north into Prenzlauer Berg, east Berlin's most picturesque residential area and Mitte's fashionable adjunct in terms of nightlife and gastronomy. The streets around Kollwitzplatz are inviting for a stroll; there is lots of activity in the 'LSD' neighbourhood around Lychener Strasse, Stargarder Strasse and Dunckerstrasse, and east Berlin's gay district is around the northern reaches of Schönhauser Allee. Moving clockwise, we next come to Friedrichshain, the most 'eastern' in feel of the inner-city districts. Its spine is the broad, Stalin-era Karl-Marx-Allee. The lively area around Simon-Dach-Strasse is the neighbourhood of choice for bohos and young radicals, and nightlife clusters around the formerly industrial area on the bank of the river Spree.

South over the river, we cross the former border into western Berlin and come to Kreuzberg, once the city's main alternative nexus and the capital of Turkish Berlin. Today life is returning to the eastern area around Schlesisches Tor, while it never left the bustling western focal point of Bergmannstrasse. The borough's northern area, where it borders Mitte, contains some important museums, such as the Deutsches Technikmuseum (p137) and the Jüdisches Museum (p138) as well as the Cold War landmark Checkpoint Charlie. West of Kreuzberg lies Schöneberg, a residential district centred around Winterfeldtplatz, with its popular twice-weekly market, and the historic gay district that stretches along and around Motzstrasse and Fuggerstrasse. Wittenbergplatz, at its north-western corner, marks the start of the west end.

Museum für Fotografie p12

North of Schöneberg, Tiergarten is centred around the huge wooded park of the same name. The district contains the diplomatic quarter, as well as the new entertainment and commercial district of Potsdamer Platz, and the neighbouring Kulturforum that is home to institutions such as the Neue Nationalgalerie (p99) and the Philharmonie (p104). Finally, there is the well-heeled district of Charlottenburg, Berlin's west end, whose main arteries are the Kurfürstendamm, an upmarket commercial avenue, and the parallel Kantstrasse. Most of the formal sights, such as the new Museum für Fotografie (p105), and west Berlin's signature landmark, the Kaiser-Wilhelm-Gedächtniskirche (p105), are in the borough's eastern end.

Don't mention the Wall

'Is there anything left of the Wall?' That's the first question asked by many visitors. The answer is: not much. A short section has been preserved on the border between Mitte and Wedding at the Gedänkstätte Berliner Mauer (p152). It's in unnaturally pristine condition (any graffiti is removed from it straight away), but is the only place where you are able to see what the various layers of defences looked like. A section of the inner Wall (the side that faced East Berlin) stands on the Friedrichshain bank of the Spree along Mühlenstrasse. Now known as the East Side Gallery, it was covered with paintings by inter-national artists in the early 1990s. And on Niederkirchnerstrasse, along the border between Kreuzberg and Mitte, there is a stretch of the Wall that has been preserved with graffiti and pockmarks inflicted by the

hammers and chisels of souvenir-chipping in the winter of 1989-90.

The area directly south of Niederkirchnerstrasse is known as the Topographie des Terrors (p138), once the site of the Gestapo headquarters. It's just one of many landmarks relating to that other dark chapter in Berlin's history, the Nazi era. Little is left extant from that time, though the tragedy of the Holocaust is memorialised all over the city in a variety of ways. The Olympia-Stadion is the biggest single structure of that period still standing.

Making the most of it

If you're planning to visit a lot of museums during your visit, then you may want to invest in a discount card. Many museums and galleries are administered by the Staatliche Museen zu Berlin (SMPK), including the Altes Museum, the Pergamonmuseum, the Gemäldegalerie (p95) and the Ethnologisches Museum (p152). SMPK offers a three-day card (€15; €7.50 reductions), which is available from any of its museums. It doesn't cover temporary exhibitions, however. Most museums are closed on Mondays but open until 10pm on Thursdays, when they are free after 6pm. For more information, visit www.smb.spk-berlin.de.

Another deal is the WelcomeCard (two days, €16; three days €22; valid for one adult and up to three children under 14), which combines free travel on public transport with reduced or free tours, boat trips and entry to museums, theatres and other attractions in both Berlin and nearby Potsdam. WelcomeCards are available from Berliner Tourismus Marketing (p186), from S-Bahn offices and from many of the city's hotels.

Monsieur Vuong p15

Eating & Drinking

Berlin has never been a great gastronomic capital, and that doesn't look likely to change any time in the near future. But to say it doesn't rank up there with Paris, Rome or New York isn't to imply that you can't dine decently here, or that things aren't steadily improving. Meanwhile, some cities would kill to have a café-life as good as Berlin's and its reputation as an excellent place for drinking is well deserved. The cafés serve breakfast all day, the bars stay open deep into the night, and the restaurants tend to be relaxed, roomy and delightfully cheap compared to other western European capitals.

Surrounded by poor agricultural land, not much use for growing anything except cabbages and potatoes, Berlin's traditional dishes have always been of the stodgy meat-and-two-veg variety. *Eisbein* is the signature local dish, a leathery-skinned and extremely fatty pig's trotter, sometimes marinated and usually served with puréed peas. You won't find it on the menu, however, in anything but the most doggedly old-school establishments. Other regional cuisines from Germanic Europe are preferable and probably better represented, such as Swabian (Schwarzwaldstuben, p71), Austrian (Austria, p135),

Swiss (Nola am Weinberg, p70) or Alsatian (Storch, p119; Gugelhof, p83).

The brevity of Germany's colonial experience has also meant no deep-rooted link with a foreign cuisine, like Britain's with India's, or Morocco's with France. Turkish food, however, which arrived with post-war 'guest workers', is now deeply embedded on the western side of town and Kreuzberg can claim to be the place where the doner kebab was invented in the early 1970s (Hasir, p125; see box p132). Berlin's other post-war culinary innovation is also a snack at street-level: the Currywurst, a pork sausage sliced and drenched in warm ketchup and curry powder. You can try the traditional version under the arches at Prenzlauer Berg's venerable Konnopke's (p84), or the upmarket organic version at west Berlin's Witty's.

Reunification has meant a more well-travelled population, and lots of cheap real estate where young restaurateurs could try out their ideas. With the arrival of the government to stimulate things at the high end, and an increasingly cosmopolitan population to encourage ethnic variety at street level, things are getting better and better. Michelin might only have awarded Berlin a total of nine stars in 2006, but at least that was two up on the year before.

Apart from reinvented German cuisine – the so-called *Neue Deutsche Küche* that is slowly giving ground to an eclecticism that would more properly be termed 'modern European' – Italian has long been well represented (Sale e Tabbachi, p140; Trattoria Paparazzi, p87) and good quality Japanese food is now common (Kuchi, p70) along with other East Asian cuisines (Pan Asia, p70; Mao Thai, p84; Edd's, p100; Monsieur Vuong p70).

SHORTLIST

Best new
- Schneeweiss (p145)
- Shiro i Shiro (p71)
- Solar (p140)
- Spindler & Klatt (p128)

See and be seen
- Borchardt (p60)
- Pan Asia (p70)
- Paris Bar (p109)

Classic cocktails
- Galerie Bremer (p108)
- Victoria Bar (p103)
- Würgeengel (p130)

Traditional dishes
- Grossbeerenkeller (p140)
- Honigmond (p69)
- Marjellchen (p109)

Modern German
- Gugelhof (p83)
- Restaurant 44 (p109)
- Storch (p119)

Vegetarian
- Abendmahl (p124)
- Kapelle (p70)

Beergardens
- Café am Neuen See (p99)
- Prater (p85)

Sausages
- Konnopke's Imbiss (p84)
- Witty's (p119)

Breakfasts
- Hazelwood (p69)
- Schönbrunn (p85)
- Tim's Canadian Deli (p119)

Haute cuisine
- Hugo's (p102)
- Margaux (p56)
- Vau (p63)

Kaffee und Kuchen
- Anna Blume (p82)
- Café Einstein (p100)

DON'T MISS

East-West fusion ideas are the latest thing to take hold, exemplifed by the Japanese-Italian menu at Shiro i Shiro (p71), the Japanese-North German fusion at Oki (p84) or the eccentric combinations at Der Imbiss W (p139). Another new gastronomic fashion is the club-restaurant, where dinner is often accompanied by live entertainment, sometimes eaten reclining on loungers rather than sitting up at tables, and is followed by a general clearing of furniture as the dining area transforms into a dancefloor. Spindler & Klatt (p125) is the best of these places, but now Bangaluu (p64) is challenging it with an even more decadent dining experience. The morning after, weekend buffet brunches are an increasingly common new feature, offered at many cafés and restaurants around the city, including Senti (p128), Café Morgenrot (p82), Hazelwood (p69) and Tee Tea Thé (p119). See box p129.

Boundaries are blurred right across the whole spectrum of eating and drinking. Restaurants often have bars, which you're welcome to use even if you've no intention of eating; and bars, in their turn, frequently serve food. Cafés by day are popular for a long breakfast, light lunch or afternoon *Kaffee und Kuchen* (coffee and cake) and then often turn into bars by night. Berliners do like a drink. The capital's changing demographics mean that cocktail bars are on the increase, but there are also still plenty of characterful dives and unpretentious watering-holes. This being Germany, beer is the main tipple, though local brews are poor in comparison to the best of Bavaria or Bohemia.

Tipping & etiquette

In restaurants, a service charge of 17 per cent is added to the bill, but, unless the service has been awful (not unheard of in Berlin), diners usually round up the total. Tips are handed directly to the server (or you tell staff how much to take) rather than left on the table. When you hand over the cash, don't say 'danke' unless you want them to keep the change.

In bars, people tend to pay their own way and drink at their own pace – partly because in many places bills are only totted up as you leave – but ceremonial rounds of tequila, vodka or Jägermeister are a feature of the Berlin night. Even though the general tendency is for bars to close earlier than they used to, hardly anywhere closes before 1am and most places stay open much later – many as long as there's still anyone in there.

Solar p15

Boss Orange Store p19

Shopping

Berlin has never had one single downtown or retail focus, and these days things are more mixed up than ever. While both the Kurfürstendamm in the west end and Friedrichstrasse in the east boast the kind of grand stores and big names characteristic of any major city, what unified Berlin has hitherto done best is to offer both space and independence to small, idiosyncratic businesses. Scattered around the city, in courtyards or otherwise barren streets, from the punky bohemia of Friedrichshain to the elegant pavements of Charlottenburg, you'll find small fashion labels and individual design operations, second-hand shops as well as doggedly eccentric specialists.

Since Berlin first sketched out its post-Wall infrastructure, the major outlines of the shopping landscape have been clear. The west end has remained the upmarket showpiece it always was. Major department stores and the flagship outlets of international brands march west from KaDeWe (p120) on Wittenbergplatz and along the Kurfürstendamm. More discreet boutiques, interior design shops and tasteful bookshops are scattered around the streets between the Ku'damm and Kantstrasse, in the area around Savignyplatz.

In the 1990s, newer department stores and more international brands sprouted in the east along Friedrichstrasse, including interesting retail concepts such as

the all-in-one cultural spot that is Dussmann das Kulturkaufhaus (p65) and the high-end designer outlet Quartier 206 (p63) as well as an elegant branch of the French department store chain Galeries Lafayette (p63). Meanwhile, in between east and west there's also the big Arkaden mall at Potsdamer Platz. And over on the other side of Mitte, south of Alexanderplatz, construction has started on an even bigger new mall.

The final big piece of the puzzle is also in Mitte: the complex of restored Jugendstil courtyards called the Hackesche Höfe. Berlin's attractive but modest answer to Covent Garden or Les Halles is the centerpiece of the Scheunenviertel, home to local designers, specialty stores and cafés, galleries and cabarets. The area fanning out from here, especially on and around the axis of Neue and Alte Schönhauser Strasse, has established itself as home to the adventurous and the eccentric, including local designers and labels such as Lisa D (p75), RespectMen (p75) and Claudia Skoda (p72) as well as everything from retro-futurist furniture shops to stores selling Third World household gizmos.

But as we say, things are getting mixed up. The Scheunenviertel's reputation for style and daring has begun to draw the likes of Hugo Boss (p72), Carhartt and Adidas to the area. Rising rents are also helping to chase small Berlin designers out of Mitte, as part of a perceptible drift both back towards the west, and eastwards into Friedrichshain. Berlin-based Japanese designer Yoshiharu Ito (p113), for example, one of a slew who made their names in Mitte in the 1990s, has moved west to Charlottenburg, where the streets around Savignyplatz and Bleibtreustrasse are beginning to

SHORTLIST

Best newcomers
- AM1 Am2 (p72)
- Boss Orange (p72)
- F95 (p148)
- Konk (p75)

Berlin designers
- Claudia Skoda (p72)
- Lisa D (p75)
- Respectmen (p75)
- Yoshiharu Ito (p113)

Department stores
- Dussmann das Kulturkaufhaus (p65)
- Galeries Lafayette (p63)
- KaDeWe (p120)

Markets
- Flohmarkt am Mauerpark (p88)
- Strasse des 17. Juni Fleamarket (p103)
- Trödelmarkt Boxhagener Platz (p148)
- Winterfeldt Markt (p120)

Hot chocolate
- Fassbender & Rausch (p63)
- Leysieffer (p113)

Best bookshops
- Bücherbogen (p110)
- Marga Schoeller Bücherstube (p113)
- ProQM (p75)
- Saint Georges (p88)

Discerning sounds
- DaCapo Records (p87)
- Gelbe Musik (p110)
- Hardwax (p130)
- Mr Dead & Mrs Free (p120)
- Space Hall (p136)

Notable eccentrics
- Another Country (p135)
- Mane Lange Korsetts (p88)
- Neurotitan (p75)
- RSVP (p75)
- Knopf Paul (p136)
- Absinthe Depot Berlin (p72)

reassert themselves as a centre of style. Meanwhile, the opening of F95 on Frankfurter Allee (p148) is a sign that Friedrichshain these days is about more than just second-hand shops and streetware.

Streetware shops and urban brands are scattered all over town, such as Big Brobot (p148) in Friedrichshain, Cherrybomb (p130) or IrieDaily (p130) in Kreuzberg, Skunkfunk (p88) on Kastanienallee. Even the west end can boast a skatewear store full of unique pieces, designed in-house, such as FourAsses Clothing (p110).

Other areas have more specialised characters. Since the late 1990s opening of the interior design mall stilwerk (p113), Kantstrasse has established itself as a clustering point for high-end household items. In Charlottenburg, Knesebeckstrasse, either side of Savignyplatz, is good for bookshops, both new and antiquarian. The bustling Bergmannstrasse hood in Kreuzberg has everything from second-hand shops to small designer outlets, music stores and bookshops. In retail, as in nightlife, Kastanienallee is a thoroughfare of the quirky and alternative, connecting the Mitte scene to that of Prenzlauer Berg. Elsewhere in the latter district, a more staid kind of stylishness prevails on and around Rykestrasse, while Dunckerstrasse has probably now usurped Kreuzberg's Bergmann/Zossener Strasse axis in terms of the best concentration of CD shops.

There are several interesting flea markets. Sunday's Flohmarkt am Mauerpark (p88) has the biggest crowd and the widest selection of stuff, though the Strasse des 17. Juni Fleamarket (p103) in the Tiergarten is the best place for collectors. The Trödelmarkt Boxhagener Platz (p148) in Friedrichshain mixes bric-a-brac with the work of local artists and T-shirt designers.

Most districts have a lively high street to meet the needs of any given day and there are still a few beautiful old neighbourhood market halls, such as those on Ackerstrasse in Mitte or Marheinekeplatz in Kreuzberg.

Opening hours

Shops generally open around 9am or 10am. The smaller and more traditional stores tend to close around 6pm, but a relatively recent relaxation of formerly draconian laws means that many bigger shops and more adventurous smaller retailers are able to stay open until 8pm. It's also now possible to go shopping on Saturday afternoons, when once all was desolate.

Credit cards are accepted ever more widely, but you'll still find a surprisingly large number of places refusing to deal with plastic. As a general rule, the more old-school the establishment, the surlier the service. But at the younger, more independent end of things, shopping can be a very friendly experience, and English is often spoken.

F95

Spindler & Klatt p24

WHAT'S BEST
Nightlife

Berlin prides itself on its nightlife and justly so, for the most part. You can stay out all night pretty much any night of the week. Late-night bars are everywhere, there are bands and DJs in just about every space that's big enough to accommodate a bar and a stage, most clubs have relaxed door policies and low admission prices and the locals like to party. It is, in short, an insomniac's dream – and a recovering addict's nightmare.

The city's reputation for nocturnal high jinks stretches right back to the Weimar years when, apart from the cabaret scene of legend, Berlin was also the first city to have anything one might

recognise as a gay community in the modern sense. It's never been a place where people were afraid to party, and even communist East Berlin had more liberal licensing laws than London. Over on the other side of the Wall, West Berlin teemed with draft-dodging youth and nihilistic artists. Very few of these people had jobs, but most of them had money for a beer or two, along with a spirit of hedonism.

It's also long been a city where music matters. Berlin concert audiences are some of the most enthusiastic in the world, every second person you meet seems to be some kind of DJ and in any half-decent late-night bar the staff will

have been chosen as much for their taste in tunes as their prowess with a cocktail-shaker.

And as with so many aspects of city life, Berlin's all-too-vivid history has an effect still felt today. In the days of division, West Berlin was an island, remote from the musical mainstream; East Berlin was remoter still. The feeling that nothing that came out of here would ever be commercial led to an attitude of confrontational experimentation – 'if no one's going to buy it, we might as well do exactly what we want'. This attitude was epitomised by Einstürzende Neubauten, still not displaced as the city's signature band long after their heyday. Though much has changed since that lot first started making music with hammers and drills, reflecting the city's post-war experience of rebuilding itself from ruin, you just know that Berlin is never going to end up in thrall to any kind of fresh-faced pop scene.

The nightlife scene really took off after the fall of the Wall, as the West Berlin avant-garde collided with a party-starved East Berlin generation on makeshift dancefloors, in spaces left accessible by the abandonment of border defences and the collapse of East German industry. The techno scene of those no-man's land years is long gone, but clubs such as Berghain (see p148 and box p147) and a planned new version of the legendary Tresor continue to open up in post-industrial spaces. Moveable parties, accessed via flyers or word-of-mouth, similarly exploit spaces not yet brought into the commercial mainstream.

But Berlin's renovation proceeds apace, and things are changing. As rents rise, most of the old squatter bars and clubs have disappeared, and the DIY aesthetic of the 1990s

SHORTLIST

Best newcomers
- 103 Club (p66)
- Berghain/Panorama Bar (p148)
- Fritzclub im Postbahnhof (p149)
- Ruder Club-Mitte (p78)
- White Trash Fast Food (p93)

Eclectic booking
- Ausland (p88)
- Kaffee Burger (p78)
- Kinzo Club (p80)
- nbi (p91)
- Rosi's (p149)

Rock on
- Knaack (p91)
- Magnet (p91)
- Mudd Club (p78)

Coolest cabaret
- BKA Theatre (p136)
- Café Theater Schalotte (p115)
- Chamäleon (p77)
- Kleine Nachtrevue (p123)
- Scheinbar (p123)

Best jazz clubs
- A-Trane (p113)
- B-Flat (p77)

Reinvented venues
- Arena (p130)
- Café Moskau (p80)
- Columbiaclub (p137)
- Watergate (p133)

Best gay joints
- Barbie Deinhoff's (131)
- Das Haus B (p149)
- Heile Welt (p122)
- Möbel Olfe (p133)
- Roses (p133)
- Tom's Bar (p123)

Dodgy dives
- Ex 'n' Pop (p122)
- Rio (p65)
- SO36 (p133)

has begun to dissipate. Meanwhile, an influx of young professional types, who until recently would never have considered Berlin as a place to live, has encouraged the spread of a kind of bland, unchallenging stylishness. It speaks volumes that one of the only perceptible new fads is for restaurant-clubs such as Spindler & Klatt (p128) or Bangaluu (p64).

It's in increasingly upmarket Mitte that the trend towards fashion and exclusive door policies is most pronounced, but even there it's not too hard to get in anywhere. Prenzlauer Berg has more variety these days, and there's still room for places like the doggedly alternative White Trash Fast Food (p93). Friedrichshain and Kreuzberg offer a more down-to-earth approach. Schöneberg has the city's biggest gay scene. Tiergarten and Charlottenburg, though, are mostly dead after dark.

No more borders

The main characteristic of the live music scene is a continuing blurring of boundaries. Just as many clubs feature a live act along with DJs, so most performance venues will have someone at the turntables before and after a show. A place like Kaffee Burger (p78) might be a literary salon one minute, a live venue the next, and end the night as a debauched disco that keeps going until rush hour. Rock and dance have cross-pollinated, as exemplifed by club-influenced rock acts such as the Robocop Kraus, and the success of Canadian settler Peaches, who helped inspire a glut of 1980s-influenced art-school playback singers hopping about to primitive electronics. The shows of old-timers such as Boy From Brazil and Cobra Killer, or theatrically inclined imports such as Snax or Angie Reed, have also taken things

back in the direction of that old Berlin tradition, cabaret.

Cabaret itself is still alive and well, though don't go out looking for the reincarnation of Liza Minnelli. The political satire sprinkled with songs and sketches that Berliners call Kabarett is largely impenetrable to outsiders. Acrobats, magicians and dancing girls are the staple of the form called Varieté – Chamäleon (p77) in the Hackesche Höfe is the best place to check this out. Drag cabaret, known as Travestie, isn't as common as many expect it to be, but you can still find a show in the old Berlin tradition at the friendly Kleine Nachtrevue (p123). A more daring kind of cabaret thrives in smaller, more out-of-the-way places such as Scheinbar (p123) in Schöneberg or Café Theater Schalotte (p115) in Charlottenburg. Look out for star turns such as Die O-Ton Piraten (clever drag musical theatre that montages famous film dialogues into irrelevant and unlikely storylines), Gayle Tufts (a charming American entertainer who mixes pop music with stand-up in a jumble of German and English) and Bridge Markland (gender-bending dance and poetry).

But while you can find clubs catering to every musical taste – from the lively post-rockabilly scene at Roadrunners Club (p93) to country at White Trash to funk and soul at Bohannon (p77) – the main sound around is minimal techno, as it has been for years. Ricardo Villalobos and Richie Hawtin (who has relocated here from Montreal) are probably the best local exponents, while other DJs, such as Kaos and Ellen Alien, have begun pushing the sound in a more electro-tinged direction. There's also wet&hard, a sort of erotic techno infused with throbbing 1970s disco basslines, best exemplified by DJ Corvin Dalek. Look out for monthly Flesh parties at the new Ruder Club-Mitte (p78) near Hackescher Markt.

Finding the party

Though we've listed the best venues, much of what goes on here is beyond the scope of a book like this: once-a-week clubs in crumbling locations, temporary collectives throwing multi-act parties and the like. Though clubs such as Berghain, Watergate (p133) and Rio (p65) stand out, much of the scene remains constantly on the move, even more so since the police began harrassing improperly licensed venues. Many clubs don't update their websites, or only post the next week's events, and party promoters move from venue to venue.

Berlin's two fortnightly listings magazines, *tip* and *Zitty*, do a good job of covering the basics, but there's always something last-minute or underground going on. Look for flyers in shops, bars and cafés, where copies of the city's two free gay magazines, *Siegessäule* and *Sergei*, can also be picked up. You could also consult *Exberliner*, Berlin's rather overwritten English-language monthly. A couple of websites that cover the local scene in German and English are www.dorfdisco.de and www.trashaspopcanbe.de. There's also lots of information, though only in German, at www.berlinonline.de. If all else fails, simply stand on the street at three in the morning and listen out for a ruckus. There's sure to be one somewhere.

Bangaluu

Konzerthaus

Arts & Leisure

With a rich and colourful theatre landscape, a growing reputation as a centre for dance and choreography, a deeply embedded cinema culture, double the normal number of classical music offerings for a city of this size and a varied calendar of international festivals in all of these areas, Berlin is undoubtedly a major performing arts capital. It doesn't hold up too well in terms of sport, though. And a serious subsidy squeeze means that many of the arts are static, if not contracting.

The classical world

The Berliner Philharmoniker (www.berliner-philharmoniker.de), based at the Philharmonie (p104) has long been one of the world's leading orchestras, and is currently going from strength to strength under Sir Simon Rattle. Pamela Rosenberg recently arrived as new intendant from the San Francisco Opera. But the Phil is only the tip of an iceberg that features six other major orchestras, a number of smaller ensembles and no fewer than three opera houses. Ingo Metzmacher recently took over from American conductor Kent Nagano as musical director of the Deutsches Symphonie Orchester (www.dso-berlin.de), known for its avant-garde programme. Ground-breaking contemporary work is also the staple of the Rundfunk-Sinfonieorchester Berlin (www.rsb-online.de) under Marek Janowski.

The old masters are well served by the Berliner Sinfonie-Orchester (www.berliner-sinfonie-orchester.de) which plays at the Konzerthaus (p63), though chief conductor

Eliahu Inbal has just been succeeded by Lothar Zagrosek, who is likely to pull the orchestra in a more contemporary direction. Of the smaller ensembles, the Deutsches Kammerorchester Berlin (www.dko-berlin.de), under manager Stefan Fragner, has an excellent reputation for working with rising-star conductors and soloists, while the Ensemble Oriol (www.ensemble-oriol.de) is a fine group with a strong emphasis on contemporary work.

The Staatsoper Unter den Linden (p60) is the grandest of the opera houses, and leaps from one success to another under intendant Peter Mussbach and the Berliner Staatskapelle – directed by Daniel Barenboim – is Berlin's finest opera orchestra. The Komische Oper (p59) strives to carve out its own niche with controversial and topical productions, while over in Charlottenburg the Deutsche Oper (p115) currently struggles to find a distinctive artistic profile. Among the city's smaller ensembles, look out for the newly founded Novoflot (www.novoflot.de), which usually presents its innovative productions at the Sophiensaele (p79). For something a little different, look out for Yellow Lounge events (www.yellowlounge.de), which feature classical DJs, top-notch VJs and intimate live performances in a nightclub context.

There are also some top-quality music festivals throughout the year, including Zeitfenster (p32) and MaerzMusik (p32) in March, for baroque and contemporary music respectively, UltraSchall (p31) for new music, the Classic Open Air (p35) concert series in the Gendarmenmarkt each July, and MusikFest Berlin (p36) in September, which brings some of the world's finest orchestras and ensembles to Berlin.

SHORTLIST

Best newcomers
- Admiralspalast (p66)
- Dokument Kino (p80)
- F40 (p137)

Classical grandeur
- Konzerthaus (p63)
- Renaissance Theater (p115)
- Staatsoper Unter den Linden (p60)

Avant-garde energy
- HAU (p140)
- Schaubühne am Lehniner Platz (p115)
- Sophiensaele (p79)
- Volksbühne (p79)

State-of-the-art
- Arsenal (p104)
- Philharmonie (p104)
- Tempodrom (p140)

Top sport settings
- Max-Schmeling-Halle (p93)
- Olympia-Stadion (p153)

DON'T MISS

Theatre & dance

Berlin has long revelled in a reputation for cutting-edge theatre which dates back to the days of Brecht and Piscator. A solid civic establishment is complemented by a lively fringe and such a general challenging of boundaries that it's become almost impossible to draw a definite boundary between dance and theatre. The two forms cohabit under one roof at the HAU (p140) and the Sophiensaele (p79), though the dance company of choreographer Sasha Waltz no longer shares space with Thomas Ostermeier's theatre company at the Schaübuhne am Lehniner Platz (p115).

The recent integration of three Kreuzberg venues under one artistic umbrella as the HAU has proved a great success. Elsewhere, the Volksbühne (p79) flies the flag for the avant-garde (look out for

Airline flights are one of the biggest producers of the global warming gas CO_2. But with **The CarbonNeutral Company** you can make your travel a little greener.

Go to **www.carbonneutral.com** to calculate your flight emissions then 'neutralise' them through international projects which save exactly the same amount of carbon dioxide.

Contact us at **shop@carbonneutral.com** or call into the office on **0870 199 99 88** for more details.

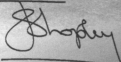

CarbonNeutral®flights

productions by Christoph Schlingensief), the Berliner Ensemble mixes modern productions of Brecht with the work of contemporary German-language writers and the Deutsches Theater is renowned for its high-class productions of the classics. English-language theatre, meanwhile, thrives at F40 (p137) in Kreuzberg. In dance, look out for site-specific productions by the now homeless Sasha Waltz and also for pieces by young choreographers Constanza Macras, Jerome Bel and Jochen Roller.

Movie scene

The Berlin International Film Festival (p32 and box p36) is one of the world's major movie events, with an International Competition featuring star-studded premières, plus a wide range of satellite events. But it's not the only film festival on the calendar. Summer's Fantasy Film Festival (p35) premières the latest in fantasy, sci-fi, splatter and horror from around the world. The same bunch are behind Verzaubert: The International Queer Film Festival (p37), which showcases gay and lesbian cinema every November and December.

Mainstream Hollywood movies are mostly dubbed into German, but the CineStar Original multiplex, housed, along with the IMAX cinema, in the Sony Center, shows films in their original language. Movies in the original English can also be found at Schöneberg's Odeon Kino (p123) and the Babylon Kreuzberg (p133). Also in the Sony Center, the two-screen Arsenal (p104) has an eclectic programme of non-mainstream cinematic fare from every corner of the globe.

Sporting events

With just one team in the German top division, Hertha BSC (p156), and no likely contenders in the lower leagues, the city that recently hosted the FIFA World Cup final has less decent football per capita than just about any comparable metropolis. It's difficult for the outsider to love Hertha, but it's not hard to get tickets for their games at the Olympia-Stadion (p153). Hertha usually qualify for the UEFA Cup, but often exit early.

By contrast, ALBA, the city's basketball team, is extremely successful and usually packs the Max-Schmeling-Halle (p93) for its games. EHC Eisbären Berlin (p156) compete creditably in the German ice-hockey league and Berlin Thunder draw huge crowds for American football games at the Olympia-Stadion. Major events on the Berlin sporting calendar are the Deutschland Pokal-Endspiel, the final of the German football cup at the Olympia-Stadion, the Qatar Ladies German Open, a clay-court tennis tournament that functions as a warm-up for the French Open and generally attracts the big names, and September's Berlin Marathon.

CineStar IMAX

timeout.com

Over 50 of the world's greatest
cities reviewed in one site.

Calendar

Tanz im August p35

The following are the pick of the annual events that take place in Berlin. Further information and exact dates can be found nearer the time in the city's two fortnightly listings magazines, *tip* and *Zitty*, or from leaflets and flyers regularly distributed to bars and restaurants around the city. Dates highlighted in **bold** are public holidays.

January

Ongoing Spielzeiteuropa (see Oct)

1 Neujahrstag (New Year's Day)

Early Jan **Tanztage**
Sophiensaele
www.tanztage.de
A two-week dance and choreography event highlighting new local talent.

Mid-late Jan **Internationale Grüne Woche**
Messegelände am Funkturm
www.gruenewoche.de
Overindulge, for ten whole days, on food and drink from Germany and around the world.

Mid Jan **UltraSchall**
Various venues
www.dradio.de/drl
Berlin's top venues host this ten-day festival of new music, which is also broadcast on the airwaves.

Late Jan **BREAD & butter**
Kabelwerke
www.breadandbutter.com
A cutting-edge fashion-industry trade fair, over three days. See also July.

Late Jan **Lange Nacht der Museen**
Citywide
www.lange-nacht-der-museen.de
For one evening in January, around 200 museums stay open late for visitors. See box p33.

February

Ongoing Spielzeiteuropa (see Oct)

Early Feb Transmediale
Akademie der Künste
www.transmediale.de
Massive three- to five-day event showcasing media art and digital culture.

Mid Feb Berlin International Film Festival
Various venues
www.berlinale.de
Major international film festival attracting A-list stars and highlighting more obscure branches of film. See box p36.

March

Mar (date varies) MaerzMusik – Festival für aktuelle Musik
Various venues
www.berlinerfestspiele.de
A festival of contemporary music from international avant-garde musicians and composers, over two to three weeks.

Mid Mar International Tourism Fair
Messegelände am Funkturm
www.itb-berlin.de
Tourism boards, travel agents and hotel chains have stalls at this five-day event.

Mar/Apr Zeitfenster – Biennale für alte Musik
Konzerthaus
www.konzerthaus.de
A one-week biennial festival of music from the 16th and 17th centuries. The next festival will take place in 2008.

April

Mar/Apr (date varies) Karfreitag (Good Friday)

Mar/Apr (date varies) Oster Montag (Easter Monday)

May

1 Tag der Arbeit (Labour Day)

May (date varies) Himmelfahrt (Ascension Day)

May (date varies) Pfingstmontag (Whit Monday/Pentecost)

May-Sept Museumsinselfestival
Museumsinsel and other venues
www.museumsinselfestival.info
Season of open-air performances, from rock and classical concerts to readings, plays and film screenings.

Early May Deutschland Pokal-Endspiel
Olympiastadion
tickets@dfb.de
Germany's domestic football cup final in the nation's showpiece arena.

Early-mid May Qatar Telecom Ladies German Open
LTTC Rot-Weiss
www.german-open.org
The world's fifth-largest international women's tennis championship.

Berlin Philharmonie at the Waldbühne p35

Long Night of the Museums

Here's a riddle. It's a cracking night out in Berlin but it has nothing to do with drinking and dancing. So what is it? It's the **Lange Nacht der Museen**, is what – the Long Night of the Museums.

Twice a year, usually a Saturday night in January and another in September, as many as 200 Berlin museums and galleries extend their opening hours until 2am to give locals and tourists a chance to go on a cut-price museum crawl. It costs just €12 a ticket (€8 reductions) for as many museum stops as you can pack in before closing time. It sounds like a bid to bring the tourists in, but the event was originally launched to give locals a chance to taste more of what the city's museums have to offer. And they appear to be lapping it up as Lange Nacht events attract tens of thousands of people and have just celebrated their first decade in business.

There are myriad collections and archives to see on the night, spanning a range of interests from plastic mould-making and sugar production to masterpieces of European art and antiquities from the ancient world. Museums are dispersed across the city, but organisers aim to simplify things by giving each Lange Nacht a theme and organising special exhibitions and itineraries within it.

The Lange Nacht normally kicks off with a 6pm speech from the mayor outside the **Rotes Rathaus** (p79), and from there, jump-on jump-off buses fan out on seven or eight circular routes, themed by interest or district. These shuttle buses, running every ten minutes, are free with a Lange Nacht ticket, as is all public transport – just as well, as the special buses are often completely packed.

And the Lange Nacht isn't just about dusty collections. Concerts, performances, screenings, lectures and discussions are all organised. Sometimes there's even food and drink. And if your legs will still carry you afterwards, the usual kind of long Berlin night will just be getting into gear when the museum doors finally close.

Loveparade

DON'T MISS

May (date varies)
Theatertreffen Berlin
Berliner Festspiele
www.berlinerfestspiele.de
Performances by winners of contemporary German-speaking theatre competition, spread over three weeks.

May/June **Karneval der Kulturen**
Kreuzberg
www.karneval-berlin.de
A colourful four-day multicultural celebration with a huge Sunday parade.

June

June **Berlin Philharmonie at the Waldbühne**
Waldbühne
www.berlin-philharmonic.com
A candle-lit open-air classical concert in an atmospheric forest theatre.

21 **Fête de la Musique**
Various venues
www.fetedelamusique.de
A regular summer solstice music event featuring a wide range of DJs and bands.

Weekend before Christopher Street Day **Schwul-Lesbisches Strassenfest**
Nollendorfplatz and around
www.regenbogenfonds.de
A gay and lesbian street fair that takes over Schöneberg every year, filling several blocks of Berlin's gay quarter.

Sat late July **Christopher Street Day Parade**
From Kurfürstendamm to the Siegessäule
www.csd-berlin.de
Berlin's big and bold gay and lesbian pride march ends up with a concert and party at the Siegessäule.

July

Ongoing Museumsinselfestival (see May)

Early July **Classic Open Air**
Gendarmenmarkt
www.classicopenair.de
This four- to seven-day big name classical music concert is held in Berlin's most exquisite square.

Mid July **Loveparade**
Strasse der 17. Juni
www.loveparade.net
The techno fest was back in business in 2006; no decision at press time for 2007. See website for information.

Mid July **BREAD & butter**
Kabelwerke
www.breadandbutter.com
The summertime sister of the January fashion fair, over three days (see Jan).

July-Aug **Deutsch-Amerikanisches Volksfest**
Truman Plaza, Hüttenweg/Clayallee
www.deutsch-amerikanisches-volksfest.de
Four weeks of fun for all the family, American style – with rodeos, popcorn, rides, hotdogs and beer.

August

Ongoing Deutsch-Amerikanisches Volksfest (see July), Museumsinselfestival (see May)

Aug (date varies)
young.euro.classic
Konzerthaus
www.young-euro-classic.de
Two weeks of concerts by youth orchestras from around Europe.

1st weekend Aug **Internationales Berliner Bierfestival**
Karl-Marx-Allee
www.bierfestival-berlin.de
Hundreds of beers from 60 countries, from stalls along Stalinist avenue.

Early Aug **Fantasy Film Festival**
CinemaxX Potsdamer Platz
www.fantasyfilmfest.com
The latest in splatter, science-fiction, fantasy, thriller and horror films.

2nd half Aug **Tanz im August**
Various venues
www.tanzimaugust.de
Germany's leading modern dance festival offers big names and new trends.

Late Aug/early Sept **Kreuzberger Festliche Tage**
Viktoriapark
www.kreuzberger-festliche-tage.de

Screen best

Berlin is gripped by the glitz and glamour of the film world for two weeks every February when the **Berlin International Film Festival** comes to town. A-list celebrities leave the warmth of winter-sun hideaways and brave the German capital's sub-zero temperatures to promote films submitted for the **Berlinale**. Making the headlines in 2006 were Sigourney Weaver, George Clooney and Meryl Streep.

At almost 60 years old, the Berlinale is one of the world's major cinema award ceremonies. The festival's various sub-sections feature more than 300 movies from five continents and even the International Competition is happy to break the mould and present its Golden and Silver Bear awards to non-Hollywood movies. Awards are handed out in all the traditional acting and filmmaking categories and there are independent prizes for specialist sectors, including a children's film section and the Teddy Award for gay and lesbian films.

The cinemas of Potsdamer Platz are the core venues of the event. Tickets – ranging from €3 to €11 – go on sale on the Monday before the start of the festival. You can buy them from the official website or from kiosks around the city, but there is a limit to how far in advance you can book. Cinemas also have tickets for the day's showings. But be prepared to spend a lot of time queuing; it's a ferociously popular event.

Two weeks of music, games, beer, food and family fun in one of Berlin's most popular parks.

September

Ongoing Kreuzberger Festliche Tage (see Aug), Museumsinselfestival (see May)

Sept (date varies) **Popkomm**
Messegelände am Funkturm
www.popkomm.de
Three-day music industry trade fair. Lots of business lunches and live acts.

Early Sept **Lange Nacht der Museen**
Citywide
www.lange-nacht-der-museen.de
Around 200 museums stay open for visitors until late. See box p33.

Early Sept **Musikfest Berlin**
Philharmonie
www.berlinerfestspiele.de
This classical music festival, with the Berlin Philharmonic and Sir Simon Rattle topping the bill in 2007, now runs for two weeks.

Mid Sept **International Literature Festival**
Haus der Berliner Festspiele and other venues
www.literaturfestival.com
Big names and new authors in a major literary feast of readings, symposia and discussions over two weeks.

Late Sept/early Oct **Art Forum Berlin Messegelände am Funkturm**
www.art-forum-berlin.de
Five-day contemporary art trade fair bringing together gallerists and artists.

Last Sun **Berlin Marathon**
Citywide
www.berlin-marathon.com
Berlin's marathon route takes runners past most of the city's major sights.

October

Ongoing Art Forum (see Sept)

Oct-Feb **Spielzeiteuropa**
Haus der Berliner Festspiele
www.berlinerfestspiele.de

Five months of new theatre and dance from across Europe.

3 Tag der Deutschen Einheit (Day of German Unity)

Mid Oct Venus Berlin
Messegelände am Funkturm
www.venus-berlin.com
Trade fair and awards ceremony for the adult entertainment industry.

Late Oct/early Nov JazzFest Berlin
Various venues
www.berlinerfestspiele.de
A wide-ranging four-day jazz event with internationally renowned artists.

November

Ongoing Spielzeiteuropa (see Oct)

1 All Saints' Day

Nov-Dec Christmas markets
Various locations
www.weihnachtsmarkt-deutschland.de
Gallons of mulled wine and stalls selling toys and gifts spill a festive mood.

Mid Nov Berliner Märchentage
Various locations
www.berlinermaerchentage.de
A three-week fairytale festival, with story-telling and musical events.

Late Nov Buss- und Bettag (Day of Repentance and Prayer)

Late Nov-mid Dec Verzaubert: International Queer Film Festival
Kino International, Karl-Marx-Allee
www.verzaubertfilmfest.com
The latest gay and lesbian films from around the world.

December

Ongoing Christmas markets (see Nov), Spielzeiteuropa (see Oct), Verzaubert: International Queer Film Festival (see Nov)

24 Heiliger Abend (Christmas Eve)
Almost everything closes from early evening as Germans retreat indoors to feast and exchange gifts.

25 Weihnachten (Christmas Day)

26 Stephanstag (St Stephen's Day/Boxing Day)

31 Berliner Silvesterlauf
Starts in the Grunewald
www.berlin-marathon.com
Traditional New Year's Eve fun run for the fit and the fearless.

31 Silvester (New Year's Eve)
Citywide
Mayhem at the Brandenburg Gate with crazed revelers tossing firecrackers all over the place, but Berlin's parks offer plenty of more sedate – and safer – events.

Karvenal der Kulturen p35

Terence Denville, 76,
Newcastle-upon-Tyne

(x) Oxfam

Hundreds of thousands of people have said *I'm in* to fight the injustice of poverty. And this kind of pressure has already made a huge difference. In Ghana, for example, most of the country's debt has been wiped out. But there's so much more to do: every day, extreme poverty kills 30,000 children. That's unacceptable. Text 'TIMEOUT' and your name to 87099. We'll let you know how to help. We can do this. We *can* end poverty. Are you in?

I give my support to help end poverty. and you know what? things actually get done

Let's end poverty together. Text 'TIMEOUT' and your name to 87099.

Itineraries

Remains of the Wall

Reunification Ramble

Not long ago, two worlds collided in the centre of Berlin. In between them was the Wall, outlining stretches of no-man's land with concrete and barbed wire. East was East and West was West and only a handful of checkpoints allowed the twain to meet. Until 9 November 1989, when it all began tumbling down. The big reunification projects are nearly all finished and the no-man's lands are now mostly filled with hotels and malls, monuments and ministries. The Wall, once the city's most famous landmark, has meanwhile been almost completely eradicated. In places it would take an archaeologist to dig up evidence that it had ever existed at all.

This itinerary – a three-kilometre (two-mile) walk – tracks the course of the Wall through downtown Berlin, from the world's most

famous checkpoint, where once Soviet and American tanks faced off across the border, to the new government quarter of the capital of unified Germany. Along the way it takes in landmark sights, new buildings and monuments and reminders of Berlin's dark and eventful history, including some surviving pieces of the Wall itself.

We start at **Checkpoint Charlie** (U6 Kochstrasse). But before stepping into the souvenir-shop bustle along Friedrichstrasse, pause to look east along Kochstrasse at the splendid pink and purple façade of the new **GSW building** on the corner of Charlottenstrasse.

Checkpoint Charlie was once a border crossing for non-Germans and Allied Forces, connecting the Russian and American sectors. Today it's just the Mitte-Kreuzberg boundary. On the east side of

Friedrichstrasse, the **Haus am Checkpoint Charlie** museum (p65) pre-dates the fall of the Wall, as does the **Café Adler** (p68) over the road – the best place to meet around here. The US Army control hut in the middle is an inaccurate reconstruction. The 'You are leaving the American Sector' sign is also fake, as are the costumed 'border guards' offering to stamp your passport (€2). There's similarly nothing left of the East German stop-and-search centre, which stood north of the junction with Zimmerstrasse, behind the hoardings that seem set to stand around the site indefinitely. Frank Thiel's photos of the last Russian and American border guards have loomed high above the scene here, from a pillar in the road, since

1998, while what remains of the checkpoint is now on display at the **Alliierten Museum** (p152).

At the junction you can see a double line of **cobblestones**. Visible for most of this walk, these mark the line of the former border Wall – the barrier that faced West Berlin, as opposed to the hinterland Wall, which stood on the East Berlin side of border defences. Follow the cobblestone line west down **Zimmerstrasse**. At No.88-91, a former industrial complex today houses a select group of commercial art galleries. The houses across on the south side were right up against the Wall – residents would step outdoors to find the Wall right in their face. The buildings near the Wilhelmstrasse corner, built

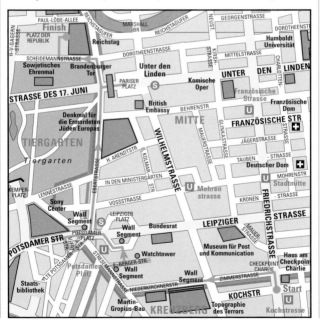

ITINERARIES

ITINERARIES

for the 1987 International Building Exhibition (IBA), were set back to allow some breathing space. On the opposite corner with Wilhelmstrasse is the **Ballon-Garten**, where a 15-minute ride up to a height of around 150 metres (500 feet) in a helium balloon ('The largest captive balloon in the world!') can be had for €19, weather permitting. There are lots of snack stands here too.

Continue the walk down **Niederkirchnerstrasse** on the other side of Wilhelmstrasse. The building on the north side was built by the Nazis as Goering's Luftfahrtsministerium (Air Ministry); today it's the Finanzamt (Inland Revenue). On the south side, behind a wire fence, is a **200-metre stretch of the Wall**, one of the longest surviving anywhere. Left pitted and threadbare by the 'wallpecker' tourists and souvenir-hunters who chiselled away at it in early 1990, it is today a protected monument. On its other side is the **Topographie des Terrors** (p68), once HQ of the Gestapo, now site of a temporary memorial and soon to house a documentation centre.

You'll pass the main entrance to the **Martin-Gropius-Bau** (p66) on the left. When the Wall was slap-bang in front of it, a side entrance had to be used. Then turn right along **Stresemannstrasse**, where the Wall ran along the road's far side. Opposite the end of Köthener Strasse, on the Erna-Berger-Strasse corner, there are a couple of slabs of **hinterland Wall**. At press time they were behind hoardings, soon to be incorporated into the foyer of a new building for the environment ministry. David Bowie's "'Heroes'" was recorded at Köthener Strasse 38. If Bowie really was inspired by seeing two lovers kiss by the Wall, then the event happened right about here. And if guards ever shot over their heads (highly unlikely), it might well have been from the surviving **watchtower** which can be found along **Erna-Berger-Strasse**, a few metres from its original position. The five-armed floodlights on waste ground to the north and south are also relics of the border defences.

Doubling back a little to Erna-Berger-Strasse 3, you can cut

Brandenburger Tor p44

British Embassy p44

ITINERARIES

through into **Leipziger Platz**, where two more slabs of hinterland Wall stand in their original location (the graffiti is more recent). Virtually nothing else visible from here existed when the Wall came down. The whole area was just one big scrubby no-man's land, and remained so until building began in the mid 1990s. The still incomplete octagon of Leipziger Platz and the streets fanning out from the towers of **Potsdamer Platz** to the west, are all part of Berlin's biggest Reunification project: a whole new quarter, straddling the line of the Wall, neither East nor West.

At Alte Postdamer Strasse 5, the **Haus Huth** was one of only two surviving pre-War buildings. Today it has the **Diekmann** restaurant (p118) on the ground floor, the **DaimlerChrysler Contemporary** gallery (p112) on the top floor, is next to a mall and stands surrounded by all the commercial and entertainment venues of what is now called the Daimler-Chrysler Quarter. Renzo Piano was the main architect here, though there are also some

buildings by Sir Richard Rogers along the edge of the park to the east. The brick-clad tower is by Hans Kollhoff.

On the other side of Potsdamer Strasse, the gloriously canopied single-structure **Sony Center**, home to the **CineStar Original** and **Arsenal** (both p122) cinemas, plus the **Filmmuseum** (p122), is the work of Helmut Jahn. The area's only other surviving pre-War structure, the former **ballroom of the Esplanade Hotel**, is on the east of the Center's impressive oval inner courtyard, protected behind glass. A small pre-moving ceremony was presided over by film director Wim Wenders, who used the ballroom to film the Nick Cave and Crime and the City Solution concert scenes for *Wings of Desire*. The movie also contained many other scenes shot around the urban desolation that made up this area back in 1987.

Today there is urban bustle that includes many eating and drinking stops. Try **Vapiano** (p120) on the corner of Ebertstrasse, next to the **Ritz-Carlton** hotel (p171). Over the road to the south, east of the entrance to Potsdamer Platz station, you'll see more slabs of Wall, bearing a small exhibit. Though standing on the line of the western Wall, these are actually pieces of hinterland Wall, placed here recently.

Continue north up Ebertstrasse. Most of the buildings on the right are embassies of the German *Länder* (states). Hitler's *Führerbunker* lay under the area north of Vossstrasse (its entrance is over on the far side, where 1980s East German housing blocks stand) but there is nothing left of it now. (See box p87.)

The Tiergarten appears on the left before the new **Denkmal für die ermordeten Jüden Europas** (Memorial to the Murdered Jews of Europe; p128) appears on the right. Take time to explore the labyrinth of concrete blocks; the entrance to the documentation centre is over at the south-east corner.

A little further north is the **Brandenburger Tor** (p127). This once stood alone in no-man's land. Now cyclists and pedestrians pass through the Gate to the new buildings of **Pariser Platz** on the eastern side. The US Embassy is

going up in the south-west corner. Michael Wilford's new **British Embassy** is round the corner on Wilhelmstrasse, behind the **Hotel Adlon** (p165). The road outside has been closed to traffic since the start of the 'War on Terror'. Other notable new buildings include Frank Gehry's **DG Bank** at No.3 and Behnisch and Partner's **Akademie der Künste** at No.4.

Back on the western side of the Gate, a right turn brings you around the corner of the Tiergarten to the **Reichstag** (p117), which has been brilliantly remodelled by Sir Norman Foster and topped with a cupola open to the public. The entrance is on the building's western side (the Wall ran behind it, to the east). Before entering, look for the stall where you can pick up a free guide to the building and panorama of **Government Quarter** buildings. If the line stretches back as far as the bottom of the steps, expect a 30-minute wait followed by airport-style security and crowded lifts. But the walk to the top of the cupola is a joy, especially at sunset.

Reichstag

KaDeWe p46

The U2 Tour

The U2 underground line connects the centres of east and west Berlin, juxtaposing their sights, department stores and sausage stands, stopping off at the new, unifying quarter that is Potsdamer Platz. On the central stretch – the oldest portion of the Berlin U-Bahn – there are some beautiful stations and something interesting to be found near just about every stop. Here we present the highlights. How much you cram into one day is a matter of stamina, specific interest and the amount of shopping you manage to acquire along the way.

First you need a ticket. The standard €2.10 BVG fare will buy you two hours' travel in one direction. A day pass for the central zones is a modest €5.80. Either is available from any of the ticket machines at any of the stations.

Start at **Zoologischer Garten**, more commonly known as 'Bahnhof Zoo' or 'Zoo Station', and as such

the title of a song by the other U2. It's no longer a stop for inter-city and international trains, but for decades this was where arrivals from the West would emerge to find – after transit through the drabness of East Germany – a surprisingly colourful commercial downtown. It's still the centre of west Berlin. **Stilwerk** (p113), the interior design mall, is a short walk along Kantstrasse. Glitzy **Kurfürstendamm**, main avenue of the west, begins two blocks to the south. And west Berlin's signature sight, the **Kaiser-Wilhelm Gedächtniskirche** (p105), a church left partially ruined to memorialise wartime destruction, is around the corner. Allow an hour or two if you want to explore the actual **Zoo** (p99), across the busy bus interchange outside the station. On the other side of the tracks, the new **Museum für Fotografie** (p105) is on Jebenstrasse.

Wittenbergplatz, the next station east, is a nicely restored art nouveau building. **KaDeWe** (p120), continental Europe's largest department store, is right outside. Opposite, on the north-west corner of the square, a fine organic Currywurst can be consumed at **Witty's** stand (p119). Beyond it, from Tuesday to Friday, there's a small farmer's market devoted to organic produce.

The train surfaces before **Nollendorfplatz**, the main station for the western gay district. **Motzstrasse**, leading south-west, is its main thoroughfare. The theatre on the square was the legendary Metropol club in the 1980s and venue for Erwin Piscator's political theatre experiments in the 1920s. It is currently dark. There are cafés and boutiques along lively Maasenstrasse, and a great market in **Winterfeldtplatz** (p116) every Wednesday and Saturday. Erich Kästner's *Emil and the Detectives* was mostly set in Nollendorfplatz, and Christopher Isherwood lived just around the corner at Nollendorfstrasse 17 when living through the times that he would later fictionalise in *Goodbye to Berlin*, the novel that provided the basis for the movie *Cabaret*. On the south-facing wall of the station is a **memorial** to gay and lesbian victims of the Nazis.

Between **Bülowstrasse** and **Gleisdreieck**, look north for a wide-angle view of Potsdamer Platz's postmodern skyline. U2, the group, recorded 'Achtung Baby!' – as Bowie recorded '"Heroes"' – at Hansa Studios, Köthener Strasse 38, a block away from **Mendelssohn-Bartholdy-Park** station. The studios are now the Meistersaal, a small concert hall for chamber music. After here, the U2 line goes back underground. This section was closed while the Wall was up, and Potsdamer Platz station lay unused underneath. Today's overground landscape is covered here in Reunification Ramble (p5).

One exit from **Stadtmitte** station you emerge on to **Friedrichstrasse**, mainstream shopping mile of the east, close to

Galeries Lafayette

Galeries Lafayette (p63) and **Quartier 206** (p63). The other exit is at the south-west corner of the **Gendarmenmarkt**. Here you'll find the **Deutscher Dom** (p60) and the **Franzözischer Dom/Huguenottenmuseum** (p60) and a profusion of upmarket venues for lunch, including **Borchardt** (p60), **Lutter & Wegner** (p63) and **Vau** (p63). You can also gorge on chocolate at **Fassbender & Rausch** (p63).

Three stops further east, the platforms at **Märkisches Museum** station are tiled with maps showing the growth of Berlin. Just east of the next stop, **Klosterstrasse**, are the only remains of the medieval Berlin wall, the Stadtmauer. Set into the 14th-century ruins is the 17th-century pub, Zur Letzten Instanz. It takes its name from the nearby law court, from which there was no further appeal. At the north end of Klosterstrasse are the ruins of the Franciscan Klosterkirche, an unrestored victim of World War II.

Alexanderplatz station is the most complex on the network and it's easy to get lost in its warren of tunnels. This is the hub of east Berlin and, overground, with its **Fernsehturm** (television tower; p79), and strange 1960s World Time Clock, the busy square still retains some of the atmosphere of a communist-era showpiece. The Haus des Lehrers on the south-east side, across Grünerstrasse, with its splendid socialist mural, has been restored, but renovation has robbed the **Galeria** department store of its communist character. The area around the fountain has been a meeting place for goths since long before the Wall came down. Across the buildings over the road on the north-east side of the square is a quotation from Alfred Döblin's modernist novel *Berlin Alexanderplatz*, spelled out in giant

type. Building work is still going on around here and 'Alex' has yet to find its final shape, but despite the cranes and goths and modern Western advertising, it's still a weirdly authoritarian space whose contours make the most sense when viewed from the heights of the Fernsehturm.

Rosa-Luxemburg-Platz is the stop for the east end of the fashionable Scheunenviertel. From here, you can walk down Rosa-Luxemburg-Strasse, past the impressive modernist bulk of east Berlin's landmark avant-garde theatre, the **Volksbühne** (p79), browse the boutiques of Münzstrasse and Alte and Neue Schönhauser Strasse, dip into the **Hackesche Höfe** and, if you're getting hungry, seek East Asian refreshment at the perennially hip **Monsieur Vuong** or **Pan Asia** (both p70).

The U2 continues north into Prenzlauer Berg. From the next stop, **Senefelderplatz**, a short walk up **Kollwitzstrasse** leads into the chic neighbourhood around Kollwitzplatz. The line emerges overground before the stop after that, **Eberswalder Strasse**, which stands at the nexus of several crucial thoroughfares. **Kastanienallee** to the south-west is the alternative artery connecting the scenes of Prenzlauer Berg and north Mitte. Danziger Strasse runs to the east and a left turn up Lychener Strasse leads into what's known, after the initials of its main thoroughfares, as the **'LSD' district**. In both of these directions there are too many cafés, bars and restaurants to list right here, but it's a perfect place to end the day, or kick off an evening. You can also try an eastern-style Currywurst at **Konnopke's Imbiss** (p84), under the overhead tracks just south of the station.

ITINERARIES

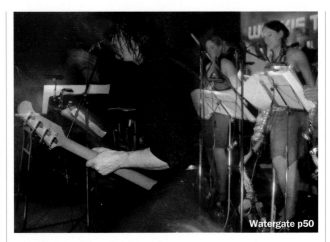

Watergate p50

All-night Crawl

Everything you've heard is true. Berlin nightlife is big, long, hard-drinking and stays up all night. Nightclubs turn into day clubs and some Saturday night places don't close their doors until it's almost Monday. A major plus for visitors is the cost. With no, or low, admission prices and the average beer costing around €3, having fun costs about half what it would in London.

By night, as by day, Berlin's districts have distinct characters. The manageable size of the inner city and an excellent and reliable 24-hour public transport network mean that it's possible to check out a variety of them in a single night – and variety is the point of this itinerary. If you can't be bothered with public transport, hail a moving cab and ask for a *Kurzstrecke* (short journey); you'll pay just €3 for a journey of up to two kilometres – an excellent way

of hopping about. And if any of our suggested places are too crowded or insufficiently convivial, you'll find plenty of other places nearby.

The area around **Hackescher Markt** in Mitte is a good place to start an evening. There are a myriad restaurants and a free show along **Oranienburger Strasse**, where ladies of the night stand in very high heels. Our itinerary begins around 11pm on a weekend night at **Ambulance** (p67), where well-presented cocktails are served in a lounge where there's room to gather and make plans. DJs play the right tunes to get the party started. You can linger in this neighbourhood for another drink at fashionable **Greenwich** (p69), just a short walk away, where you can kick back on lime-coloured leather or perch at the bar and admire the fishtanks to a soft techno soundtrack – but there's never much happening here early in the evening.

Jump into a cab for a *Kurzstrecke* to **Veteranenstrasse** and the nightlife of north Mitte. Have a beer at **Bergstübl** (p67), an old working-class local with retro furniture and seductive back rooms, popular with scenesters, gays and eccentrics. Alternatively, have a game of *Kicker* (table football) next door at **FC Magnet** (p69), a former communist club turned football bar.

A short stroll up Veteranenstrasse brings us to **Zionskirchplatz**, where a Romanesque church lends the square a touch of class. The traditional stop here is **Kapelle** (p70), a roomy and comfortable café named after the clandestine anti Nazi organisation that used to meet in the cellar. In a less traditional mood, try **Ick Koof mir Dave Lombardo wenn ich reich bin** (I'll buy myself Dave Lombardo when I'm rich; Zionskirchstrasse 34), a laid-back whiter-than-white café-bar named after the drummer from Slayer. It's far from being a heavy-metal joint, though, and serves a profusion of lemonade varieties.

Around the corner, you'll hit the hippest street in town: **Kastanienallee**. Once full of punks and squatters, it has been steadily gentrifying but has never quite relinquished its alternative character. There are so many places along here that we defy anyone to have a drink in every bar. First stop is **103** (p66), an L-shaped, orange-lit bar that is one of Kastanienallee's prime places to see and be seen. A little further on you'll cross the **Prenzlauer Berg** and find the punk-funk **Café Morgenrot** (p82) on the right-hand side, still packing them in. Next up, back on the left, is **Schwarz Sauer** (p87), 103's competition as Kastanienallee's most popular hangout. Beyond the junction with Oderberger Strasse, we arrive at **Bastard@Prater** (p90) – an ugly room but often

offering an early dance to reggae, ragga and dancehall. A little further up, diagonally over the road, **An einem Sonntag im August** (p82) is our last stop on Kastanienallee. An eccentric retro affair, it has big mirrors, gold stage curtains, green floral wallpaper and weekend DJs.

Kastanienallee winds up at the junction by **Eberswalder Strasse U-Bahn** station. There are plenty of snack options around here. Cross under the railway tracks and head up the street diagonally opposite, Pappelallee. On the left-hand side you'll find **Klub der Republik** (p84), a big and boisterous first-floor bar at the top of a rickety staircase. The music is retro, the beers are many and various and a no-nonsense good time is had by all. Further up Pappelallee, turn right into Raumerstrasse and you'll arrive at **Helmholtzplatz**, another nexus of local nightlife. Head left around the square to **Wohnzimmer** (p87), a quirkily cool 'living-room' with a shabby, worn-out feel.

Schwarz Sauer

From here, call a cab. Or walk back down Dunckerstrasse to Danziger Strasse and catch the M10 tram in the direction of Warschauer Strasse. Get off at Grünberger Strasse/Warschauer Strasse, cross the road, head east down Grünberger and turn right into the **Simon-Dach-Strasse**. Welcome to Friedrichshain's nightlife strip, a bubbly bohemian stew of new-age punks, anarchic radicals and rock-grunge types. As on Kastanienallee, you can pick from assorted flavours. These vary from the murals and heavy rock at **Paule's Metal Eck** (p145) through cocktails amid plastic furniture and coloured neon at **Künstliche BEATmung** (p145).

Another right turn brings us back on to Warschauer Strasse, and here the itinerary forks. You can jump into a cab and take a *Kurzstrecke* to nearby **Berghain/Panorama Bar** (see p148 and box p147) and carry on through the morning there. Or you can turn left down Warschauer for a stroll amid the crowd crossing over Warschauer Brücke. At the junction with Mühlenstrasse look to the right and you'll spy some remaining slabs of Berlin Wall, covered in paintings, known as the **East Side Gallery**. Walk over the **Oberbaumbrücke**, which crosses the river Spree and the former East-West border into **Kreuzberg**.

The first building on your left was once part of the border post but is now **Watergate** (p133), a paradise of techno and electronica spread over two floors and equipped with one of Berlin's best sound systems. You can dance right at the water's edge and watch the sun come up over the river through big picture windows.

If you still have stamina, there are plenty more places further up **Falckensteinstrasse** or left along **Schlesische Strasse**. But if the night is done, turn right to Schlesisches Tor U-Bahn station. There are snack options here, or you can take the U-Bahn one stop to Görlitzer Bahnhof and walk up **Oranienstrasse**. The smell of bread emanates from 24-hour **Melek Pastanesi** (Oranienstrasse 28) or enjoy kebabs or lentil soup at various Turkish cafés. German cafés and weekend buffet brunches (see box p129) get going around 10am.

Greenwich p48

Berlin by Area

Altes Museum p53

Mitte

The centre of Berlin – historically, culturally, scenically and also administratively – Mitte is what it says on the tin: the 'middle'. Unter den Linden and Friedrichstrasse are its two main axes, running respectively east-west and north-south. Friedrichstrasse is a narrow and busy commercial artery. The Linden is a grand avenue lined with solemn public buildings, and eventually arrives, after changing its name, at Alexanderplatz – centre of old East Berlin and a key urban hub. South and east of here are scattered points of interest. The main action is to the north of the borough, in the narrow lanes of the Scheunenviertel and beyond.

Unter den Linden & Museumsinsel

Unter den Linden runs east from the Brandenburg Gate, passing museums and embassies, opera houses and cathedrals. The name comes from the lime trees (Linden) that shade the central walkway. Its 18th- and 19th-century neo-classical and baroque buildings were mostly rubble after World War II, but the majority have been restored or rebuilt. The Linden arrives at Museumsinsel, the island in the Spree where Berlin was born and, as the name suggests, home to some important collections. On the south side of the street, on the far side of the river, the Palast der Republik, once home to the East German parliament, was slowly being demolished as this guide goes to press. It will eventually be replaced by a reconstruction of the old Prussian Stadtschloss.

Sights & museums

Alte Nationalgalerie

Bodestrasse 1-3 (2090 5801/www. smb.spk-berlin.de). S5, S7, S9, S75 Hackescher Markt. **Open** 10am-6pm Tue, Wed, Fri-Sun; 10am-10pm Thur. **Admission** €8; €4 reductions. No credit cards. **Map** p55 D3 ❶
The Old National Gallery is a grand home to one of Germany's largest collections of 19th-century art. Among the 440 paintings and 80 sculptures, German artists such as Adolph Menzel, Caspar David Friedrich, Max Liebermann and Carl Spitzweg are well represented. There are also some first-rank early Impressionist works.

Altes Museum

Am Lustgarten (2090 5245/www. smb.spk-berlin.de). S5, S7, S9, S75 Hackescher Markt. **Open** 10am-6pm Tue, Wed, Fri-Sun; 10am-10pm Thur. **Admission** €8; €4 reductions. No credit cards. **Map** p55 D3 ❷
Opened as the Royal Museum in 1830, the Old is one of Schinkel's finest buildings, with a magnificent entrance rotunda where vast neon letters declare that 'All Art has been Contemporary'. This place is currently home to the Ägyptisches Museum (Egyptian Museum), whose most celebrated exhibit is the bust of Nefertiti, which dates from around 1350 BC. The collection also includes the 'Berlin Green Head', dating from around 500 BC, and a piece of papyrus with the only known example of Cleopatra's handwriting. The Altes Museum's normal displays have been pared down to make room for all this, but temporary exhibitions are still held here.

Berliner Dom

Am Lustgarten (2026 9133/guided tours 2026 9119/www.berliner-dom. de). S5, S7, S9, S75 Hackescher Markt. **Open** *Apr-Sept* 9am-8pm Mon-Sat; noon-8pm Sun. *Oct-Mar* 9am-7pm Mon-Sat; noon-7pm Sun. **Admission** €5; €3 reductions. No credit cards. **Map** p55 D3 ❸
The dramatic Berlin Cathedral celebrated its centenary in 2005. Built in Italian Renaissance style, the building was razed to the ground during World War II and remained a ruin until 1973, at which point restoration work finally began. Crammed with Victorian detail and statues of eminent German Protestants, its lush 19th-century interior is worth visiting for the crypt containing around 90 sarcophagi of Hohenzollern notables, or to clamber up for splendid views from the cupola. Guided tours every 45 minutes from 10.30am to 3.30pm.

Brandenburger Tor

Pariser Platz. S1, S2 Unter den Linden. **Map** p54 B4 ❹
Constructed in 1791, and designed by Carl Gotthard Langhans after the Propylaea gateway into ancient Athens, the Brandenburg Gate was built as a triumphal arch. The Quadriga statue, a four-horse chariot driven by Victory and designed by Johann Gottfried Schadow, sits on top. It has had an eventful life. When Napoleon conquered Berlin in 1806 he carted the Quadriga off to Paris and held it hostage until his defeat in 1814. The Tor was badly damaged in World War II, and during subsequent renovations, the GDR removed the Prussian Iron Cross and turned the Quadriga around so that the chariot faced west. The current Quadriga is a 1958 copy, and was stranded in no-man's land for 30 years. The Tor was the scene of much celebration while the Wall came down, and after that there had to be further repairs. The Iron Cross was replaced and the Quadriga was turned back to face into Mitte again.

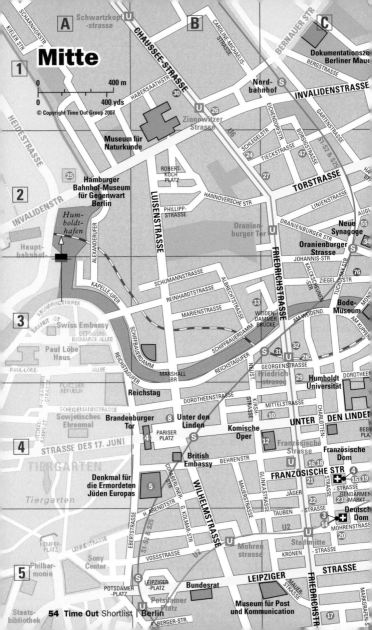

Mitte

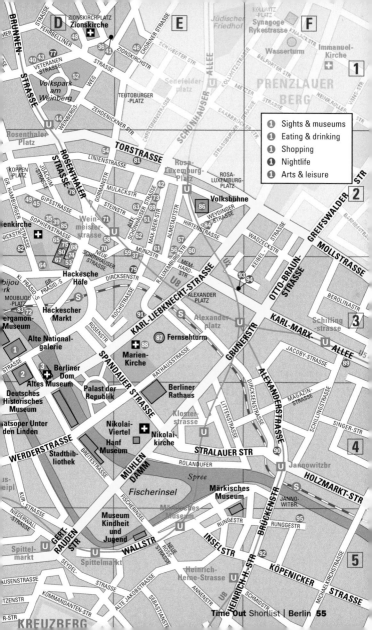

KREUZBERG

Legend:
- ① Sights & museums
- ① Eating & drinking
- ① Shopping
- ① Nightlife
- ① Arts & leisure

Denkmal für die ermordeten Juden Europas

Cora-Berliner-Strasse 1 (2639 4336/ www.holocaust-denkmal.de). U2, S1, S2, S26 Potsdamer Platz. **Open** *Information centre* 10am-8pm daily. **Admission** free. **Map** 54 B4 **⑤**

After years of controversy, Peter Eisenmann's 'field of stelae' – 2,711 of them, arranged in undulating rows over a whole city block – with its attendant information centre to memorialise 'the Murdered Jews of Europe', was opened in May 2005. Each of the concrete slabs has its own foundation, and they tilt at differing angles. There's no vantage point or overview – to engage with the thing you need to walk into it. The gaps between the stelae aren't wide enough for two people walking side by side; you are meant to explore on your own. It's spooky in places, especially on overcast days and near the middle, where many feel a sense of confinement. The information centre is underground and accessed from stairs at the south-east corner. It's like a kind of secular crypt, containing a sombre presentation of facts and figures about the Holocaust's Jewish victims.

Deutsches Historisches Museum

NEW *Zeughaus, Unter den Linden 2 (203 040/www.dhm.de). U6 Französische Strasse.* **Open** 10am-6pm daily. **Admission** €4. No credit cards. **Map** p55 D4 **⑥**

In a former armoury, the revamped Museum of German History was unveiled in June 2006. It extends over three floors and focuses on crucial points in German history, starting from the age of Germanic tribes around 1000 BC. There are also 'topic rooms' dealing with such subjects as 'The Relationship between the Sexes' or 'Changes in Work and Profession'. Temporary exhibitions are held in the splendid new wing by IM Pei on the west side of the complex. 'Farbe der Geschichte', an exhibition about flags, runs from Sept 2007. 'Neuvos Mundos', about the German

author of westerns, Karl Mai, runs from Oct 2007 to Feb 2008. The shop has an excellent selection of historical postcards and reproduction posters. See also box p78.

Pergamonmuseum

Am Kupfergraben (2090 5566/www. smb.spk-berlin.de). U6, S1, S2, S5, S7, S9, S75 Friedrichstrasse. **Open** 10am-6pm Tue, Wed, Fri-Sun; 10am-10pm Thur. **Admission** €8; €4 reductions. No credit cards. **Map** p55 D3 **⑦**

One of the world's major archaeological museums, the Pergamon contains three big draws. The first highlight is the Hellenistic Pergamon Altar. This dates from as far back as 170-159 BC, when Pergamon was one of the major cities of Asia Minor; huge as it is, the museum's re-creation is only one third of its original size. The altar's outstanding feature is the stunning original frieze that once wound around its base. Even more architecturally impressive is the two-storey Roman Market Gate of Miletus, erected in AD 120. The third big attraction is the blue- and ochre-tiled Persian Gate of Ishtar, dating from 605-562 BC. There are other gems, but it's an admirably digestible and focused place. Upcoming highlights include 'Dschazira', an exhibition examining the culture of Mesopotamia, until 2 Sept 2007, and 'Sammlerglück aus dem Orient', with items from the Keir Collection, from 15 May to 31 August 2007. The Pergamon is also home to the Museum für Islamische Kunst (Museum of Islamic Art). Renovations, which will happen in stages, begin in 2008.

Eating & drinking

Margaux

Unter den Linden 78, entrance in Wilhelmstrasse (2265 2611/www. margaux-berlin.de). S1, S2 Unter den Linden. **Open** 7-10.30pm Mon-Thur; noon-2pm, 7-10.30pm Fri, Sat. **€€€€**. **French. Map** p54 B4 **⑧**

This top-flight restaurant features Michael Hoffmann's slightly avant-garde take on classic French cooking, exemplified by dishes such as stewed

Brandenburger Tor p53

OUR CLIMATE NEEDS
A HELPING HAND TODAY

Be a smart traveller. Help to offset your carbon emissions from your trip by pledging Carbon Trees with Trees for Cities.

All the Carbon Trees that you donate through Trees for Cities are genuinely planted as additional trees in our projects.

Trees for Cities is an independent charity working with local communities on tree planting projects.

www.treesforcities.org   Tel 020 7587 1320

Trees for Cities
Charity registration number 1059

shoulder of venison seasoned with coriander, anise and saffron. The spacious interior is lit by glowing columns of honey-hued onyx, which reflect in the black marble floors. An extraordinary wine list includes around 30 vintages of Château Margaux.

Tadschikische Teestube

In the Palais am Festungsgraben, Am Festungsgraben 1 (204 1112). U6, S1, S2, S5, S7, S9, S75 Friedrichstrasse. **Open** 5pm-midnight Mon-Fri; 3pm-midnight Sat, Sun. No credit cards. **Café**. Map p54 C3 ⑨

An improbable gift from the Soviet Union in the early 1980s, the Tajik Tearoom is an extraordinary throwback. Sip exotic teas while lounging on the floor with samovars, low tables, plentiful rugs and cushions. It's a little faded nowadays, but worth the detour. Excellent snacks and light meals.

Shopping

Berlin Story

Unter den Linden 40, Mitte (2045 3840/www.berlinstory.de). U6 Französische Strasse. **Open** 10am-7pm daily. Map p54 C4 ⑩

You won't find a better stock of Berlin-related books in German and English: everything from novels with Berlin settings to non-fiction volumes on history and culture, plus historical maps, posters, videos, CDs, postcards and souvenirs. There's a free film to watch in the back, next to the small café.

Kunst & Nostalgie Markt

Museumsinsel, by Deutsches Historisches Museum (0171 710 1662). U6, S1, S2, S5, S7, S9, S75 Friedrichstrasse. **Open** 11am-5pm Sat, Sun. Map p55 D3 ⑪

Spread out along the riverbank, this is one of the few places where you can still find true GDR relics, with anything from old signs advertising coal briquettes to framed pictures of Honecker, but it's mostly stalls selling paintings and handicrafts.

Arts & leisure

Komische Oper

Behrenstrasse 55-7 (202 600/tickets 4799 7400/www.komische-oper-berlin. de). U6 Französische Strasse. Map p54 C4 ⑫

Denkmal für die ermordeten Juden Europas p56

After its founding in 1947, the Komische Oper made its name by breaking with the old operatic tradition of 'costumed concerts' – singers standing around on stage – and putting an emphasis on 'opera as theatre', with real acting skill demanded of its young ensemble.

Staatsoper Unter den Linden

Unter den Linden 7, Mitte (203 540/ tickets 2035 4555/www.staatsoper-berlin. de). U2 Hausvogteiplatz. **Map** p55 D4 🆁
The Staatsoper was founded as Prussia's Royal Court Opera in 1742, and designed along the lines of a Greek temple. The present building is a 1955 reconstruction, the façade faithfully copying that of Knobelsdorff's original structure. The elegant interior gives an immediate sense of past glory, with huge chandeliers and elaborate wall paintings.

South of Unter den Linden

Before getting into its ceremonial stride, the Linden crosses Friedrichstrasse. By day, this is a bustling commercial street of grand hotels and new department stores. By night, there's not much going on except for trade from the clutch of fine restaurants on and around the Gendarmenmarkt, the area's sightseeing centrepiece. Friedrichstrasse continues south into Kreuzberg at what was once Checkpoint Charlie (see p138).

Sights & museums

Deutscher Dom

Gendarmenmarkt, entrance in Markgrafenstrasse (2273 0431/ www.deutscherdom.de). U2, U6 Stadtmitte. **Open** 10am-10pm Tue; 10am-6pm Wed-Sun. **Admission** free. **Map** p54 C5 🆔
Both this church and the Französischer Dom were built in 1780-85 by Carl von Gontard, in imitation of Santa Maria in

Montesanto and Santa Maria dei Miracoli in Rome. The Deutscher Dom was intended for Berlin's Lutheran community. Its neo-classical tower is topped by a 7m (23ft) gilded statue representing Virtue. Inside is an exhibition on the history of Germany's parliamentary system.

Französischer Dom/ Hugenottenmuseum

Gendarmenmarkt (229 1760/ www.franzoesische-kirche.de). U2, U6 Stadtmitte. **Open** noon-5pm Tue-Sat; 11am-5pm Sun. **Admission** €2; €1 reductions. No credit cards. **Map** p54 C4 🆖
Built in the early 18th century for Berlin's French Protestant community, the church was later given a baroque tower, which offers fine views. An exhibition on the history of the Huguenots is within, plus another devoted to the church's history, particularly the effects of World War II – it was bombed during a Sunday service in 1944.

Eating & drinking

Borchardt

Französische Strasse 47 (8188 6262). U6 Französische Strasse. **Open** 11.30am-late daily. €€€. **French**. **Map** p54 C4 🆗
In the late 19th century the original Borchardt opened next door at No.48. It became the place to be for politicians and society folk, but was destroyed in World War II. Now Roland Mary and Marina Richter have reconstructed a highly fashionable, Maxim's-inspired bistro that serves respectable French food. The kitchen closes at midnight.

Entrecôte Fred's

Schutzenstrasse 5 (2016 5496/www. entrecote.de). U2, U6 Stadtmitte. **Open** noon-midnight Mon-Fri; 6pm-midnight Sat. €€€. **French**. **Map** p54 C5 🆘
Steak and frites in a brasserie ambience close to Checkpoint Charlie. The food is simple but well prepared and Fred's Special Sauce, a mixed herb

Quartier 206 p63

Admirable palace

The latest face-lift for a venerable venue.

After almost a decade in the slumps, the historic **Admiralspalast** re-opened its doors in summer 2006 with a sell-out extended run of Brecht and Weill's *The Threepenny Opera* (originally staged just over the river at what is now the Berliner Ensemble). Ongoing building work did not deter the public from enjoying anew this century-old cultural complex, which has seen many a facelift since its initial opening as an ice arena in 1911. Whatever the look, the emphasis has always been on racy entertainment throughout the night and day: bars, reviews, dancing girls, restaurants casinos, bowling alleys, ballrooms and one of Berlin's first cinemas.

The legacy of the last 100 years is still on show because the Admiralspalast rather miraculously survived wartime bombing intact. In the Grand Café, the most recent influx of construction workers found five ceilings, one under the other, each from a different era. Today's taste is for a mix of old and new. You can walk through a 1930s foyer to a brand-new bar designed with the shape of a violin in mind. Coats are hung in the new cloakroom on original pegs. Other key fixtures and fittings from the golden days remain, such as an immense 490-bulb chandelier hanging from the ceiling of the 1,760-seat theatre. Hitler's former loggia, which had its own bar and sleeping area, and which used to protrude rudely way over the stalls, have been reined in.

Round-the-clock entertainment is once again on the cards. In addition to the main theatre and café, there are two smaller stages for live theatre and readings, a clubroom being developed for party nights, and plans for a fourth-floor spa, to make the most of a natural water source almost 3,000 metres below ground level. It will soon flow into the sauna/wellness area, which will have a Finnish feel, not least because Finnair has agreed to fly in fresh rejuvenating mud every morning.

remoulade, is excellent. The extensive wine list encompasses all French regions and there are half bottles. Professional service, classic desserts and plenty of room.

Lutter & Wegner

Charlottenstrasse 56 (202 9540/www. lutter-wegner-gendarmenmarkt.de). U2, U6 Stadtmitte. **Open** 11am-3am daily. **€€€. Modern European. Map** p54 C4 ⓭

This place has it all: history (an early Berlin wine merchant, its sparkling wine became known as Sekt, now the common German term); atmosphere in its elegant rooms; great German/Austrian/French cuisine and excellent service. The wine list is legendary and if the prices look high, head for the bistro, where the same list holds sway along with perfect salads, cheese and ham plates.

Vau

Jägerstrasse 54-5 (202 9730/www. vau-berlin.de). U6 Französische Strasse. **Open** noon-2.30pm, 7-10pm Mon-Sat. **€€€€. Modern European. Map** p54 C4 ⓳

This young but mature Michelin-starred restaurant occupies a tunnel-like space remodelled by architect Meinhard von Gerke – designer of Berlin's Tegel airport. Chef Kolja Kleeberg presents (often quite literally) an eclectic menu. The house perennial *Kartoffelschmarrn*, a torn-up potato pancake served with brown butter, chives, sour cream and caviar, is a savoury reimagining of a traditional dessert. Turnabout is likewise fair play with the *Caprese Vau*, a dessert of mozzarella, strawberries in olive oil and basil sorbet.

Shopping

Fassbender & Rausch

NEW *Charlottenstrasse 60 (2045 8440/www.fassbender-rausch.de). U2, U6 Stadtmitte.* **Open** 10am-8pm Mon-Fri; 10am-6pm Sat; noon-6pm Sun. **Map** p54 C5 ⓴

Though the logo says 'since 1863' (the founding date of Fassbender), these two old chocolate companies didn't amalga-

mate until the 1990s. This vast flagship venue opened in 2005. Downstairs is delicious chocolate in every configuration, plus huge chocolate replicas of the Brandenburg Gate and the Reichstag. Upstairs there's a café and a restaurant with a full dinner menu – every item of which contains chocolate.

Galeries Lafayette

Französische Strasse 23, Mitte (209 480/www.galerieslafayette.de). U2, U6 Stadtmitte. **Open** 10am-8pm Mon-Sat. **Map** p54 C4 ㉑

This Jean Nouvel glass block houses a refreshing shopping experience: great clothes, frequent sales on the upper floors, a good selection of accessories and cosmetics at street level and, best of all, a basement food hall where you'll feel transported to Paris among fresh cheeses, chocolates, wines, breads and condiments.

Quartier 206

Friedrichstrasse 71, Mitte (2094 6240/www.quartier206.de). U2, U6 Stadtmitte. **Open** 10.30am-7.30pm Mon-Fri; 10am-6pm Sat. **Map** p54 C4 ㉒

Reminiscent of New York City's Takashimaya and designed by that city's Calvin Tsao, this upmarket store offers not just the most lusted-after designers, but also their definitive items. Cult cosmetics and centuries-old perfumes are on the ground floor; upstairs is devoted to women's and men's fashion, plus a home-living section with sinfully expensive design items.

Arts & leisure

Konzerthaus

Gendarmenmarkt 2, Mitte (203 092 101/www.konzerthaus.de). U6 Französische Strasse. **Map** p54 C4 ㉓

This 1821 gem by Schinkel has three main spaces for concerts. Organ recitals in the large concert hall are a treat, played on the massive Jehmlich organ at the back of the stage. The Berliner Sinfonie-Orchester is based here, presenting a mixture of the classic, the new and the rediscovered.

The Deutsches Sinfonie Orchester and Berliner Staatskapelle also play here, and there are informal concerts in the cosy Musik Club in the depths of the building.

North along Friedrichstrasse

North of Unter den Linden, Friedrichstrasse begins to fizzle a little after passing the station and former border post of the same name. There are several theatres dotted about as it runs on, forming the boundary between the Scheunenviertel to the east and the government quarter to the west.

Sights & museums

Brecht-Weigel-Gedänkstätte

Chausseestrasse 125 (283 057 044/ www.adk.de). U6 Oranienburger Tor. **Open** *Guided tours* Every 30mins 10-11.30am Tue, Wed, Fri; 10am-noon, 5-6.30pm Thur; 9.30am-1.30pm Sat. Every hr 11am-6pm Sun. **Admission** €3; €1.50 reductions. No credit cards. **Map** p54 B2 ㉔

Bertolt Brecht's home from 1948 until his death in 1956 has been preserved exactly as he left it. Tours of the house last 30 minutes and give interesting insights into the life and reading habits of the playwright and poet. Brecht's second wife, actress Helene Weigel, continued living in the house until she died in 1971, and her recipes are served at the Kellerrestaurant downstairs. Phone ahead to arrange a tour in English.

Hamburger Bahnhof, Museum für Gegenwart

Invalidenstrasse 50-51 (397 8340/ www.smb.spk-berlin.de). S5, S7, S9, S75 Lehrter Bahnhof. **Open** 10am-6pm Tue, Wed, Fri; 10am-10pm Thur; 11am-8pm Sat; 11am-6pm Sun. **Admission** €8; €4 reductions. No credit cards. **Map** p54 A2 ㉕

The Museum of Contemporary Art is housed in a former railway station. The exterior features a stunning light installation by Dan Flavin; inside, the big draw is currently the gradual unveiling of the controversial Friedrich Christian Flick Collection – a staggering 2,000 works from around 150 late 20th century artists – in a series of themed exhibitions. There are other exhibitions too: a Brice Marden exhibition runs until June 2007; 'Schmerz', an exhibition about 'art, religion, medicine', until 5 Aug 2007. Plus there's a great bookshop.

Eating & drinking

Bangaluu

NEW *Invalidenstrasse 30 (8096 93077/www.bangaluu.com). U6 Zinnowitzer Strasse.* **Open** 7pm-late Tue-Sat. €€€. **Modern European**. **Map** p54 B1 ㉖

Live music, white leather loungers, a foot and shoulder massage and repartee with resident drag queen host Mataina are pleasurable accompaniments to a ten-dish international cuisine menu that, like an airline ticket, is cheaper the earlier you book. There's also a candle-lit cocktail bar and a dancefloor for afterwards.

Weinbar Rutz

Chausseestrasse 8 (2462 8760/www.rutz-weinbar.de). U6 Zinnowitzer Strasse. **Open** 5pm-midnight Mon-Sat. €€€€. **Wine bar**. **Map** p54 C2 ㉗

The impressive ground-floor bar has a whole wall showcasing wines from around the globe – not obscure New World vintages, but the best of the best. The second-floor restaurant serves a limited nouvelle cuisine menu. Snacks are available downstairs; booking essential.

Shopping

Berliner Antik- & Flohmarkt

Bahnhof Friedrichstrasse, S-Bahnbogen 190-203 (208 2655/www.antikmarkt-berlin.de). U6, S1, S2, S3, S5, S7, S9, S75 Friedrichstrasse. **Open** 11am-6pm Mon, Wed-Sun. **Map** p54 C3 ㉘

Over 60 dealers are gathered in renovated arches under the S-Bahn tracks east of Friedrichstrasse station along Georgenstrasse. Expect to find furniture, jewellery, paintings and vintage clothing, some of it from the 1920s and '30s.

Dussmann das KulturKaufhaus

Friedrichstrasse 90 (202 50/www. kulturkaufhaus.de). U6, S1, S2, S5, S7, S9, S75 Friedrichstrasse. **Open** 10am-10pm Mon-Sat. **Map** p54 C3 ㉙
Intended as a 'cultural department store', this spacious four-floor retailer mixes books with CDs, videos with magazines, and has internet terminals, an interactive video-viewing room and a DVD shop. Lots of bargains and remainders too.

Nightlife

Rio

Chausseestrasse 106 (no phone/www. rioberlin.de). U6 Zinnowitzer Strasse.

Open 11.30pm-late Sat. No credit cards. **Map** p54 B1 ㉚
The DJs in the front room of this former restaurant can get a bit indulgent, but the dancefloor in the back usually moves to the best electro in Berlin, as well as hosting local heroes such as Cobra Killer and Kissogram. It's a big and well-liked place, perhaps because it retains a gritty, debauched charm while also managing to glam it up a bit.

Tränenpalast

Reichstagufer 17 (2061 0011/www. traenenpalast.de). U6, S1, S2, S5, S7, S9, S75 Friedrichstrasse. **Open** varies. No credit cards. **Map** p54 C3 ㉛
In the days of division this was the entrance to the Friedrichstrasse checkpoint and the exit from East Berlin, scene of many a sad farewell and hence the name: 'Palace of Tears'. Shows in this historical landmark range from cabaret and stand-up to chansons, jazz concerts and tango events.

Shiro i Shiro p71

Arts & leisure

Admiralspalast

NEW *Friedrichstrasse 101 (3253 3130/tickets 4799 7499/www.admirals palast.de). U6, S1, S2, S5, S7, S9, S75 Friedrichstrasse.* **Map** p54 C3 **32**
See box p62.

Berliner Ensemble

Bertolt-Brecht-Platz 1 (2840 8116/ www.berliner-ensemble.de). U6, S1, S2, S5, S7, S9, S75 Friedrichstrasse. **Map** p54 B3 **33**
Constructed in 1891, and still with an elaborate period interior, the Berliner Ensemble is best known for its association with Brecht – first during the Weimar period (this was where *The Threepenny Opera* was first staged in 1928) and later under the Communists when Brecht ran the place from 1948 until his death eight years later. Under current intendant Claus Peymann, expect a repertoire where modern productions of Brecht rub shoulders with pieces by living German and Austrian writers.

Scheunenviertel & Mitte Nord

The Scheunenviertel ('Barn District') stands just beyond the line of the medieval city wall, and is Berlin's historic Jewish quarter. Bounded by Friedrichstrasse to the west, Oranienburger Strasse to the south, Alte Schönhauser Strasse to the east and Torstrasse to the north, it is a district of uncharacteristically narrow streets, dotted with commercial art galleries, eccentric shops, fashionable bars and designer cafés. The contemporary scene spills beyond into the area that is becoming known as Mitte Nord, and from the nexus of nightlife around Veteranenstrasse and Zionskirchplatz, it climbs up Kastanienallee and on towards Prenzlauer Berg.

Sights & museums

Neue Synagoge

Centrum Judaicum, Oranienburger Strasse 28-30 (8802 8451/www. cjudaicum.de). S1, S2 Oranienburger Strasse. **Open** Sept-Apr 10am-6pm Mon-Thur, Sun; 10am-2pm Fri. *May-Aug* 10am-8pm Mon, Sun; 10am-6pm Tue-Thur; 10am-5pm Fri. **Admission** €3; €2 reductions. No credit cards.
Map p54 C2 **34**
Built in 1857-66 as the Berlin Jewish community's showpiece, the New Synagogue was attacked during Kristallnacht in 1938, but not too badly damaged – Allied bombs did far more harm in 1945. The façade remained intact and the Moorish dome has been rebuilt. Inside is a permanent exhibition about Jewish life in Berlin and a glassed-in area protecting the ruins of the sanctuary. The dome is also open to visitors in summer.

Sammlung Hoffmann

Sophienstrasse 21 (2849 9121/www.sophie-gips.de). U8 Weinmeisterstrasse. **Open** (by appointment only) 11am-4pm Sat. **Admission** €6. No credit cards.
Map p55 D2 **35**
Erika and Rolf Hoffmann's private collection of international contemporary art includes a charming floor installation by Swiss video artist Pipilotti Rist and work by Douglas Gordon, Felix Gonzalez-Torres and AR Penck. The Hoffmanns offer guided tours through their apartment every Saturday by appointment – felt slippers supplied.

Eating & drinking

103

Kastanienallee 49 (4849 2651). U8 Rosenthaler Platz. **Open** 9am-2am Mon-Fri; 10am-2am Sat, Sun. No credit cards. **Bar. Map** p55 D1 **36**
Well-lit and airy (for Berlin), this L-shaped bar competes with Schwarz Sauer to be the primary Kastanienallee hangout. The food is generally excellent, an odd mix of Asian and Italian. But more importantly, it's the perfect

summer location to sit outside with a beer and watch well-coiffed local freaks strut their stuff.

Alt-Berlin

Munzstrasse 23 (no phone/www.heinzundinge.de) U8 Weinmeisterstrasse. **Open** 8pm-late daily. No credit cards. **Bar**. **Map** p55 E2 ③

An old-style Berlin Kneipe (pub) that's been left that way – wood-panelling, nasty ornaments – in contrast to the self-consciously stylish renovations usual around here. Young crowd, though, and entertaining staff. No phone? 'Too modern!' If the bar in front looks full, there's seating in the back.

Ambulance

Oranienburger Strasse 27 (no phone). S1, S2 Oranienburger Strasse. **Open** 7pm-late daily. No credit cards. **Bar**. **Map** p54 C2 ③

A surprisingly discreet cocktail bar situated on the Oranienburger tourist strip, only the cocktail sign above the door gives the game away. Inside

there's a smart, comfortable lounge decked in warm red and cream. The bar staff are friendly and never forget the fresh fruit, while DJs get the party going at weekends.

Barcomi's

Sophienstrasse 21, Sophie-Gips-Höfe, 2 Hof (2859 8363/www.barcomi.de). U8 Weinmeisterstrasse. **Open** *Winter* 9am-8pm Mon-Thur; 10am-9pm Fri-Sun. *Summer* 9am-10pm Mon-Sat; 10am-10pm Sun. No credit cards. **Café**. **Map** p55 D2 ③

Prominent in the renovated courtyard downstairs from the Sammlung Hoffmann (see p66), and serving American-style coffee and snacks and light meals, Barcomi's is a deservedly popular stop for lunch or an afternoon break.

Bergstübl

Veteranenstrasse 25 (4849 2268). U8 Rosenthaler Platz. **Open** 4pm-6am Mon-Fri; noon-6am Sat, Sun. No credit cards. **Bar**. **Map** p55 D1 ④

Claudia Skoda p72

Hackesche Höfe p19

Perhaps the most popular spot on popular Veteranenstrasse and certainly the oddest. A former fascist hangout, with old wood panelling still intact, it's now owned by an African and popular with a cruisy gay crowd. But the clientele is resolutely mixed, with hipsters sharing small tables with hardcore alkies and neighbourhood eccentrics, while an eclectic selection of DJs spin over a lousy sound system.

Der Imbiss W

Kastanienallee 49 (4849 2657). U8 Rosenthaler Platz. **Open** *Winter* noon-11.30pm daily. *Summer* noon-midnight daily. **€**. **Fusion**. No credit cards. **Map** p55 D1 ㊶

Owned by 103 (p66), the bar next door, this vogueish place is named after Gordon W, a minor celebrity chef from Canada, who devised its wacky fusion menu of 'naan pizzas', 'rice shells' and international 'dressings'. The food is clever but it's not always that well executed.

Erdbeer

Max-Beer-Strasse 56 (no phone). U2 Rosa-Luxemburg-Platz. **Open** *Summer* 2pm-late daily. *Winter* 6pm-late daily. No credit cards. **Bar**. **Map** p55 E2 ㊷

The name means 'strawberry', and this spacious and dingy bar has earned a reputation for its powerful and delicious fresh fruit drinks. There are other eccentric mixtures on offer, as well as the usual beer offering, plus nightly DJs of wildly differing styles and quality.

FC Magnet

Veteranenstrasse 26 (no phone/www. fcmagnet.de). U8 Rosenthaler Platz. **Open** 8pm-late daily. No credit cards. **Bar**. **Map** p55 D1 ㊸

The slacker entrepreneurs behind FC Magnet have taken an old social club and created a fashionable football bar complete with its own team. Though the drinks aren't exceptional, people pack in at weekends to play Kicker (table football) under a giant photograph of Franz Beckenbauer.

Gorki Park

Weinbergsweg 25 (448 7286/www. gorki-park.de). U8 Rosenthaler Platz. **Open** 9.30am-2am daily. No credit cards. **Café**. **Map** p55 D1 ㊹

A tiny Russian-run café with tasty and authentic snacks – blini, borscht and the like. Guests range from students and loafers to the occasional guitar-toting Ukrainian and scenesters having a quiet coffee before heading down to pose at more centrally located bars. The interesting weekend brunch buffet includes a range of warm dishes, but the vodka selection is disappointing.

Greenwich

Gipsstrasse 5 (2809 5566). U8 Weinmeisterstrasse. **Open** 8pm-6am daily. No credit cards. **Bar**. **Map** p55 D2 ㊺

It's not long since East Berlin nightlife was mostly squats serving cheap beer and industrial vodka. But when club pioneer Cookie opened this place, still referred to as 'Cookie's Bar', the city began its half-hearted romance with glam-flecked exclusivity. Of course, this being Berlin, an ironed shirt will probably get you in. The interior looks like a set from *Barbarella*.

Hazelwood

Choriner Strasse 72 (4432 4635/www. hazelwood-berlin.de). U8 Rosenthaler Platz. **Open** 6pm-late Tue-Fri; 10am-4pm, 6pm-late Sat, Sun. No credit cards. **American**. **Map** p55 E1 ㊻

See box p57.

Honigmond

Borsigstrasse 28 (2844 5512/www. honigmond-berlin.de). U6 Zinnowitzer Strasse. **Open** 7.30am-1am daily. **€€**. **German**. **Map** p54 C2 ㊼

This quiet neighbourhood place serves up traditional German food alongside an innovative menu that ranges from kangaroo to Swiss fondue. Noteworthy are the *Königsberger Klöpse* (east Prussian meatballs in a creamy caper sauce) and a very good Caesar salad. Excellent wine list and remarkable home-made bread (and butter!). There's a small hotel upstairs (see p165).

Kapelle

Zionskirchplatz 22-4 (4434 1300/ www.cafe-kapelle.de). U8 Rosenthaler Platz. **Open** 9am-3am daily. No credit cards. **Café. Map** p55 D1 ㊽

A comfortable, high-ceilinged café/bar across from the Zionskirch, Kapelle takes its name from Die Rote Kapelle, 'the Red Orchestra'. This was a clandestine anti-fascist organisation and in the 1930s and '40s the Kapelle's basement was a meeting place for the resistance. The menu features organic meat and vegetarian dishes, and proceeds are donated to local charities.

Kuchi

Gipsstrasse 3 (2838 6622/www.kuchi. de). U8 Weinmeisterstrasse. **Open** noon-midnight Mon-Thur; 12.30pm-12.30am Fri, Sat; 6pm-midnight Sun. **€€. Japanese. Map** p55 D2 ㊾

It's the quality of the ingredients here that makes the food special. And it isn't just fish that you'll find in the sushi rolls: one maki is filled with chicken, mandarin oranges and poppy seeds. Delicate tempura, yakitori chicken hearts or shiitake mushrooms are all excellently served by a young, cool and multinational team. Packed at lunchtime.

Maxwell

Bergstrasse 22 (280 7121/www. mxwl.de). U8 Rosenthaler Platz or S1, S2, S25 Nordbahnhof. **Open** 6pm-midnight daily. **€€€. Modern European. Map** p54 C1 ㊿

In a beautiful neo-gothic former brewery – tucked in a peaceful courtyard with summer tables – chef and proprietor Uwe Popall presides over a relaxed and tasteful space while offering a light, eclectic menu. His philosophy of colourful simplicity – letting local and seasonal ingredients be themselves – is popular with members of the art scene as well as the younger diplomatic crowd. It's one of our favourites too.

Monsieur Vuong

Alte Schönhauser Strasse 46 (3087 2643/www.monsieurvuong.de). U2
Rosa-Luxemburg-Platz. **Open** noon-midnight Mon-Sat; 2pm-midnight Sun. **€€.** No credit cards. **Vietnamese. Map** p55 E2 ㉛

Something of an institution now, this Scheunenviertel fixture serves fresh and tasty Vietnamese soups and noodles. A couple of daily specials supplement a handful of regular dishes. Cheap, cheery and stylish, but often packed to the rafters.

Nola's am Weinberg

Veteranenstrasse 9 (4404 0766/ www.nola.de). U8 Rosenthaler Platz. **Open** 10am-2am daily. **€€€. Swiss. Map** p55 D1 ㉜

The food in this former park pavilion is hearty fare, such as venison goulash with mushrooms and spinach noodles, or rösti with spinach and cheese with fried eggs. The goat's cheese mousse with rocket starter is large enough for two. With a little thought put in, it is possible to eat quite cheaply here. Quiet terrace as well as a spacious bar and dining-room.

Pan Asia

Rosenthaler Strasse 38 (2790 8811/www. panasia.de). U8 Weinmeisterstrasse or S5, S7, S9, S75 Hackescher Markt. **Open** noon-1am daily. **€€. East Asian. Map** p55 D3 ㉝

In a pleasant courtyard off busy Rosenthaler, with tables outside in summer, this is a fashionably minimalist place to see, be seen and eat modern Asian food. Japanese beers and Chinese teas complement excellent wun tun, kimchi salad and a variety of soups and wok dishes. A self-conscious crowd, unbelievable bathrooms and inconsistent service.

Perlweiss

NEW *Torstrasse 89 (no phone). U8 Rosenthaler Platz.* **Open** 9pm-late Tue-Sat. No credit cards. **Bar. Map** p55 D2 ㉞

This L-shaped cocktail and party bar decorated in dazzling white (the name, 'pearl white', is a German toothpaste brand) focuses on soul and funk music and has a vaguely 1970s theme. Fresh flowers on the bar and on the tables

B-Flat p77

provide a contrasting wave of colour. Perlweiss is a good rendezvous for a pre-clubbing drink.

Schwarzwaldstuben

Tucholskystrasse 48 (2809 8084/ www.schwarzwaldstuben-berlin.de). S1, S2 Oranienburger Strasse. **Open** 9am-11pm Mon-Fri; 9am-midnight Sat, Sun. **€€. German**. No credit cards. **Map** p54 C2 🖘

This casually chic Swabian restaurant wears its mounted deer head ironically. The food is excellent: soups are hearty, standout entrées include the *Schäuffele* with sauerkraut, and the *Flammkuchen* is good. Try the Rothaus Tannenzapfle beer on tap.

Shiro i Shiro

NEW *Rosa-Luxemburg-Strasse 1 (4930 9700/www.shiroishiro.com). U2 Rosa-Luxemburg-Platz.* **Open** *Breakfast* 7.30am-11am. *Lunch* noon-3pm. *Dinner* 7-11.30pm. *Bar* 7pm-3am. **€€€€. Fusion**. **Map** p55 E2 🖘

The food is splendid in this bright, white restaurant beneath the Lux 11 hotel (p166). Japanese/Mediterranean hybrid dishes colourfully juxtapose fine ingredients, individually prepared, and listed that way on the menu: 'Lobster/grape/coconut pilaf/lobster bisque' or 'Sole/lavender/ravioli/spinach/green asparagus'. There's wonderful sashimi and an excellent wine list. Downsides are cramped dining areas, nothing for vegetarians and hurried service. Go for the tables near the open kitchen, rather than those by the noisy bar, or head for the absurdly long table between the two.

Susuru

NEW *Rosa-Luxemburg-Strasse 17 (211 1182/www.susuru.de) U2 Rosa-Luxemburg-Platz.* **Open** noon-10pm Mon-Fri; noon-11pm Sat. No credit cards. **€€€. Japanese**. **Map** p55 E2 🖘

Choose from the modest menu of Japanese dishes offered here (mostly noodle soups) and a big selection of juices and teas under a huge cloud-like lampshade constructed from lots of smaller Philippe Starck lampshades. It's a low-key place but the food is tasty; try the *gyoza*. There's a no smoking policy throughout.

Bohannon p77

Shopping

Absinthe Depot Berlin

Weinmeisterstrasse 4 (281 6789/ www.erstesabsinthdepotberlin.de). U8 Weinmeisterstrasse. **Open** 4pm-midnight Mon-Fri; 1pm-midnight Sat. No credit cards. **Map** p55 D2 ❺❽
Potent absinthes, mainly from western Europe (no Czech stuff), line the walls. The smiling owner may invite you for a tasting session, otherwise boutique bottles can be consumed at a stand-up table.

AM1 AM2

NEW *Münzstrasse 21 (3088 1945). U8 Weinmeisterstrasse.* **Open** noon-8pm Mon-Fri; noon-6pm Sat. **Map** p55 E2 ❺❾
Two stores featuring the clothes of Greek designer Kostas Murkurdis. Womenswear is in the first courtyard, menswear in the second. The designs, a sexy mix of quality fabrics and the fitted item, are only available in Berlin and Japan and command exorbitant prices.

Blush

Rosa-Luxemburg-Strasse 22 (2809 3580/www.blush-berlin.com). U2 Rosa-Luxemburg-Platz. **Open** noon-8pm Mon-Fri; noon-7pm Sat. **Map** p55 E2 ❻⓿
This small shop's selection of lingerie in lace and silk is beautiful and well-chosen. There are imports from France and Italy, as well as German brands.

Boss Orange Store

NEW *Max-Beer-Strasse 2-4 (8471 07880). U8 Weinmeisterstrasse.* **Open** 11am-8pm Mon-Sat. **Map** p55 E2 ❻❶
Hugo's leisure label presents classy, casual clothing for men and women in a revamped former canteen. A one-off item range downstairs, in-store tailor, coffee bar and themed changing rooms (bathroom, living-room, library and greenhouse) add to the fun.

Claudia Skoda

Alte Schönhauser Strasse 35 (280 7211). U8 Weinmeisterstrasse. **Open** noon-8pm Mon-Fri; noon-7pm Sat. **Map** p55 E2 ❻❷

Berlin's most established womenswear designer has extended her range to include men – designs for both sexes are offered here. Using high-tech yarns and innovative knitting techniques, the collections bear her signature combination of stretch fabrics and graceful drape effects.

Elternhaus

Alte Schönhauser Strasse 14 (2759 6900/www.elternhaus.com). U8 Weinmeisterstrasse. **Open** 1-7pm Mon-Fri; noon-6pm Sat. No credit cards. **Map** p55 E2 ⊛

Elegant streetwear created by an artist and design collective out of Hamburg. Witty but untranslatable German slogans are printed across beautifully tailored T-shirts for men, women and children. Also keyrings, bags and beautiful military-style jackets.

Fiona Bennett

Grosse Hamburger Strasse 25 (2809 6330/www.fionabennett.com). S3, S5, S7, S9, S75 Hackescher Markt. **Open** 10am-6pm Mon-Wed; 10am-8pm Thur, Fri; noon-6pm Sat. **Map** p55 D3 ⊛

British-born Fiona Bennett's hats could be considered as works of art. She has mastered the sloping, wide brim and crafts horned headdresses, feathered fedoras, and hats reminiscent of insects or sea urchins. For all their beautiful theatrics, they still have a classic feel.

Fishbelly

Sophienstrasse 7 (2804 5180/www. fishbelly.de). U8 Weinmeisterstrasse. **Open** 12.30-7pm Mon-Fri; noon-6pm Sat. **Map** p55 D2 ⊛

Often compared to London's Agent Provocateur, this tiny shop located in the Hackesche Höfe (p19) has a range of extravagant undergarments by designers such as Dolce & Gabbana Intimo, Capucine Puerari and Christian Dior. The shop's own-brand line of imaginative lingerie is making its own mark, and is definately worth checking out.

Fernsehturm p79

BERLIN BY AREA

Konk

NEW *Kleine Hamburger Strasse 15 (2809 7839/www.konk-berlin.de) S1, S2 Oranienburger Strasse.* **Open** noon-8pm Tue-Sat. No credit cards. **Map** p55 D2 ⑯

This elegant boutique features avant-garde womenswear from Berlin designers. There are bold colours and designs for an immediate impact, as well as classic styles given a modern makeover. Approach from the southern end of the street (it's split in two by a sports field).

Lisa D

Hackesche Höfe, Rosenthaler Strasse 40-41 (282 9061/www.lisad.com). U8 Weinmeisterstrasse or S3, S5, S7, S9, S75 Hackescher Markt. **Open** 11am-7.30pm Mon-Sat. **Map** p55 D3 ⑰

Austrian-born Lisa D is well known on the Berlin fashion scene and was one of the first to move into the Hackesche Höfe. Expect long, flowing womenswear in subdued shades from this avant-garde designer.

Neurotitan

Rosenthaler Strasse 39 (3087 2576/ www.neurotitan.de). S3, S5, S7, S9, S75 Hackescher Markt. **Open** noon-8pm Mon-Sat. No credit cards. **Map** p55 D2 ⑱

At the end of an alley and up on the second floor, this is one of Berlin's most interesting book and music stores. It's good for handmade and small-press art books, original artwork and small label CDs and vinyl.

ProQM

Alte Schönhauser Strasse 48 (2472 8520/www.pro-qm.de). U8 Weinmeisterstrasse. **Open** noon-8pm Mon-Fri; noon-6pm Sat. **Map** p55 E2 ⑲

The artist owners offer a well-informed and cosmopolitan selection of new and used books and periodicals on architecture, art, design, pop culture, town planning and cultural theory. Many of the titles are in English.

RespectMen

Neue Schönhauser Strasse 14 (283 5010). U8 Weinmeisterstrasse.

Open noon-8pm Mon-Fri; noon-7pm Sat. **Map** p55 D2 ⑳

Dirk Seidel and Karin Warburg's menswear seems traditionally tailored on the rail, yet shows a body-conscious, contemporary cut when worn. Trousers, jackets, suits and coats can be made to order. They also stock Bikkembergs and Paul Smith.

RSVP

Mulackstrasse 14 (2809 4644/www. rsvp-berlin.de). U8 Weinmeisterstrasse. **Open** noon-7pm Tue-Fri; noon-6pm Sat. **Map** p55 D2 ㉑

This tiny store offers an enticing selection of stationery for the aesthete. Items carefully laid out on their shelves include Moleskine notebooks, exotic erasers, almond glue from Italy, Koh-i-noor pencils, art deco scissors, Mead Composition books, Japanese document clips and Kaweco Sport cartridge pens.

T&G

Monbijouplatz 10 (2809 5143). S5, S7, S9, S75 Hackescher Markt. **Open** 11am-8pm Mon-Fri; 10am-6pm Sat. **Map** p55 D3 ㉒

Bold and enjoyably pretentious, Tools & Gallery features fashion for men and women from the likes of Givenchy, Alexander McQueen and Vivienne Westwood, with menswear especially strong. The gallery got left behind in their old Rosenthaler Strasse location.

Trainer

Alte Schönhauser Strasse 50 (9789 4610/www.solebox.de). U8 Weinmeisterstrasse. **Open** 1-7.30pm Mon-Fri; 1-6pm Sat. **Map** p55 E2 ㉓

Trainer is the place for rare and collectable limited-edition Pumas, Nikes or Adidas, shoes that are no longer available in New York or London. Japanese tour groups have been known to descend like locusts and buy out the entire store. Sales staff are helpful and well informed.

Walking Large

Rosenthaler Strasse 32, Mitte (2804 1751/www.walking-large.de). U8

Weinmeisterstrasse. **Open** noon-8pm
Mon-Fri; 11am-8pm Sat. No credit cards.
Map p55 D2 ⁷⁴

This minimalist shoebox of a shoe
shop specialises in sleek and trendy
urban brands of trainers. Look for
footwear from the likes of Gola, Vans,
Triple5Soul, PF Flyers, Bikkembergs,
Asics and Converse.

Whisky & Cigars

Sophienstrasse 8-9 (282 0376/
www.whisky-cigars.de). S3, S5, S7,
S9, S75 Hackescher Markt. **Open**
11am-7.30pm Mon-Fri; 11am-6pm Sat.
Map p55 D2 ⁷⁵

Two friends who share a love of single
malts are behind this shop, which
stocks 450 whiskies from around the
world, and cigars from Cuba, Jamaica
and Honduras. They hold regular tasting and smoking evenings and also run
a delivery service.

Nightlife

2BE

Ziegelstrasse 23 (2630 9610/www.
2be-club.de). S1, S2 Oranienburger
Strasse or U6 Oranienburger Tor.
Open 11pm-late Fri, Sat. No credit
cards. **Map** p54 C3 ⁷⁶

Regular DJs specialise in hip hop at
this venue and club, with some reggae
and dancehall thrown in. There's also
a live act or two every month and big-
name spinners such as Grandmaster
Flash and DJ Premier do pass
through. It's a big space with a dancefloor, an outside area and several
understaffed bars.

Acud

Veteranenstrasse 21 (449 1067/
www.acud.de). U8 Rosenthaler
Platz. **Open** varies. No credit cards.
Map p55 D1 ⁷⁷

A massive complex with an alterna-tive pedigree, containing a cinema, a theatre and a gallery as well as a dancefloor that's mostly devoted to reggae, breakbeat and drum 'n' bass. The cinema programme is interesting, mostly independent and low-budget films. There's something on most nights and it's a popular spot for ston-ers, particularly the dingy bar.

B-Flat

Rosenthaler Strasse 13 (2838 6895/ www.b-flat-berlin.de). U8 Rosenthaler Platz. **Open** *from 9pm daily. No credit cards.* **Map** p55 D2 ⓐ
Maintaining a large piano-bar feel, this elegant and roomy jazz bar manages to get a decent local hero in once in a while, but its strongest nights tend to feature singers. Free Wednesday night jam session from 9pm.

Bohannon

Dircksenstrasse 40 (6950 5287/ www.bohannon.de). U2, U5, U8, S5, S7, S9, S75 Alexanderplatz or S5, S7, S9, S75 Hackescher Markt. **Open** 10pm-late Mon, Thur-Sat. No credit cards. **Map** p55 E3 ⓐ
The name, a nod to funk legend Hamilton Bohannon, indicates its driving musical principle. Billed as offering 'soulful elec-tronic clubbing', this basement location features two dancefloors and regular sets by the likes of Berlin's own Jazzanova or guest DJs such as Keb Darge.

Chamäleon

Hackesche Höfe, Rosenthaler Strasse 40-41 (400 0590/www.chamaeleon berlin.de). S5, S7, S9, S75 Hackescher Markt. **Open** *Performances 8.30pm Mon, Wed, Thur; 8.30pm, midnight Fri, Sat; 7pm Sun. No credit cards.* **Map** p55 D2 ⓐ

Sage Club p80

A new history

Back when the Wall fell, Berlin suddenly found itself with two of everything. Two national galleries, two parliament buildings, two central stations – and two competing versions of German history. The Federal Republic was planning its own history museum; East Germany had the Museum der deutschen Geschichte, presenting the Marxist-Leninist take on events in Zeughaus on Unter den Linden.

That building now houses the **Deutsches Historisches Museum** (German Historical Museum; p56), which, after 15 years of careful planning and agonised deliberation, is finally presenting the unified version of German history. The exhibition, which opened in June 2006, offers a comprehensive and rather breathtaking tour through the past, from the age of Germanic tribes around 1000 BC to the reunification period of 1989-94.

'Time columns' guide you around the experience with artefacts, artwork and costumes adding colour to earlier periods. Film footage, propaganda posters and newsreels document the modern era. Two exhibits of note are models of the planned Great Hall of the People, showpiece for the intended Nazi capital of Germania, and an intricate and deeply moving model of Crematorium II from Auschwitz.

While on the premises, don't miss the museum's stunning new wing by IM Pei, of Louvre pyramid fame, used to house temporary exhibitions.

Stunning acrobats combined with music theatre is the focus at this beautiful old cabaret theatre. As Hackesche Höfe becomes increasingly commercialised, there's a risk that this place may get blanded out. But for now it attracts a very diverse audience and is the most comfortable and affordable revue house.

Kaffee Burger

Torstrasse 60 (2804 6495/www. kaffeeburger.de). U2 Rosa-Luxemburg-Platz. **Open** 8pm-late Mon-Thur; 9pm-late Fri, Sat; 7pm-late Sun. No credit cards. **Map** p55 E2 **③**

Best known as home of the popular twice-monthly Russendisko, Kaffee Burger's eclectic programme runs the cultural gamut from readings and lectures, through film screenings and live music to DJs in every idiom. The decor has been left intact from GDR days. The crowd is mixed and international; drinks are cheap.

Mudd Club

Grosse Hamburger Strasse 17 (4403 6299/www.muddclub.de). S5, S7, S9, S75 Hackescher Markt. **Open** varies; call for information. No credit cards. **Map** p55 D2 **②**

This brick-lined basement space is owned by Steve Mass, who founded the original NYC club of yore. Band booking emphasises loveable losers such as Mark Lanegan or the Dirty Three, but there are East European connections too.

Ruder Club-Mitte

NEW *Kleine Präsidentenstrasse 157-158, am Monbijoupark (no phone/ www.ruderclub-mitte.de). S5, S7, S9, S75 Hackescher Markt.* **Open** 10pm-6am Thur-Sat. No credit cards. **Map** p55 D3 **③**

Dark and slightly difficult-to-find cavern (it's under the S-Bahn arches facing the river on the edge of the park) with an excellent soundsystem for harder-edged electronic music of various genres – from nu-beat EBM and techno to wet&hard parties presented by the Flesh label. No minimal techno, and not many people over 30.

Arts & leisure

Kino Babylon Berlin-Mitte
Rosa-Luxemburg-Strasse 30 (242 5076/www.babylonberlin.de). U2 Rosa-Luxemburg-Platz. No credit cards. **Map** p55 E2 ㉞

This former East German premier theatre is in a landmark building by Hans Poelzig, who designed the classic German silent film *The Golem*. After years of renovation, it's back to its full Weimar glory and worth a visit just for that. The cosy auxiliary kino around the corner offers more original-language programming and assorted surprises.

Sophiensaele
Sophienstrasse 18, Mitte (information 2789 0030/tickets 283 5266/www.sophiensaele.com). U8 Weinmeisterstrasse or S5, S7, S9, S75 Hackescher Markt. No credit cards. **Map** p55 D2 ㉟

Expect a contemporary programme of dance, theatre, music and opera, with up-and-coming groups from around the world. If avant-garde is ever crowd-pleasing, then this is where you'll find it. The largest of the off-theatres, Sophiensaele is a venue for an assortment of theatre and dance festivals.

Volksbühne
Rosa-Luxemburg-Platz, Linienstrasse 227 (247 6772/www.volksbuehne-berlin.de). U2 Rosa-Luxemburg-Platz. **Map** p55 E2 ㊱

Christoph Schlingensief's productions at east Berlin's premier avant-garde theatre (the name means 'People's Stage') guarantee a love/hate reaction. The wood-panelled stage has also played host to the likes of Franz Ferdinand and Aphex Twin. The building is home to the hip, eclectic Roter and Grüner Salons. Former after-hours hangouts for the East German theatre elite, these two very different halls retain their old-style decor and reek of nostalgia in spite of hosting a wide range of indie acts, DJs and other events.

With the **Fernsehturm** (television tower) visible from all over the city, and with its role as a major public transport hub, Alexanderplatz is a point of orientation. The **Rotes Rathaus** on its western side is the city's (red) town hall. Alexanderplatz proper is the square on the other side of the S-Bahn tracks, a vast open space whose communist and Weimar buildings are still being renovated. Among the housing blocks to the south, a huge mall is under construction. There are scattered points of interest between here and Kreuzberg, and east along Karl-Marx-Allee to Friedrichshain.

Sights & museums

Fernsehturm
Panoramastrasse 1A (242 3333/www.berlinerfernsehturm.de). U2, U5, U8, S5, S7, S9, S75 Alexanderplatz. **Open** Mar-Oct 9am-1am daily. Nov-Feb 10am-midnight daily. **Admission** €6.80; €3.50 reductions. **Map** p55 E3 ㊲

Built in the late 1960s, the 365m (1,198ft) Television Tower intended to be an assertion of communist dynamism and modernity, and became one of the central symbols of the East German capital. Today its ball-on-spike shape is one of Berlin's signature graphic images. Take an ear-popping trip up to the observation platform; the view is unbeatable night or day, and there's a revolving restaurant.

Marienkirche
Karl-Liebknecht-Strasse 8 (242 4467/www.marienkirche-berlin.de). U2, U5, U8, S5, S7, S9, S75 Alexanderplatz. **Open** Apr-Oct 10am-6pm daily. Nov-Mar 10am-4pm daily. **Admission** free. **Map** p55 E3 ㊳

Begun in 1270, this is one of Berlin's few remaining medieval buildings. Just inside the door is a wonderful 1485

Dance of Death fresco, while the 18th-century Walther organ is considered that famous builder's masterpiece.

Nightlife

Café Moskau

Karl-Marx-Allee 34 (2463 1626/ www.das-moskau.com). U2, U5, U8, S5, S7, S9, S75 Alexanderplatz or U5 Schillingstrasse. No credit cards. **Map** p55 F3 69

This marvel of socialist architecture was once the hotspot for party appa-ratchiks. These days its array of spaces host a variety of regular one-nighters and one-off events, from left-field fashion shows to world-class DJs – and the downstairs dancefloor is a surprisingly intimate place to see them. The Sunday GMF gay night is always packed.

Golden Gate

Dircksenstrasse 77-8 (no phone/ www.goldengate-berlin.de). U8, S5, S7, S9, S75 Jannowitzbrücke. **Open** from 11pm Fri, Sat. No credit cards. **Map** p55 F4 90

Located beneath Jannowitzbrücke U-Bahn, Golden Gate is accessed from that station's exit in Schicklerstrasse (look for where the bicycles are parked). Down below you'll find plenty of drunken locals crowded into a small space with an informal living-room feel. There's a varied selection of DJs and a tiny stage that sometimes hosts surprisingly popular bands, such as Comets on Fire, as well as electro-cabaret events.

Kinzo Club

Karl-Liebknecht-Strasse 11 (2887 3883/www.kinzo-berlin.de). U2, U5, U8, S5, S7, S9, S75 Alexanderplatz. **Open** 11pm-late Thur-Sat. No credit cards. **Map** p55 E3 91

This minimalist, cutting-edge club is on the cusp of nightlife and media arts, boasting top DJs such as Chica and the Folder, Erobique, Le Hammond Inferno or Eric D of Whirlpool Productions, plus VJ sets, film screenings and sound art. The place has a gay vibe, though all types show up.

Sage Club

Köpenicker Strasse 76 (278 9830/www. sage-club.de). U8 Heinrich-Heine-Strasse. **Open** 10pm-late Thur; 11pm-late Fri-Sun. No credit cards. **Map** p55 F5 92

A warrenous complex of half-a-dozen dancefloors and bars under Heinrich-Heine-Strasse station, catering to a youngish, fashion-conscious crowd. Nights are themed: Thursday is rock, Friday R&B and hip hop, Saturday house and electro, Sunday techno. In a separate part of the complex, the Cantina Berlin Barcelona hosts club nights.

Sternradio

Alexanderplatz 5 (2462 59320/ www.sternradio-berlin.de). U2, U5, U8, S5, S7, S9, S75 Alexanderplatz. No credit cards. **Map** p55 E3 93

Named after an old East German radio brand and located in a typical late 1960s edifice, this place was considered déclassé until punters started grooving on the Ostalgie of the architecture. So now it's popular – even sort of hip. The DJ menu varies from techno to hip hop.

Week12End Club

Alexanderplatz 5, 12th floor (no phone/ www.week-end-berlin.de). U2, U5, U8, S5, S7, S9, S75 Alexanderplatz. **Open** 11pm-late Thur, Fri, Sat. **Map** p55 E3 94

Super-chic but only moderately pretentious club on the 12th floor of an office building. Biggish names often take the turntables, such as Richie Hawtin or the 2ManyDJs and DFA crews, and occasionally there are live acts too. Whatever's on, it's almost worth visiting just for the location and view.

Arts & leisure

Dokument Kino

NEW *Rungestrasse 20, Mitte (2759 5895/www.dokument-kino.de). U8 Heinrich-Heine-Strasse or U8, S5, S7, S9, S75 Jannowitzbrücke*. No credit cards. **Map** p55 F5 95

The newest addition to Berlin's off-cinemas shows all documentaries all the time, on potentially any subject you can name. Located in a cosy upstairs space on the border of Mitte and Kreuzberg.

Saint Georges p88

Prenzlauer Berg

Prenzlauer Berg spreads up the hill north-east of Mitte. A residential district and the most beautiful borough of east Berlin, it is devoid of landmark sights but has a busy cultural life and several focal points. The area around Kollwitzplatz and the Wasserturm (water tower) along Knaackstrasse has a sedate but convivial scene of cafés and restaurants. More alternative venues are clustered in the 'LSD' area around Lychener Strasse, Stargarder Strasse and Duncker Strasse. Kastanienallee is the area's most happening main thoroughfare, and blends into the Mitte North nightlife quarter at its southern extremity. At its northern end, Kastanienallee meets Schönhauser Allee, Prenzlauer Berg's main street. This leads north into east Berlin's gay district.

Eating & drinking

8mm

Schönhauser Allee 177B (4050 0624/www.8mmbar.com). U2 Senefelderplatz. **Open** 9pm-late daily. No credit cards. **Bar**. Map p83 B3 ❶

Here the attractive, young and poor go for that fifth nightcap into incoherence at around 6am and local scenesters rub shoulders with anglophone expats. There seems to be more hard alcohol consumed in this purple-walled dive than in your average Berlin hangout and, yes, sometimes films are shown, should anyone still be in a fit state to watch them.

Gugelhof

An einem Sonntag im August

NEW *Kastanienallee 103 (4405 1228). U2 Eberswalder Strasse.* **Open** 9am-late daily. No credit cards. **Café/bar**. **Map** p83 B2 ②

Named after a song by Berlin's Element of Crime, this mixed and friendly café/bar with its show-stealing 1970s am-dram interior (love the gold curtains!) is one of Kastanienallee's quirkiest, attracting a happy, dressed-down crowd.

Anna Blume

Kollwitzstrasse 83 (4404 8749/ www.cafe-anna-blume.de). U2 Eberswalder Strasse. **Open** 8am-2am daily. **Café**. **Map** p83 B2 ③

Café and florist rolled into one and named after a dada poem by Kurt Schwitters. The pastries are expensive but of high quality, the terrace is a good spot in summer, and the subdued interior, not surprisingly, smells of flowers.

Becketts Kopf

Pappelallee 64 (0162 237 9418). U2 Eberswalder Strasse. **Open** 8pm-4am Tue-Sun. No credit cards. **Bar**. **Map** p83 B1 ④

The head of Samuel Beckett stares from the window of this red-walled, intimate spot, which prides itself on expert cocktails and a variety of scotches and whiskeys. Prices are about average for mixed drinks in Berlin (around €7.50) but quality is several notches above.

Café Morgenrot

Kastanienallee 85 (4431 7844). U2 Eberswalder Strasse. **Open** 10am-1am Tue-Fri; 11-3am Sat, Sun. No credit cards. **Café**. **Map** p83 A2 ⑤

See box p129.

Café Oberwasser

Zionskirchstrasse 6 (448 3719). U8 Bernauer Strasse/tram M1 Zionskirchplatz. **Open** 6pm-late Mon-Sat. **€€**. No credit cards. **Russian/vegetarian**. **Map** p83 A2 ⑥

This cosy bistro-type restaurant with dim lighting and overstuffed furniture may look a bit second-hand but after a drink or two it feels like having dinner in the attic of some faded aristocrat. The food is a mostly vegetarian combination of Russian and non-Russian cuisine, freshly prepared.

EKA

*Dunckerstrasse 9 (4372 0612/www.
eka-leka.de). U2 Eberswalder Strasse.*
Open noon-late daily. No credit cards.
Café. Map p83 B1 **7**
This comfortable café resembles a 1940s
US soda shop reimagined as a livery sta-
ble. Berlin always finds a way to sneak
beer into an afternoon of coffee and
cake, and EKA is no exception, serving
both Bock and Portuguese brews.
Although in no way set up for it, it also
manages to sneak in a DJ sometimes.

Entweder Oder

*Oderberger Strasse 15 (448 1382/www.
cafe-eo.de). U2 Eberswalder Strasse.*
Open 10am-11.30 daily. **€€**. No credit
cards. **German**. Map p83 A2 **8**
German food with a light touch: roasts,
grilled fish and the occasional schnitzel
cosy up to fresh salads and simple pota-

to side dishes. The menu changes daily
and everything is organic. Connected to
the underground art scene back in the
days of the Wall, this place still rotates
new work by local artists.

Gugelhof

*Knaackstrasse 37 (442 9229/www.
gugelhof.de). U2 Senefelderplatz.* **Open**
4pm-1am Mon-Fri; 10am-1am Sat, Sun.
€€€. **German**. Map p83 B2 **9**
A mature Alsatian restaurant that
pioneered the Kollwitzplatz scene in the
1990s. The food is refined but filling, the
service formal but friendly and the furnishings comfortably worn in. The
Backöfe – lamb, pork and beef marinated in riesling, stewed and presented in
an earthenware pot with root vegetables
– shows the kitchen at its most characterful. Alsatian tartes flambées and a
good wine list are further draws.

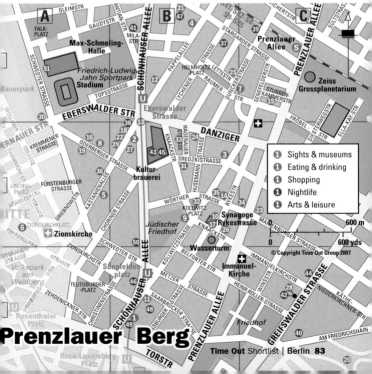

Hausbar

Rykestrasse 54 (no phone). U2 Senefelderplatz. **Open** 7pm-5am daily. No credit cards. **Bar**. **Map** p83 B2 ⑩
Bright red and gold, with a cherub-filled sky on the ceiling, this small pocket of fabulousness seats about 15 people at a push. Hausbar is more fun than many of the more pretentious cafés nearby, and it's particularly inviting at three or four in the morning.

I Due Forni

Schönhauser Allee 12 (4401 7333). U2 Senefelderplatz. **Open** noon-1am daily. **€€**. No credit cards. **Italian**. **Map** p83 B3 ⑪
The punky staff look more likely to bounce you than tease your tastebuds. But in a city of cheap pizzas baked by Turks or Palestinians pretending to be Italian, the stone-oven pizza here stands out for being authentic and very tasty.

Klub der Republik

Pappelallee 81 (no phone). U2 Eberswalder Strasse. **Open** 8pm-4am daily. No credit cards. **Bar**. **Map** p83 B1 ⑫
Accessed via a wobbly staircase in the courtyard, this spacious bar manages to mix the best of the retro design craze with the sort of lively revelry associated with the east in the mid 1990s. The range of beers is gratifyingly wide and the DJs are top notch, playing anything from 1960s soul to jazz fusion to electronica.

Konnopke's Imbiss

Under U-Bahn tracks, corner of Danziger Strasse/Schönhauser Allee (442 7765). U2 Eberswalder Strasse. **Open** 6am-8pm Mon-Fri; noon-7pm Sat. **€**. No credit cards. **German**. **Map** p83 B1 ⑬
This justly famous sausage stand under the U2 line has been managed by the Ziervogel family since 1930 and introduced the Currywurst to East Berlin in 1960. Lunching workers, politicians after the common touch, passing scenesters – everyone eats at Konnopke's.

Mao Thai

Wörther Strasse 30 (441 9261). U2 Senefelderplatz. **Open** noon-midnight daily. **€€€**. **Thai**. **Map** p83 B2 ⑭
Charming service and excellent food comes with a 'to whom it may concern' testimonial from the Thai ambassador, framed on the stairs down to the lower level. Classics such as *tom kai gai*, green papaya salad with peanuts, vegetarian spring rolls, and glass noodle salad with minced pork are all spectacular. Well established, comfortable and friendly.

Miro

Raumerstrasse 29 (4473 3013). S8, S41, S42, S85 Prenzlauer Allee. **Open** 10am-late daily. **€€**. **Turkish**. **Map** p83 C1 ⑮
This cool, roomy place serves Anatolian specialities and well-priced drinks. The menu is long and intriguing, with many vegetarian possibilities, legions of starters and a good salad selection – all of which arrive in generous proportions.

Oki

Oderberger Strasse 23 (4985 3130). U2 Eberswalder Strasse. **Open** 3pm-11pm Tue-Sun. **€€**. No credit cards. **German/Japanese**. **Map** p83 A2 ⑯
This small, bright local successfully fuses north German food with Japanese delights in dishes such as potato soup with shiitake mushrooms or *Tafelspitz* with stir-fried vegetables and rice. It sounds odd but it's excellent. Traditional sashimi, sushi, tempura and udon noodles are also on the small menu.

Pasternak

Knaackstrasse 22-4 (441 3399/ www.restaurant-pasternak.de). U2 Senefelderplatz. **Open** 10am-1am daily. **€€**. **Russian**. **Map** p83 B2 ⑰
Small bar and Russian restaurant that's often crammed, which can be irritating at some tables – try for one in the small side room. The atmosphere is friendly and the food fine and filling. Kick off with borscht or the ample fish plate, then broach the hearty beef stroganoff.

Eisdieler p88

Prater

Kastanienallee 7-9 (448 5688/www. pratergarten.de). U2 Eberswalder Strasse. **Open** 6pm-1am Mon-Sat; noon-1am Sun. €€. No credit cards. **German**. Map p83 B2 ⑬

This huge and immaculately restored swing-era beerhall attracts a smart, high-volume crowd. The big wooden tables, beer-swilling lustiness and primeval platefuls of meat and veg can almost make you feel like you're in Munich. In summer the shady beer garden makes for an all-day buzz. Brunch is served from 10am to 4pm at weekends. The Bastard@Prater (p90) club is part of the same complex.

Razzia in Budapest

Oderberger Strasse 38 (4862 3620/ www.razzia-in-budapest.de). U2 Eberswalder Strasse. **Open** 7pm-late daily. No credit cards. **Bar**. Map p83 A2 ⑲

East Berlin not Ost enough for you? This wood-panelled spot boasts a 'Hungarian' feel that veers from cosy to crazed. There's Böhmisches dark

beer on tap, and ten house cocktails with names such as 'Sommer in Budapest' and 'Razzia'. Weekend DJs serve up a diet of oldies.

Schönbrunn

Am Schwanenteich, im Volkspark Friedrichshain (4679 3893). Tram M4. **Open** 10am-1am Mon-Fri; 10am-2am Sat, Sun. **Café**. Map p83 C3 ⑳

Actually over the border in Friedrichshain, but more part of the Prenzlauer Berg scene, this is a fashionable refurbishment of the old park café by the lake. The concrete front has been left as it was, but the lounge within is furnished in retro style, and the music and food made modern. On a sunny afternoon, older park-goers take their beer on the terrace next to the in-crowd having breakfast.

Schwalbe

Stargarder Strasse 10 (4403 6208/ www.schwalbeberlin.de). U2, S8, S41, S42, S85 Schönhauser Allee. **Open** 4pm-2am Mon-Fri; 3pm-4am Sat; 3pm-2am Sun. No credit cards. **Café/bar**. Map p83 B1 ㉑

Furniture p88

Schwalbe is about as swish as a football bar gets, offering German and Italian league games in a fashionable café environment where you can have coffee and cake instead of beer, for a change. Downstairs, there are three crowded Kicker (table football) tables and DJs on Saturday.

Schwarz Sauer

Kastanienallee 13 (448 5633). U2 Eberswalder Strasse. **Open** 8am-6am daily. No credit cards. **Bar.** **Map** p83 B2 ㉒

Possibly the most popular bar on Kastanienallee and currently the main meeting place for those who inhabit the twilight zone between Prenzlauer Berg and Mitte. Strangely, its ambience is sort of plain, its waitstaff Berlin surly, and its food and drink merely adequate. But in summer the outside tables overflow day and night. In winter a tolerance for cigarette smoke is helpful.

Tea Room

NEW *Marienburger Strasse 49 (4403 1983/www.tearoomberlin.com). Tram M2 Marienburger Strasse.* **Open** noon-10pm Mon-Fri; noon-11pm Sat. No credit cards. **Café/cocktail bar.** **Map** p83 C2 ㉓

This beautiful but eccentric New Yorker-run hybrid offers tea and cocktails (and cocktails made with tea) as well as sandwiches on unusual breads and excellent dim sum. Eat and drink at the handsome bar, or take advantage of tables outside, out back, or in the non-smoking side room.

Trattoria Paparazzi

Husemannstrasse 35 (440 7333). U2 Eberswalder Strasse. **Open** 6pm-1.30am daily. **€€€.** No credit cards. **Italian.** **Map** p83 B2 ㉔

Behind the daft name and ordinary façade is one of Berlin's best Italians. Cornerstone dishes are *malfatti* (pasta rolls seasoned with sage) and *strangolapretti* ('priest stranglers' of pasta, cheese and spinach with slivers of ham), but pay attention to the daily specials. House wines are excellent, though there are few other choices. Booking is essential.

Wohnzimmer

Lettestrasse 6 (445 5458). U2 Eberswalder Strasse. **Open** 10am-4am daily. No credit cards. **Café.** **Map** p83 B1 ㉕

This shabbily elegant 'living room' has a bar-like structure made from an inspired ensemble of kitchen cabinets. Threadbare divans and artsy bar girls make this the perfect place to discuss Dostoevsky's works with career students over a tepid borscht. Evening light from candelabra reflects on gold-sprayed walls; daytimes can, however, be sluggish.

Yes

NEW *Knaackstrasse 14 (no phone/www.yes-berlin.de). U2 Knaackstrasse.* **Open** 8pm-late Mon-Sat. No credit cards. **Bar.** **Map** p83 B2 ㉖

This cosy bar has been designed with love by its young architect owner, usually to be found pouring Schweinfurter Brauhaus from the tap, or explaining that he imported the tables from Madrid. A low-key but welcome addition to the Wasserturm area.

Shopping

DaCapo Records

Kastanienallee 96 (4434 0290). U2 Eberswalder Strasse. **Open** 11am-7pm Tue-Fri; 11am-4pm Sat. **Map** p83 B2 ㉗

A pricey but wide selection of used vinyl that includes lots of old releases from the East German label Amiga. There are also plenty of rare 1950s 10-inch albums and jazz 45s.

D-Fens

Greifswalder Strasse 224 (4434 2250/www.d-fens-berlin.de). Tram M4 Am Friedrichshain. **Open** noon-7pm Mon-Fri; noon-3pm Sat. No credit cards. **Map** p83 C3 ㉘

This small DJ shop in a revamped garage specialises in house, electro, trance, techno and disco. Owner Ralph Ballschuh, a DJ himself, is happy to turn up the volume on any track you wish. D-Fens is tricky to find – your best bet is to follow the signs for the Knaack club (p91).

Eisdieler

Kastanienallee 12 (2839 1291/
www.eisdieler.de). U2 Eberswalder
Strasse. **Open** noon-8pm Mon-Fri;
noon-7pm Sat. **Map** p83 B2 ㉙
Five young designers pooled their
resources and each manages a label
under the Eisdieler banner – clubwear,
second-hand gear, casualwear and
street style. Till Fuhrmann's jewellery,
crafted from silver and wood, is particularly distinctive.

Flohmarkt am Mauerpark

Bernauer Strasse 63-4 (0176 2925
0021). U2 Eberswalder Strasse.
Open 7am-5pm Sun. **Map** p83 A1 ㉚
One of the biggest and busiest flea markets for everything from cheap Third
World fashion to cardboard boxes of
black-market CDs. It's probably better
for household knick-knacks and local
delicacies than it is for vintage finds.
There's a family vibe.

Furniture

Sredzkistrasse 22 (4434 2157).
U2 Eberswalder Strasse. **Open** 12.30-
7pm Tue, Fri; 2-7pm Wed; 12.30-8pm
Thur; 12.30-4pm Sat. No credit cards.
Map p83 B2 ㉛
This is a reasonably priced and well-
thought-out selection of retro furniture, TVs, radios and lamps. Lots of
plastic in burnt orange and brown and
luscious olive green, and a huge,
enjoyable range of wallpaper from the
1960s and '70s.

Kollwitzplatz Market

Kollwitzplatz. U2 Senefelderplatz. **Open**
11am-4pm Thur, Sat. **Map** p83 B2 ㉜
Open-air food markets are still rare in
the east. This one is a small, unassum-
ing organic market. Steaming punch
and wholegrain cinnamon waffles
make it *gemütlich* in winter, but it's
more lively in summer.

Mane Lange Korsetts

Hagenauer Strasse 13 (0179 201
2602/www.manelange.de). U2
Eberswalder Strasse. **Open** by
appointment only. No credit cards.
Map p83 B2 ㉝

Lovely original corsets in lush materials are handmade on the premises
by local designer Mane Lange.
Bustiers come off the rack; bespoke
orders require a fitting but are completed in 24 hours.

Saint Georges

Wörther Strasse 27 (8179 8333/
www.saintgeorgesbookshop.com).
Tram M2 Marienburger Strasse.
Open 11am-8pm Mon-Fri; 11am-7pm
Sat. **Map** p83 C2 ㉞
Comfortable leather couches are provided for browsing a decent and
reasonably priced selection of second-
hand English-language books. Lots of
biographies and contemporary lit, and
a good turnover of dog-eared classics.

Scuderi

Wörther Strasse 32 (4737 4240).
U2 Senefelderplatz. **Open** 11am-7pm
Mon-Fri; 11am-3pm Sat. **Map** p83 B2 ㉟
The four women who share this space
work magic with gold, silver, pearls,
stones and hand-rolled glass, creating
lightweight jewellery that makes a
strong statement.

Skunkfunk

Kastanienallee 19 & 20 (4403 3800/
www.skunkfunk.com). U2 Eberswalder
Strasse. **Open** noon-8pm Mon-Fri;
noon-7pm Sat. **Map** p83 A2 ㊱
Spanish urban label with adjacent
stores that house men's and women's
wear in lush cotton, fruity to earthy
colours, and asymmetric styles.
Jackets are streamlined and men's
jeans baggy and beautifully tailored.
The name is on everything, sometimes
a little obvious, sometimes within a
charming detail.

Nightlife

Ausland

Lychener Strasse 60 (447 7008/
www.ausland-berlin.de). U2
Eberswalder Strasse. **Open** varies.
No credit cards. **Map** p83 B1 ㊲
A tiny basement run by a bunch of
nutty bohos offering experimental
music – noise, free jazz, avant-folk and

Icon p91

live electronica – plus film and installations. It can get packed when a top act, such as Acid Mothers Temple, stops by. Note that concerts begin one hour later than the time posted – on principle, apparently. There's usually a DJ after the show.

Bastard@Prater
Kastanienallee 7-9 (4404 9669/ www.praterteam.de). U2 Eberswalder Strasse. **Open** varies. No credit cards. **Map** p83 B2 ❸❽

Connected to the Prater beer garden (p85), this many-chandeliered spot veers between first-rate indie rock tunes, over-the-hill and up-and-coming underground hip hop and DJ nights favouring hardcore gabba, ragga and jungle music.

Duncker
Dunckerstrasse 64 (445 9509/ www.dunckerclub.de). U2 Eberswalder Strasse or S8, S41, S42, S85

Prenzlauer Allee. **Open** 9pm-late Mon; 10pm-late Tue, Thur, Sun; 11pm-late Fri, Sat. No credit cards. **Map** p83 C1 ❸❾

A GDR-era institution in a neo-Gothic building, where time seems to stand still. Monday is Goth night, while the rest of the week is devoted to music ranging from the 1960s to modern-day indie and electro.

GeburtstagsKlub
Am Friedrichshain 33 (4202 1406/ www.geburtstagsklub.de). Tram M4 am Friedrichshain. **Open** 11pm-late Mon, Fri, Sat. No credit cards. **Map** p83 C3 ❹❶

House, breakbeats, electro, funk and disco music boom loud in this subterranean establishment, decorated with light and slide projections. Reggae, ragga and dancehall feature on Monday nights. There are also monthly drag performances.

Knaack

Icon

*Cantianstrasse 15 (4849 2878/
www.iconberlin.de). U2 Eberswalder
Strasse.* **Open** 11pm-late Tue;
11.30pm-late Fri, Sat. No credit
cards. **Map** p83 B1 ④

A tricky-to-locate entrance in the courtyard leads to an interesting space cas-
cading down into a long stone cellar
with an intense dancefloor space, imaginative lighting, good sound and a separate bar. Sounds vary from breakbeat
and drum 'n' bass to reggae and hip
hop. Ninja Tune DJs have a monthly
night, and jungle legends such as
Grooverider often spin.

Knaack

*Greifswalder Strasse 224, Prenzlauer
Berg (concerts 442 7061/club 442
7060/www.knaack-berlin.de). Tram
M4 Hufelandstrasse.* **Open** *Bar* 6pm-
late daily. *Club* 8pm-late Wed; 9pm-late
Fri, Sat. No credit cards. **Map** p83 C3 ④

Follow the Rammstein-ish bar to the
back, enter a narrow hallway, and
you'll find a small, dark club. Knaack
books an eclectic array of excellent acts,
from the Rapture to RA the Rugged
Man to Michael Hurley. It also hosts
free nights of local bands, which are
usually less impressive. Disco upstairs.

Kulturbrauerei

*Schönhauser Allee 35 (443 1515/
www.kesselhaus-berlin.de). U2
Eberswalder Strasse.* **Open** varies.
No credit cards. **Map** p83 B2 ④

There's an assortment of venues within
this enormous former brewery which,
with its outdoor bars and barbecues, can
resemble a cross between a medieval
fairground and a school disco.
Kesselhaus, Maschinehaus and Palas
are the three venues linked to the
Kulturbrauerei proper (unlike nbi; see
below) and host diverse acts in a similar
vein. Kesselhaus is the largest, drawing
its biggest crowds for reggae concerts.

Magnet

*Greifswalder Strasse 212/3, Prenzlauer
Berg (4400 8140/www.magnet-club.de).
Tram M4 Hufelandstrasse.* **Open** 8pm-
late daily. No credit cards. **Map** p83 C3 ④

Once a jazz club, this venue has
become one of the biggest bookers
of up-and-coming *NME*-type indie
bands. Recent renovations have
improved the sight lines, though it can
still be difficult to navigate a peek
when the place fills up.

nbi

NEW *Kulturbrauerei, Schönhauser
Allee 36 (4405 1681/www.neue
berlinerinitiative.de). U2 Eberswalder
Strasse.* **Open** 6pm-late daily. No
credit cards. **Map** p83 B2 ④

Recently moved to the Kulturbrauerei,
the latest space for this electroclub pioneer is a pink box sprinkled with furniture in the *Wohnzimmer* style.
Excellent sound system, though, and
several nights per month are given to
labels and promoters such as Monika
and RepeatRepeat, which leads to such
surprises as Einstürzende Neubauten
popping in. The space doesn't lend
itself to dancing, so electronic music
has been de-emphasised.

Pfefferbank

*Schönhauser Allee 176A (281
8323/www.pfefferbank.de). U2
Senefelderplatz.* **Open** 11pm-late Fri,
Sat. No credit cards. **Map** p83 B3 ④

Behind a semi-hidden door located
near the main entrance to the massive
Pfefferberg brewery complex, a reviv-
ified booking policy is bringing au
courant DJs and live acts, such as
Optimo and the Locust, to this under-
attended, bunker-like spot. With
nightlife starting to pool along the bottom of Schönhauser Allee, this place is
finally finding its feet.

Pick Ab!

*Greifenhagener Strasse 16 (445 8523).
U2, S8, S41, S42, S85 Schönhauser
Allee.* **Open** 10pm-6am Mon-Fri, Sun;
10pm-noon Sat. No credit cards.
Map p83 B1 ④

This late-night cruise bar was decorated by someone with very camp taste.
The place fills up best during the winter months, when the heated back-
rooms are more comfortable for
cruising than the freezing parks.

BERLIN BY AREA

Let's get trashed

Underground stalwart White Trash makes even more noise.

Having received a record 168 complaints about the noise, **White Trash Fast Food** (p93) has abandoned the poky former Chinese restaurant it occupied on Torstrasse and reopened in vast new premises at the bottom of Schönhauser Allee.

The brand remains the same: an alternative bar with a rebellious attitude specialising in country and rock 'n' roll. It's just that now there's much more room for it, including a cave-like basement club space called Diamond Lounge where they can crank up the volume as loud as they damn well please. And there is still decent food – comprised of burgers and Tex-Mex – though it was never exactly fast in the first place.

Trash decor includes two Chinese lions guarding the entrance, and a pagoda and mural inside, all brought along from the old place. Original features here, dating from its time as an Irish pub, include the pillars, arches and stairwells of the bar area, which spreads across three levels. White Trash has added its own touch – blood-red paint, specially mixed for the establishment.

A formerly snooty door policy (they notoriously refused entry to Bruce Willis) has been relaxed a bit in the interest of filling the place. The hardcore, hard-drinking clientele of rowdy intellectuals and tattooed rebels has become a little diluted by straighter types. But there's still usually a long queue to get in and White Trash can still justly take pride in a certain authenticity – you might not like country music, but at least you know you're going to hear the good stuff.

In essence, White Trash is just the latest incarnation of a scene that stretches back decades. Underground bars full of radical country fans in black leather have been a feature since the days when Nick Cave assembled the band that still backs him today. (The last hold-out on the western side is the notorious Ex 'n' Pop (p122) on Potsdamer Strasse.)

A continuing White Trash tradition is the tattoo service, now occupying the shop next door. A tattoo costs nothing if you have their name within the design – a lifetime souvenir of a big night out.

Kulturbrauerei p91

Roadrunners Club

*Saarbrücker Strasse 24 (448 5755/
www.roadrunners-paradise.de). U2
Senefelderplatz.* **Open** 8pm-late Fri,
Sat. No credit cards. **Map** p83 B3 ➍➑
It takes a bit of wandering around the
grounds of a disused brewery to find
this club decked out in 1950s
Americana, but it's worth it for fans of
rockabilly, country, surf, burlesque
and suchlike. The stage is small, but
there's plenty of room for dancing – to
both live acts and DJs.

White Trash Fast Food

NEW *Schönhauser Allee 6-7 (no
phone/www.whitetrashfastfood.com).
U2 Senefelderplatz.* **Open** 4pm-late
daily. No credit cards. **Map** p83 B3 ➍➒
Recently relocated to this enormous red-
draped edifice, Berlin's hardest-drinking
alternative nightlife institution is going
from strength. The drunken expat white
trash of White Trash appear set on
world domination, with multiple floors,
a *Flintstones*-style cave in the basement,
nightly DJs (who can finally crank up
the country and electro without the
neighbours complaining), gutter-
dwelling live acts and the usual, above-
average American cuisine of sadly
shrinking proportions. See box p92.

Zentrale Randlage

*Schönhauser Allee 172 (no phone/
www.zentrale-randlage.de). U2
Senefelderplatz.* **Open** varies.
No credit cards. **Map** p83 B2 ➎➊
A prime exponent of the clubhouse
trend, with old couches and a serving
hatch rather than a bar. It wouldn't
immediately strike you as a party
space – the entrance suggests a high-
school gym – but it packs for live acts
and local DJs. Music ranges from
avant-jazz to electro-rock, but weekends are for dancing.

Arts & leisure

Max-Schmeling-Halle

*Am Falkplatz (443 045/tickets 4430
4430/www.max-schmeling-halle.de).
U2 Eberswalder Strasse or U2, S8,
S41, S42, S85 Schönhauser Allee.*
Map p83 A1 ➎➊
Named after the German boxer who
knocked out the seemingly invincible
Joe Louis in 1936, this state-of-the-art
indoor arena is better known as the
home of Berlin's basketball hotshots
ALBA (www.albaberlin.de). The 11,000-
capacity hall hosts a variety of international sporting events, rock concerts
and conferences.

Neue Nationalgalerie p99

Tiergarten

Tiergarten takes its name from the huge, wooded park that is the district's central feature. A former hunting-ground for the Prussian electors, it was severely damaged during World War II, had all its trees chopped down for firewood in the desperate winter of 1945-46, and was slowly restored thereafter. During the Cold War, the Wall ran down its eastern side. Now the Tiergarten is once again the link between Mitte and Charlottenburg, a beautiful park that, even when full of joggers, cyclists and sunbathers, rarely feels very crowded.

At the park's north-eastern end is the **Reichstag**, the new government quarter and Berlin's futuristic new **Hauptbahnhof**. At its south-west corner is Berlin's **Zoo**, and east of that the diplomatic district, now replete with gleaming new embassies. The postmodern towers and arcades of **Potsdamer Platz** lie at the south-eastern corner, spilling over the border into Mitte and Kreuzberg.

Sights & museums

Bauhaus Archiv
Klingelhöferstrasse 14 (254 0020/ www.bauhaus.de). Bus M29, 100, 187. **Open** 10am-5pm Mon, Wed-Sun. **Admission** €6-€7; €3-€4 reductions. No credit cards. **Map** p96 C4 ❶
Walter Gropius, founder of the Bauhaus, designed the elegant white building that now houses this absorbing design museum. The permanent exhibition presents furniture, ceramics, prints, sculptures, photographs and sketches created at the Bauhaus between 1919 and 1933 (when the school was closed by the Nazis). There

are also first-rate temporary exhibitions and an interesting gift shop offering 250 items for home or office.

DaimlerChrysler Contemporary

Alte Potsdamer Strasse 5 (2594 1420/ www.sammlung.daimlerchrysler.com). U2, S1, S2, S25 Potsdamer Platz. **Open** 11am-6pm daily. **Admission** free. **Map** p97 F4 ②

DaimlerChrysler's collection is serious stuff. It has stuck to the 20th century, and covers abstract, conceptual and minimalist art; its collection numbers around 1,300 works from artists such as Josef Albers, Max Bill, Walter de Maria, Jeff Koons and Andy Warhol, which the gallery rotates in themed portions.

Filmmuseum Berlin

Sony Center, Potsdamer Strasse 2 (300 9030/www.filmmuseum-berlin. de). U2, S1, S2, S25 Potsdamer Platz. **Open** 10am-6pm Tue, Wed, Fri-Sun; 10am-8pm Thur. **Admission** €6; €4 reductions. No credit cards. **Map** p97 E3 ③

This well-designed exhibition space chronicles the history of German cinema. Striking exhibits include the two-storey-high video wall of disasters from Fritz Lang's adventure films and a morgue-like exhibition space devoted to films from the Third Reich. The main attraction, though, is the Marlene Dietrich collection – personal effects, home movies, designer clothes and correspondence. Exhibitions are often accompanied by films at the Arsenal cinema (p104) downstairs.

Gemäldegalerie

Stauffenbergstrasse 40 (266 2101/ www.smb.spk-berlin.de). U2, S1, S2, S25 Potsdamer Platz. **Open** 10am-6pm Tue, Wed, Fri-Sun; 10am-10pm Thur. **Admission** €8; €4 reductions. No credit cards. **Map** p97 E4 ④

The Picture Gallery's first-rate early European painting collection features a healthy selection of the biggest names in Western art. Highlights are the Dutch and Flemish pieces. There are around 20 Rembrandts and a couple of Franz Hals's finest works. Other highlights include a version of Botticelli's *Venus Rising* and Correggio's brilliant *Leda with the Swan*. An exhibition of Karl Schinkel's frames runs until 31 July 2007.

Café Einstein p100

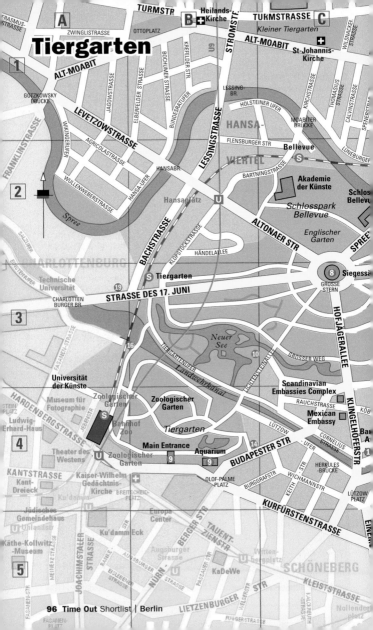

Tiergarten

Map legend:
- **1** Sights & museums
- **1** Eating & drinking
- **1** Shopping
- **1** Nightlife
- **1** Arts & leisure

Labels on map:

D | **E** | **F**

1

Krankenaus D. Bell. Vollzuganst.
Von-Ostzky-Park
OTTO-DIX-STRASSE
LESSER-URY-WEG
INVALIDENSTRASSE
Haupt-bahnhof
ALT-MOABIT
W-BRANDT-ST
KRONPRINZENUFER
MOLTKEBR.
MOABITSTRASSE
WERFTSTRASSE
LÜNEBURGER STRASSE
KULTSTRASSE
Swiss Embassy
OTTO-VON-BISMARCK ALLEE
SCHIFFBAUERDAMM
LUISENSTR
MARIENSTR
Bundeskanzleramt
PAUL-LÖBE-
ALLEE
Paul Löbe Haus
PLATZ DER REPUBLIK
REICHSTAGUFER
MARSHALL-BR
MARSHALL-BR
Haus der Kulturen der Welt **5**
Die Schlange
Spree
JOHN-FOSTER-DULLES-ALLEE
20
YITZHAK-RABIN-STRASSE
H-V-GAGERN-STRASSE
SCHEIDEMANNSTRASSE
7 Reichstag
PARISER PLATZ
BEHRENSTR
British Embassy

2

Unter den Linden

Brandenburger Tor

Sowjetisches Ehrenmal

STRASSE DES 17. JUNI

Tiergarten

Denkmal für die Ermordeten Jüden Europas

H-ARENDT-STR
G-KOLMAR-STR
EBERTSTRASSE

3

WILHELMSTR

MITTE

VOSSSTRASSE

KEMPER PLATZ
LENNÉSTRASSE
Sony Center **17**
LEIPZIGER PLATZ
LEIPZIGER STR

Kunstgewerbe-Museum
Philhar-monie
23
3 **21**
POTSDAMER-PLATZ
Bundesrat
Potsdamer Platz

Gedenkstätte Deutscher Widerstand
Gemälde-galerie
24
4
Staats-bibliothek
St-Matthäus
22
POTSDAMER STR
ALTE POTSDAMER STR
STRESEMANNSTRASSE
S-BERGER-STR
2 **12**

Japanese Embassy
HIROSHIMASTR.
HILDEBRAND STRASSE
STAUFFENBERGSTR
SIGISMUND-STRASSE
6
Neue Nationalgalerie
MARLENE DIETRICH-PLATZ
LINKSTR
Martin-Gropius-Bau

4

REICHPIETSCHUFER
REICHPIETSCH UFER
SCHÖNEBERGER UFER
Mendelssohn-Bartholdy-Park
BERNBURGER STR
ASKANISCHER PLATZ
GRUSEL KABINETT
Anhalter Bhf

Potsdam-Brücke
G-C-MARSHALL-BRÜCKE
POTSDAMER STR
AM KARLSBAD
Mendelssohn-Bartholdy-Park
Schöneberger STRASSE

5

LÜTZOWSTRASSE
DERFFLINGER STRASSE
GENTHINER STRASSE
KLUCKSTRASSE
13
15
LÜTZOWSTRASSE
SCHÖNEBERGER UFER
Gleis-dreieck
MÖCKERNSTR
KREUZBERG

18
Kurfürsten-strasse
NDORF-PLATZ
ZIETENSTRASSE
LOWSTR
KURFÜRSTENSTRASSE

0 — 400 m
0 — 400 yds

© Copyright Time Out Group 2007

Siegessäule

Haus der Kulturen der Welt

John-Foster-Dulles-Allee 10 (397 870/www.hkw.de). S5, S7, S9, S75 Bellevue/bus 100. **Open** 10am-9pm Tue-Sun. **Admission** varies. No credit cards. **Map** p97 E2 ⑤

The House of World Cultures mounts spectacular large-scale exhibitions on subjects such as contemporary Indian art, Bedouin culture or the Chinese avant-garde. The programme also involves film festivals, readings, lectures, discussions, concerts and dance performances. A unique Berlin cultural institution. Decent café too.

Neue Nationalgalerie

Potsdamer Strasse 50 (266 2651/ www.smb.spk-berlin.de). U2, S1, S2, S25 Potsdamer Platz. **Open** 10am-6pm Tue, Wed; 10am-10pm Thur; 10am-8pm Fri; 11am-8pm Sat, Sun. **Admission** €8; €4 reductions. No credit cards. **Map** p97 E4 ⑥

The building was designed in the 1960s by Mies van der Rohe, and houses German and international paintings from the 20th century. It's strong on expressionism, with works by Kirchner, Heckel and Schmidt-Rottluff. There are Cubist pieces from Picasso, Gris and Léger, Neue Sachlichkeit paintings from George Grosz and Otto Dix, and Bauhaus work from Paul Klee and Wassily Kandinsky. The permanent collection goes into storage for big shows, like the exhibition of 19th-century French masterpieces from MOMA New York, which runs from 1 June to 7 Oct 2007. A Jannis Kounellis exhibition runs from 26 Oct 2007 to 3 Feb 2008.

Reichstag

Platz der Republik (2270). S1, S2, S25 Unter den Linden. **Open** 8am-midnight daily; last entry 10pm. **Admission** free. **Map** p97 F2 ⑦

Infamously gutted by fire on 27 February 1933 – an event the Nazis used as an excuse to suspend basic freedoms and increase their dictatorial power – today, after its renovation by Sir Norman Foster, the Reichstag is again home to the Bundestag (German parliament), and open to the general public. A trip to the top of the dome is a must, but beware of the queues. After airport-style security, a lift whisks you to the roof, and from there ramps lead to the top of the dome, affording fine views.

Siegessäule

Strasse des 17. Juni Fleamarket (391 2961). S5, S7, S9, S75 Bellevue. **Open** *Summer* 9.30am-6.30pm Mon-Thur; 9.30am-7pm Fri, Sat. *Winter* 9.30am-5pm Mon-Thur; 9.30am-6pm Fri, Sat. **Admission** €2.20; €1.50 reductions. No credit cards. **Map** p96 C3 ⑧

Constructed in 1871-3 to commemorate Prussian military campaigns, the Victory Column was originally planted in front of the Reichstag, and was moved here in 1938. On top of the column is an 8m (26ft) gilded Goddess of Victory by Friedrich Drake; captured French cannons and cannonballs, sawn in half and gilded, provide the decoration of the column proper. Be warned: it's 285 steps up to the viewing platform.

Zoologischer Garten & Aquarium

Hardenbergplatz 8 (254 010/www. zoo-berlin.de). U2, U9, S5, S7, S9, S75 Zoologischer Garten. **Open** *Zoo* 9am-6.30pm daily in summer; 9am-5pm daily in winter. *Aquarium* 9am-6pm daily. **Admission** *Zoo* €11; €5.50-€8 reductions. *Aquarium* €9; €4.50-€7 reductions. *Combined admission* €16.50; €8.50-€13 reductions. No credit cards. **Map** p96 B4 ⑨

Germany's oldest zoo and one of the world's largest opened in 1841 and houses almost 14,000 creatures. It's beautifully landscaped and there are plenty of places for a coffee, beer or snack. The aquarium can be entered either from within the zoo or from its own entrance on Olof-Palme-Platz by the Elephant Gate. More than 500 species of fish, insects and reptiles are arranged over three floors in beautiful tanks.

Eating & drinking

Café am Neuen See

Lichtensteinallee 2 (254 4930). S5, S7, S9, S75 Tiergarten. **Open** Mar-Oct 10am-11pm daily. **Beergarden.** **Map** p96 B3 ⑩

Berlin's best beergarden is on the shore of a small Tiergarten lake, difficult to approach by public transport, but wonderfully placed for an after-stroll break. All human life is here, drinking beer at long tables under trees, and maybe tucking into one of their excellent pizzas. Rowboats for hire too.

Café Einstein

Kurfürstenstrasse 58 (261 5096/ www.cafeeinstein.com). U1, U2, U3, U4 Nollendorfplatz. **Open** 9am-1am daily. **Café.** **Map** p96 C5 ⑪

Red leather banquettes, parquet flooring and the crack of wooden chairs all contribute to the old Viennese café experience at Einstein. Fine Austrian dishes are produced alongside nouveau cuisine specialities, or simply order Apfelstrudel and coffee and soak up the vibe of this 1878 villa. The garden is a lovely spot for breakfast or lunch in the summer.

Diekmann im Weinhaus Huth

Alte Potsdamer Strasse 5 (2529 7524/www.j-diekmann.de). U2, S1, S2, S25 Potsdamer Platz. **Open** noon-midnight daily. €€€. **French.** **Map** p97 F4 ⑫

Decent, stylish dining in the only surviving pre-war structure on Potsdamer Platz. The staff are well drilled, there's a small terrace to complement the smart dining-room, the wine list has around 120 vintages, and the food is good for the price.

Edd's

Lützowstrasse 81 (215 5294). U1 Kurfürstenstrasse. **Open** 11.30am-3pm, 6pm-midnight Tue-Fri; 5pm-midnight Sat; 2pm-midnight Sun. €€€. No credit cards. **Thai.** **Map** p97 D5 ⑬

Advance bookings are essential at this comfortable and elegant Thai restaurant, where a husband-and-wife team please their customers with well balanced but somewhat spicy creations. Try the banana flower and prawn salad or duck No.18, double cooked and very tasty.

Arsenal cinema p104

Hauptbahnhof

Since May 2006 Berlin has had a new gateway. The new **Hauptbahnhof** (central station; p94), with its delicately gridded barrel vault covering the east-west overground tracks, now dominates the skyline north of the government quarter. One of the last of the post-Wall unifying projects to be completed, and the largest station in Europe, it's not just a link between the two halves of the city, nor even between the two halves of Germany, but exists as a hub for the entire north European railway network.

The site was chosen partly as a convenient spot to intersect the east-west lines with (underground) lines running north and south, and partly because it's on the border between east and west Berlin, whose old main stations it replaces. But in some ways it's a curious location. Arriving at Bahnhof Zoo, the traveller used to step out into a downtown bustle. Here one arrives in a kind of no-man's land between the river, the Humboldthafen, some sports facilities and a dull residential district. There's a nice view of the skyline to the south – the revamped Reichstag and the new Bundeskanzleramt – but it's a taxi or train ride to get anywhere else. The station doesn't even yet connect to the U-Bahn network.

But there are plenty of facilities to hand. Hauptbahnhof's 14 platforms use only two of the station's five levels. The rest are filled with shops, restaurants and coffee bars, information offices and car-rental agencies. It's like a mall with trains running through the middle.

It's also yet another blow to the old west end, which has been watching life dribble away eastwards for the last decade and a half.

Still, roomy and well organised, Hauptbahnhof beats the hell out of arriving or leaving via the depressing Schönefeld airport. That, in turn, is the site of Berlin's next big infrastructure project: Berlin-Brandenburg International, which is scheduled to open its runways in 2011.

BERLIN BY AREA

Potsdamer Platz p94

Hugo's

Hotel Intercontinental, Budapester Strasse 2 (2602 1263/www.hugos-restaurant.de). U2, U9, S5, S7, S9, S75 Zoologischer Garten. **Open** 6-10.30pm Mon-Sat. €€€€. **Modern European**. Map p96 B4 ⓔ

Hugo's is probably Berlin's best restaurant right now, and has the awards to prove it. Chef Thomas Kammeier juxtaposes classic haute cuisine with an avant-garde new German style. Dishes such as cheek of ox with beluga lentils and filled calamares, goose liver with mango, and Canadian lobster salad bring out the best of a mature kitchen.

Joseph Roth Diele

Potsdamer Strasse 75 (2636 9884). U1 Kurfürstenstrasse. **Open** 10am-midnight Mon-Fri. No credit cards. **Café**. Map p97 E5 ⓕ

A traditional Berlin book café that pays homage to the inter-war Austrian Jewish writer Joseph Roth, who moved to Berlin in 1920. Decorated in ochre tones, it's an amiable place with comfortable seating, offering teas, coffees, wines, beers, snacks and stunning value light meals.

Schleusenkrug

Müller-Breslau-Strasse/Unterschleuse (313 9909/www.schleusenkrug.de). S5, S7, S9, S75 Tiergarten. **Open** *Winter* 10am-6pm daily. *Summer* 10am-1am daily. No credit cards. **Bar/beergarden**. Map p96 A3 ⓖ

A bar and beer garden situated directly on the canal in the Tiergarten, with easy listening, mod and indie pop nights. During the day the place retains much of its original flavour, hinging on nautical themes and large glasses of Pils.

Vapiano

NEW *Potsdamer Platz 5 (2300 5005). U2, S1, S2, S25 Potsdamer Platz.* **Open** 10am-1am Mon-Sat; 10am-midnight Sun. €€. **Italian**. Map p97 F3 ⓗ

Collect a swipe card on your way in, use it to 'pay' for freshly prepared pasta, pizza, salads or desserts, and settle up on your way out. The counter queues at Vaplano show how much the Berlin branch of this new German chain is appreciated – the food is good, and there's plenty of seating available in the light, bright premises on Potsdamer Platz.

Victoria Bar

Potsdamer Strasse 102 (2575 9977/www.victoriabar.de). U1 Kurfürstenstrasse. **Open** 6.30pm-3am Mon-Thur, Sun; 6.30pm-4am Fri, Sat. No credit cards. **Bar**. **Map** p97 D5 ⑬

This funky grown-up cocktail bar on Potsdamer Strasse has subdued lighting, restrained colours, a relaxed crowd and staff who work well together and who know what they're mixing. Leave your coat in the cloakroom, order your favourite cocktail at the long bar and listen to jazzy sounds.

Shopping

Strasse des 17. Juni Fleamarket

Strasse des 17. Juni, Tiergarten (2655 0096). U2 Ernst-Reuter-Platz or S3, S5, S7, S9, S75 Tiergarten. **Open** 10am-5pm Sat, Sun. **Map** p96 A3 ⑲

On the stretch west of the S-Bahn station, rows of stalls with everything from high-quality, early 20th-century objects with prices to match, to a jumble of vintage and alternative clothing, old furniture, second-hand records and books. Interesting stuff, but cramped, single-file aisles.

Nightlife

Tipi Das Zelt

Grosse Querallee, between the Bundeskanzleramt & Haus der Kulturen der Welt, Tiergarten (0180 327 9358/www.tipi-das-zelt.de). Bus 100, 248 Platz der Republik. **Open** *Performances* 8.30pm Tue-Sat; 3pm, 8pm Sun. **Map** p97 E2 ⑳

A circus tent in the Tiergarten, situated near to the Bundeskanzleramt, with cool international cabaret performers, such as Italian Ennio and his amazing paper costumes, along with England's Tiger Lillies.

Philharmonie p104

Arts & leisure

Arsenal

Sony Center, Potsdamer Strasse 2, Potsdamer Platz, Tiergarten (2695 5100/www.fdk-berlin.de). U2, S1, S2, S25 Potsdamer Platz. No credit cards. **Map** p97 E3 ㉑

The Arsenal's brazenly eclectic programming ranges from classic Hollywood flicks to contemporary Middle Eastern cinema, from Russian art films to Italian horror movies, from Third World documentaries to silent films with live accompaniment. The two state-of-the-art screening rooms are in the Sony Center, placing it in the belly of the great Hollywood Beast – probably right where we need it.

CinemaxX Potsdamer Platz

Potsdamer Strasse 5, Potsdamer Platz, Tiergarten (2592 2111/www.cinemaxx. de). U2, S1, S2, S25 Potsdamer Platz. No credit cards. **Map** p97 F4 ㉒

The biggest multiplex in town with 19 screens, two or three of which usually show something in English. Bland mall surroundings for mainstream Hollywood programming, but a key venue for film festivals.

CineStar Original

Potsdamer Strasse 4, Potsdamer Platz, Tiergarten (2606 6400/www.cinestar. de). U2, S1, S2, S25 Potsdamer Platz. No credit cards. **Map** p97 E3 ㉓

This comfortable nine-screen multiplex shows films exclusively in their original languages, mostly English. Despite a few random sparks of creativity, it is basically mainstream Hollywood fare.

Philharmonie

Herbert-von-Karajan-Strasse 1, Tiergarten (2548 8999/www.berlin-philharmonic.com). U2, S1, S2, S25 Potsdamer Platz. **Open** Box office 9am-6pm daily. **Map** p97 E3 ㉔

Berlin's most famous concert hall, home to the world-renowned Berlin Philharmonic Orchestra, was designed by Hans Scharoun and opened in 1963. Its reputation for superb acoustics is accurate, but it does depend on where you sit. The Berliner Philharmoniker was founded in 1882 and has been led by some of the world's great conductors. Its greatest fame came under Herbert von Karajan between 1955 and 1989. Since 2002 it has been under the leadership of the popular Sir Simon Rattle. The Berlin Phil gives about 100 performances during its August to June season.

Tiergarten – the park p94

Kaiser-Wilhelm-Gedächtniskirche

Charlottenburg

The focal points of Berlin's well-heeled west end are the tacky commercial cauldron around Zoologischer Garten (known as Zoo Station or Bahnhof Zoo), and the grand avenue of international brands and upmarket shopping that is the **Kurfürstendamm**. Most of the life of this district is to be found on the streets between the **Ku'damm** and almost-parallel **Kantstrasse** to the north, especially on and around **Savignyplatz**.

Sights & museums

Kaiser-Wilhelm-Gedächtniskirche

Breitscheidplatz (218 5023/www. gedaechtniskirche-berlin.de). U2, U9, S5, S7, S9, S75 Zoologischer Garten. **Open** 9am-7pm daily. Guided tours 1.15pm, 2pm, 3pm Mon-Sat. **Admission** free. **Map** p107 E2 ❶

The neo-Romanesque Kaiser Wilhelm Memorial Church, built in 1891-5, is one of Berlin's best-known sights. Much of it was destroyed in a 1943 air raid and it was left that way to serve as a reminder of war. Inside is an art nouveau-style ceiling mosaic of the Hohenzollerns' pilgrimage, plus a cross made of nails from the destroyed Coventry Cathedral. The tower is flanked by drab concrete extensions, yet inside the wraparound blue stained glass is quite stunning.

Museum für Fotografie

NEW *Jebensstrasse 2 (266 2188/ www.smb.spk-berlin.de). U2, U9, S5, S7, S9, S75 Zoologischer Garten.* **Open** 10am-6pm Tue-Sun. **Admission** €6. No credit cards. **Map** p107 D1 ❷

Shortly before his fatal 2004 car crash, Berlin-born Helmut Newton established a foundation, donated over 1,000 of his photographs to it, and came to an arrangement with the Prussian Heritage Foundation. This new museum, now the largest photographic gallery in the city, was the result. Six colossal nudes, modelled on Nazi propaganda photos, glare down as you enter this former casino. The ground floor has a permanent exhibition of his 'Personal Property' (memorabilia, and a reconstruction of his study). The second floor houses rotating exhibitions of his work. There's also a huge attic for exhibitions by other photographers – visitors can expect themes like 'Simone Mangos: The Ideology of Memory' (running 1 May-31 July 2007) and 'Staged photography' (running 31 May-12 August 2007) – plus a great bookshop and café. See also box p109.

Story of Berlin

Kurfürstendamm 207-8 (8872 0100/www.story-of-berlin.de). U1 Uhlandstrasse. **Open** 10am-8pm daily; last entry 6pm. **Admission** €9.80; €8 reductions. No credit cards. **Map** p107 C2 **③**

A huge space filled with 20 themed displays, labelled in German and English, that tell the history of Berlin. Underneath all this is a huge nuclear shelter, built in the 1970s. It's still fully functional and holds up to 3,500 people. Guided tours are included in the entry fee.

Eating & drinking

Diener

Grolmanstrasse 47 (881 5329). S5, S7, S9, S75 Savignyplatz. **Open** 6pm-2am daily. No credit cards. **Bar**. **Map** p107 C2 **④**

This authentically old-style Berlin bar is named after a famous boxer, and the walls are adorned with faded murals showing hunting scenes and photographs of famous Germans you won't recognise. You could almost be in 1920s Berlin. Almost.

First Floor

Hotel Palace, Budapester Strasse 45 (2502 1020/www.firstfloor.palace.de). U2, U9, S5, S7, S9, S75 Zoologischer Garten. **Open** noon-3pm, 6-10.30pm Mon-Sat. **€€€€. Modern European**. **Map** p107 E2 **⑤**

Now under hot young chef Mathias Bucholz, this is the place for refined French/European cuisine such as Bresse pigeon served with chanterelles and a ragoût of potatoes, venison stuffed with

Zoo Station p105

Legend:
- Sights & museums
- Eating & drinking
- Shopping
- Nightlife
- Arts & leisure

Charlottenburg

Aquarium

Europa Center

OLOF-PALME PLATZ

Bahnhof Zoo

Zoologischer Garten

Zoologischer Garten

Kaiser-Wilhelm Gedächtnis-Kirche

Kurdamm Eck

Museum für Fotographie

Universität der Künste

Ludwig-Erhard-Haus

Theater des Westens

Kant-Dreieck

Jüdisches Gemeindehaus

Käthe-Kollwitz-Museum

Savignyplatz

Trinitatis-Kirche

Deutsche Oper

Bismarck-strasse

© Copyright Time Out Group 2007

400 m
400 yds

Florian

foie gras, or *loup de mer* and Breton lobster served with saffron and tomato confit. One of Berlin's top tables.

Florian

Grolmanstrasse 52 (313 9184/ www.restaurant-florian.de). S5, S7, S9, S75 Savignyplatz. **Open** 6pm-3am daily. **€€€. German. Map** p107 C2 ⑥
Florian has been serving fine south German food for a couple of decades now. The cooking is hearty, the service impeccable. Yes, staff will put you in Siberia if they don't like your looks, but they'll welcome you back if you're good.

Gabriel

Jüdisches Gemeindehaus, Fasanenstrasse 79-80 (882 6138). U1, U9 Kurfürstendamm. **Open** 11.30am-3.30pm, 6.30-9.30pm Mon-Thur, Sun. **€€.** No credit cards. **Jewish. Map** p107 D2 ⑦
Enter the Jewish Community Centre through airport-style security and head one floor up to this excellent kosher restaurant. On offer is a full range of Jewish central and east European specialities, including some of the best *pierogi* in Berlin. There's also a limited range of beers and Israeli wines.

Galerie Bremer

Fasanenstrasse 37 (881 4908). U3, U9 Spichernstrasse. **Open** 8pm-late Mon-Sat. *Gallery* 2-6pm Tue-Fri; 11am-1pm Sat. No credit cards. **Bar. Map** p107 C3 ⑧
In the back room of a tiny gallery, this bar has the air of a well-kept secret. The room is painted in deep, rich colours and has a beautiful ship-like bar designed by Hans Scharoun, architect of the Philharmonie (p104) and Staatsbibliothek. Service is unfailingly courteous; cocktails are perfectly mixed.

Julep's

Giesebrechtstrasse 3 (881 8823/www. juleps-berlin.de). U7 Adenauerplatz. **Open** 5pm-1am Mon-Thur, Sun; 5pm-2am Fri, Sat. **€€. American. Map** p107 A3 ⑨
The fusion flavours of contemporary American cuisine are done just right with dishes such as duck prosciutto or quesadillas with rhubarb and apple chutney, teriyaki chicken with lemongrass and basmati rice or Cajun-style red snapper. The Caesar salad is a classic, and desserts include chocolate brownies made with Jack Daniels.

Marjellchen

Mommsenstrasse 9 (883 2676).
S5, S7, S9, S75 Savignyplatz. **Open**
5pm-midnight daily. €€€. **German.**
Map p107 B2 ⑩
There aren't many places like this
around any more. It serves specialities
from East Prussia, Pomerania and
Silesia in an atmosphere of old-fashioned *Gemütlichkeit*. Beautiful bar, great
service and the larger-than-life owner
sometimes recites poetry or sings.

Paris Bar

*Kantstrasse 152 (313 8052). S5, S7,
S9, S75 Savignyplatz.* **Open** noon-2am
daily. €€€. **French. Map** p107 C2 ⑪
Owner Michel Wurthle's friendship
with Martin Kippenberger and other
artists is obvious from the art hanging
everywhere in this old-school salon.
This is one of Berlin's tried and true
spots. It attracts a crowd of rowdy reg-
ulars, and newcomers can feel left out
when seated in the rear. The food, as it
goes, isn't nearly as good as the staff
make out, and the service is often rude.

Restaurant 44

*Swissôtel, Augsburger Strasse
44 (2201 02288). U1, U9
Kurfürstendamm.* **Open** noon-
2.30pm, 6-10.30pm daily. €€€€.
French/German. Map p107 D2 ⑫
Chef Tim Raue offers two separate
menus: one traditional French, the
other radical Neue Deutsche Kuche.
The latter includes the likes of sandal-
wood goat's cheese with lobster tail, or
schnitzel with apple and beetroot salad
and a remoulade of white truffle. Cool
and comfortable room, elegantly
framed desserts, and a fine selection of
wines by the glass.

Schwarzes Café

*Kantstrasse 148 (313 8038). S5, S7,
S9, S75 Savignyplatz.* **Open** 24hrs
daily; closed for cleaning 6-10am Tue.
No credit cards. **Café. Map** p107 C2 ⑬
Open all hours for breakfasts and
meals, it was once all black and anar-
chistically inclined (hence the name)
but the political crowd moved on
decades ago and the decor has been

Prussian Helmut

A new museum reflects Newton's Berlin roots.

'Many of my fashion
photographs,' noted the
late Helmut Newton in his
Autobiography, 'were taken in
places that remind me of my
childhood.' That childhood was
spent in Berlin, and many of the
photos are now on display at the
Museum für Fotografie (p105).

As a horny teenager in the
1930s, Newton (then Neustädter)
had an eye for the ladies and
a passion for cameras. He
served his apprenticeship in
Charlottenburg at the studio of
fashion photographer Yva, in a
building that is now the Hotel
Bogota. As an intelligent young
Jew, he also knew that time was
running out, and fled Germany in
1938. Yva was also Jewish, and
perished at the Majdanek
concentration camp.

Establishing himself in Paris,
Newton became an international
figure. But wherever he worked,
the stamp of Berlin remained.
There's an ambiguous whiff of
both Weimar decadence and the
theatrical aspects of Nazism
in his fascination with cross-
dressing and deviant sex, the
noir quality of his black-and-
white images, the intensity
and detachment of his portraits.

Newton never lost his affection
for Berlin, and in the end came
back for good. He's buried at
the Städtische Friedhof III in
Schöneberg – also the last
resting-place of another 1930s
exile who was into cross-
dressing, one Marlene Dietrich.

brightened. Service can get over-stretched if it's crowded, such as early on a weekend morning when clubbers stop for breakfast on their way home.

Shopping

Antonie Setzer
Bleibtreustrasse 19 (883 1350/www.antoniesetzer.de). S3, S5, S7, S9, S75 Savignyplatz. **Open** 10am-7pm Mon-Fri; 10am-6pm Sat. **Map** p107 C3 ⓮
The stock and labels change seasonally here, but the fashion for women is intelligently selected from designers such as Prada, D&G, Miu Miu, Coach and Maliparmi.

Bücherbogen
Savignyplatz Bogen 593 (3186 9511/www.buecherbogen.com). S3, S5, S7, S9, S75 Savignyplatz. **Open** 10am-8pm Mon-Fri; 10am-6pm Sat. **Map** p107 C2 ⓯
Under the railway arches near Savignyplatz S-Bahn, this is Berlin's art-book central. As well as books on or by a wide selection of international artists and movements, there are excellent architecture and film sections, and a good stock of discounted art books.

Budapester Schuhe
Kurfürstendamm 43 (8862 4206). U1 Uhlandstrasse. **Open** 10am-7pm Mon-Fri; 10am-6pm Sat. **Map** p107 C3 ⓰
This is the largest of several Berlin branches, offering the latest by the likes of Prada, D&G, Sergio Rossi, JP Tod's and Miu Miu. At Kurfürstendamm 199 you'll find a conservative range for men. At the Bleibtreustrasse branch, prices are slashed by up to 50% for last year's models and hard-to-sell sizes.
Other locations: Bleibtreustrasse 24 (881 7001); Kurfürstendamm 199 (8811 1707).

dopo_domani
Kantstrasse 148 (882 2242/www.dopo-domani.com). S3, S5, S7, S9, S75 Savignyplatz. **Open** 10.30am-7pm Mon-Fri; 10am-6pm Sat. **Map** p107 C2 ⓱
Combining an interior design practice with a well-stocked interior design shop, the focus at dopo_domani is on Italian

outfitters and the presentation creates a space you'll dream of calling your own. A temple for design aficionados.

FourAsses Clothing
Lietzenburger Strasse 56 (7889 8317/www.fourasses.com). U1, U9 Kurfürstendamm. **Open** noon-8pm Mon-Fri; noon-6pm Sat. **Map** p107 D3 ⓲
Styles for skaters, snowboarders and surfers designed by the threesome who run the store – and who can be found skating on their in-store mini-ramp when there's no work to be done. Own-brand hoodies, jeans, jackets and T-shirts are all limited editions. Skate shows on Saturday.

Gadget-Gadget
NEW *Meinekestrasse 22 (8872 4582/www.gadget-gadget.com). U1, U9 Kurfürstendamm.* **Open** 10-8pm Mon-Sat. **Map** p107 D3 ⓳
German has no real equivalent of the word 'gadget', and English owner Piers Headley's fun selection of tech toys, games, tools and computer and iPod accessories is the only shop of its kind in Berlin. Useful for assorted travel items, including every imaginable kind of adaptor, transformer and charger.

Gelbe Musik
Schaperstrasse 11 (211 3962). U9 Spichern Strasse. **Open** 1-6pm Tue-Fri; 11am-2pm Sat. **Map** p107 D3 ⓴
One of Europe's most important avant-garde music stores has racks of mini-malist, electronic, world, industrial and extreme noise. Rare vinyl and import CDs, music press and sound objects make for absorbing browsing.

Harvey's
Kurfürstendamm 56 (883 3803/www.harveys-berlin.de). U7 Adenauerplatz. **Open** 11am-8pm Mon-Sat. **Map** p107 B3 ㉑
Frieder Bahnisch has been selling cut-ting-edge men's labels for 20 years. He stocks Japanese designers, both estab-lished and up-and-coming (UnderCover and Number 9 alongside Yamamoto and Comme des Garçons), plus Belgian label Martin Margiela.

Paris Bar p109

Galerie Bremer p108

Ito

*Wielandstrasse 31 (4404 4490/www.
itofashion.com). S3, S5, S7, S9, S75
Savignyplatz.* **Open** 11am-7pm Mon-
Sat. **Map** p107 B3 ㉒
See box p114.

Leysieffer

*Kurfürstendamm 218 (885 7480/
www.leysieffer.de). U1 Uhlandstrasse.*
Open 10am-7pm Mon-Sat; 10am-4pm
Sun. **Map** p107 D2 ㉓
Beautifully packaged confitures, teas,
jams and chocolates offered in this
Berlin outlet of a west German confec-
tioner make perfect gifts. There's a café
upstairs and a bakery attached.

Marga Schoeller Bücherstube

*Knesebeckstrasse 33 (881 1112/1122).
S3, S5, S7, S9, S75 Savignyplatz.*
Open 9.30am-7pm Mon-Wed; 9.30am-
8pm Thur, Fri; 9.30am-5pm Sat.
Map p107 C2 ㉔
Rated Europe's fourth-best indepen-
dent literary bookshop by *The
Bookseller*, this excellent establish-
ment, founded in 1930, includes a self-
contained English-language section
that's one of Berlin's most interesting.
Staff are sweet and helpful.

Mientus Studio 2002

*Wilmersdorfer Strasse 73 (323
9077/www.mientus.com). U7
Wilmersdorfer Strasse.* **Open**
10am-7pm Mon-Sat. **Map** p107 A2 ㉕
Mientus Studio stocks clean cuts
for sharp men from a range of collections including Dsquared, Neil Barrett,
Helmut Lang, Miu Miu, Andrew
Mackenzie and German rave labels.
Other locations: Bleibtreustrasse 24
(882 3786); Schlüterstrasse 26 (323
9077); Kurfürstendamm 52 (323 9077).

Patrick Hellmann

*Bleibtreustrasse 36 (882 6961/www.
patrickhellmann.com). S5, S7, S9, S75
Savignyplatz.* **Open** 9.30am-7pm Mon-
Fri; 9.30am-6pm Sat. **Map** p107 C3 ㉖
Prolific Berlin retailer with five other
stores to his name, specialising in international chic for men and women. A
bespoke tailoring service offers men

the choice of the Hellmann design
range in a variety of fabrics, including
some by Ermenegildo Zegna.
Other locations: Fasanenstrasse
29 (881 1985); Kurfürstendamm 53
(882 2565).

Planet

*Schlüterstrasse 35 (885 2717). U1
Uhlandstrasse.* **Open** 11am-7.30pm Mon-
Fri; 11am-6pm Sat. **Map** p107 B3 ㉗
Owners Wera Wonder and Mik Moon
have been kitting out the club scene
since 1985. Their DJ friends pump
out music to put you in club mode,
and the shop brims with sparkling
Spandex shirts, fluffy vests and dance-
durable footwear.

Riccardo Cartillone

*Savignyplatz 4 & 5 (3150 3327/
www.riccardocartillone.com). S3,
S5, S7, S9, S75 Savignyplatz.* **Open**
10am-8pm Mon-Sat. **Map** p107 C2 ㉘
For both women and men, probably the
most popular international shoe designer
in Berlin. No.4 stocks last season's styles
at reduced prices; No.5 sports the newest
collections. Cartillone's winter boots are
famously comfortable. There are also soft
leather summer shoes, heeled and flat, in
elegant, original colours.

stilwerk

*Kantstrasse 17 (315 150/www.
stilwerk.de). S3, S5, S7, S9, S75
Savignyplatz.* **Open** 10am-8pm Mon-
Fri; 10am-6pm Sat. **Map** p107 C2 ㉙
This huge, glassy haven of good taste
was opened in 1999 as a theme mall
for high-end products and continues
to anchor the Kantstrasse area. There
are over 50 retailers, purveying modern furnishings, state-of-the-art
kitchens, high-tech lighting and luxurious bathroom fittings among a vast
assortment of interior items by every
major player from Alessi to Zanussi.

Nightlife

A-Trane

*Bleibtreustrasse 1 (313 2550/
www.a-trane.de). S5, S7, S9, S75
Savignyplatz.* **Open** 9pm-2am

New home for Ito

The fashion icon goes west.

Yoshiharu Ito, an impish fashion designer in his early 40s and a fixture on the Berlin scene for over 15 years sits outside his new shop on Wielandstrasse and ponders why he never returned to Japan. 'The fashion [in Berlin] was horrible,' he recalls, then brightens. 'But the people were wild!'

Ito had arrived from Tokyo to study music, but fashion was his other passion. Scanning the clashing colours and cuts worn by young Berliners in the late 1980s, he concluded that Berlin could use some Japanese style and clarity.

He began producing his own collections, influenced by other Japanese designers such as Yamamoto and Commes des Garçons. Like other young Berlin-based designers such as Fiona Bennett, Lisa D and RespectMen, Ito made his name in the up-and-coming Mitte scene of the mid '90s. While the streets of the Scheunenviertel were throbbing with new energy, he opened a shop on Augustrasse and there, until very recently, he remained.

The problem with Mitte these days, Ito will tell you, is that it's no longer the sole preserve of the young, individual designer. It's being overrun by brands that would formerly have stayed around the Ku'damm – Boss, Adidas, Cahartt. Ito decided to move in the other direction, joining a perceptible westwards scene-shift.

Mitte was all bustle and hustle. His new surroundings allow him space to think. 'Fashion has two sides,' he reflects. 'There is hype and surface. But as I get older I think more about the other side, about patterns and technique.'

Ito's current collections for men and women (he's stronger in menswear) hinge on elegant but comfortable designs in practical materials. Stylish and simple, with clear lines but eccentric twists, they sit well among the grown-up international fashions of Berlin's west end. Ito is no longer an up-and-comer. He's arrived.

Mon-Thur, Sun; 9pm-late Fri,
Sat. Performances 10pm daily.
Map p107 C2 ③⓪
This upscale jazz bar is a bit ostenta-
tious, but there are half-decent concerts
most nights and occasionally a big name
for a longer run. Herbie Hancock,
Wynton Marsalis and Arthur Blythe
have all passed through. Late-night jam
sessions run from 12.30am on Saturdays
and Sundays. Book for anything else.

Cafe Theater Schalotte
*Behaimstrasse 22 (341 1485/www.
schalotte.de). U7 Richard-Wagner-
Platz.* **Open** *Performances* (usually)
8.30pm Thur-Sat. No credit cards.
Map p107 A1 ③①
There's sometimes excellent cabaret in
this convivial café-theatre, plus live
music, readings and other performances. Every November, the place
hosts its own international a cappella
festival, with instrument-less musical
performers from around the world.

Quasimodo
*Kantstrasse 12A (312 8086/www.
quasimodo.de). U2, U9, S5, S7, S9, S75
Zoologischer Garten.* **Open** *Concerts*
10pm Tue-Sun (doors open 1hr before
show). No credit cards. **Map** p107 D2 ③②
Historically West Berlin's premier
jazz venue, this smoky basement spot
appears close to severing its connections to the genre entirely. It still gets
some good acts, though, both local
and international.

Arts & leisure

Deutsche Oper
*Richard-Wagner-Strasse 10 (343
8401/www.deutscheoperberlin.de).
U2 Deutsche Oper.* **Map** p107 A1 ③③
With roots dating back to 1912, the
Deutsche Oper built its present 1,900-
seat hall in 1961, and carried the operatic torch for West Berlin during the
Wall years. It has lost out in profile to
the Staatsoper since Reunification, but
retains a reputation for blockbuster
productions of the classics. Unsold
tickets are available at a discount half
an hour before performances.

Renaissance Theater
*Knesebeckstrasse 100, corner
Hardenbergstrasse (312 4202/www.
renaissance-theater.de). U2 Ernst-
Reuter-Platz.* **Map** p107 C1 ③④
Some of Germany's best-known performers appear in this landmark building, with a major hit being Judy
Winter's one-woman show about
Marlene Dietrich. It claims to be the
only art deco theatre left in Europe,
which makes it a great backdrop to
the chansons evenings that are
served up with a full dinner in the
upstairs salon.

Schaubühne am
Lehniner Platz
*Kurfürstendamm 153 (890 023/www.
schaubuehne.de). U7 Adenauerplatz
or S5, S7, S9, S75 Charlottenburg.*
Map p107 A3 ③⑤
One of the places to be for the theatrical in-crowd, offering modern drama
from young authors played by great
stage actors. The programme is
almost exclusively contemporary
drama and dance, including some
English-language works, and Thomas
Ostermeier's internationally renowned
productions of Ibsen.

stilwerk p113

Pinguin Club p118

Schöneberg

The largely residential district of Schöneberg is both culturally and geographically halfway between Kreuzberg and Charlottenburg. The area around Winterfeldtplatz, with its twice weekly market, is lively with cafés and shops. The scene continues south down Goltzstrasse. Motzstrasse has been a gay area since the 1920s (gay and lesbian victims of the Holocaust are commemorated on a plaque outside Nollendorfplatz station) and remains the boys' main drag. Wittenbergplatz, at Schöneberg's north-west corner, is home to **KaDeWe**, continental Europe's biggest department store, famous for its six-floor food hall. From here, Tauentzienstrasse runs west into the Ku'damm, marking the beginning of west Berlin's main shopping mile.

Eating & drinking

Green Door

Winterfeldtstrasse 50 (215 2515/ www.greendoor.de). U1, U2, U3, U4 Nollendorfplatz/bus 2, 5, 19, 26. **Open** 6pm-3am Mon-Thur; 6pm-4am Fri, Sat; 8pm-3am Sun. No credit cards. **Bar**. **Map** p117 B2 ➊

It really does have a green door, and behind it there's a whole lotta cocktail shaking going on at the curvy bar – the drinks menu is impressively long. A good location off Winterfeldtplatz.

Habibi

Goltzstrasse 24, on Winterfeldtplatz (215 3332). U1, U2, U3, U4 Nollendorfplatz. **Open** 11am-3am Mon-Thur, Sun; 11am-5am Fri, Sat. €. No credit cards. **Middle Eastern**. **Map** p117 B2 ➋

The best branch of a small chain serving excellent Middle Eastern specialities including falafel, kibbeh, tabouleh

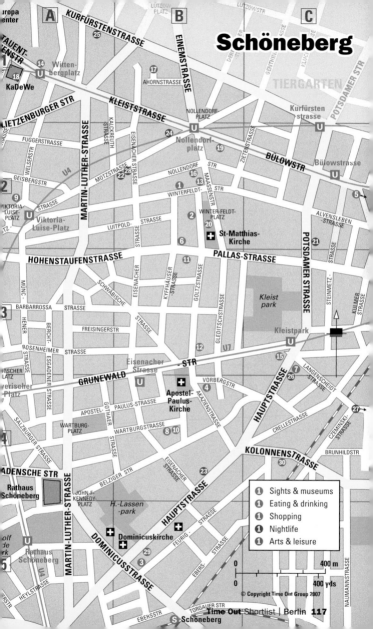

Schöneberg

A | **B** | **C**

KURFÜRSTENSTRASSE
EINEMSTRASSE

TIERGARTEN

KaDeWe

WITTENBERGPLATZ

AHORNSTRASSE

KLEISTSTRASSE

NOLLENDORF-
PLATZ

Kurfürsten
strasse

LIETZENBURGER STR

FUGGERSTRASSE

Nollendorf-
platz

BÜLOWSTR

Bülowstrasse

MARTIN-LUTHER-STRASSE

WELSERSTR

GEISBERGSTR

MOTZSTRASSE

NOLLENDORF
STR

ALVENSLEBEN
STRASSE

Viktoria-
Luise-
Platz

WINTERFELDT-

WINTER-
FELDT-
PLATZ

St-Matthias-
Kirche

HOHENSTAUFENSTRASSE

LUITPOLD-

PALLAS-STRASSE

POTSDAMER STRASSE

BARBAROSSA

EISENACHER

SCHWÄBISCHE

KYFFHÄUSER-
STRASSE

GOLTZSTRASSE

GLEDITSCHSTRASSE

Kleist
park

STEINMETZ

KÜLMER
STRASSE

STRASSE

ROSENHEIMER

FREISINGERSTR

STRASSE

Kleistpark

Eisenacher
Strasse

GRUNEWALD-
STR

VORBERGSTR

LANGENSCHEIDT
STRASSE

HAUPTSTRASSE

Apostel-
Paulus-
Kirche

AKAZIENSTRASSE

APOSTEL-

PAULUS-STRASSE

CRELLESTRASSE

CZENINSKI-
STRASSE

WARTBURG-
PLATZ

WARTBURGSTRASSE

EISENACHER STRASSE

BRUNHILDSTR

Rathaus
Schöneberg

SALZBURGER STRASSE

BELZIGER STR

KOLONNENSTRASSE

MARTIN-LUTHER-STRASSE

JOHN-F-
KENNEDY-
PLATZ

H.-Lassen
-park

HAUPTSTRASSE

FEURIG.

STRASSE

1	Sights & museums
1	Eating & drinking
1	Shopping
1	Nightlife
1	Arts & leisure

Rathaus
Schöneberg

DOMINICUSSTRASSE

Dominicuskirche

EBERSSTR

0   400 m
0   400 yds

© Copyright Time Out Group 2007

and various combination plates. Wash it all down with freshly squeezed juice and finish up with a complimentary tea and one of the wonderful pastries. Light, bright and well run.
Other locations: Akazienstrasse 9 (787 4428).

India Haus
Feurigstrasse 38 (781 2546/www. restaurant-indiahaus.de). U4, S41, S42, S45, S46 Innsbrucker Platz or S1, S41, S42, S45, S46 Schöneberg. **Open** 2pm-midnight Mon-Fri; noon-midnight Sat, Sun. **€€**. **Indian**. Map p117 B5 **3**
Proximity to the English-language Odeon Kino cinema (p123) round the corner redeems an out-of-the-way location, but food is good here and a long menu offers many vegetarian choices. The almond soup is excellent and the Malay kofta delicious. Weekend buffets cost around €7. The cheaper *Imbiss* is attached.

La Cocotte
Vorbergstrasse 10 (7895 7658/ www.lacocotte.de). U7 Eisenacher Strasse. **Open** 6pm-1am Tue-Sun. **€€€**. No credit cards. **French**. Map p117 B4 **4**

Storch

A friendly, gay-owned French restaurant where good cooking is enhanced by a sense of fun and occasional themed events – such as the Beaujolais nouveau being welcomed by a 'rustic chic' buffet and a programme of 1980s French pop and accordion music. Vegetarians aren't forgotten, there's a nice terrace and the toilets are absolutely beautiful.

Munch's Hus
NEW *Bülowstrasse 66 (2101 4086/www.munchshus.de). U2 Bülowstrasse.* **Open** 10am-1am daily. **€€**. **Norwegian**. Map p117 C2 **5**
Berlin's only Norwegian restaurant features daily specials that are a bit like the rounded German meal – potatoes and greens accompany most dishes – but with a twist that usually involves dill. Creamy, fresh soups and delicious fish dishes are their speciality, but light sandwiches and salads are also available.

Mutter
Hohenstaufenstrasse 4 (216 4990). U1, U2, U3, U4 Nollendorfplatz. **Open** 10am-4am daily. **Café**. Map p117 B2 **6**
This is a big place with two bars, an enormous selection of drinks, breakfasts until 6pm, a sushi bar from 6pm, plus other snacks throughout the day. It can be difficult to find a seat on weekend nights, when dance music plays in the front bar while more sedate sounds soothe the café area behind. The spectacular corridor to the toilets is worth a visit in itself.

Petite Europe
Langenscheidtstrasse 1 (781 2964). U7 Kleistpark. **Open** 5pm-1am daily. **€€**. **Italian**. Map p117 C3 **7**
You may have to wait for a table in this friendly place, but the turnover's fast. Weekly specials are first-rate, as are the pasta dishes. Salads could be better and none of this is haute cuisine, but it's all well made, hearty and inexpensive.

Pinguin Club
Wartburgstrasse 54 (781 3005/ www.pinguin-club.de). U7 Eisenacher Strasse. **Open** 9pm-4am daily. No credit cards. **Bar**. Map p117 B4 **8**

Though a little past its heyday, this speakeasy-style bar remains one of Berlin's finest and friendliest institutions. It's decorated with original 1950s Americana and rock 'n' roll memorabilia, the owners all have punk roots and good sounds are a feature. Take your pick from 156 spirits.

Potemkin

Viktoria-Luise-Platz 5 (2196 8181). U4 Viktoria-Luise-Platz. **Open** 8am-1am Tue-Sun. No credit cards. **Café.** Map p117 A2 ⑨

Film stills and the likes of *Battleship Potemkin* director Sergei Eisenstein adorn the walls, and the red and black decor has an appropriately constructivist feel. Breakfasts also sport titles of Eisenstein films, from the basic 'Ivan the Terrible' to 'Viva Mexico' with marinated chicken breast served with pineapple and cheese on toast. There's also a daily lunch special and snacks such as mozzarella rolls stuffed with serrano ham.

Storch

Wartburgstrasse 54 (784 2059/ www.storch-berlin.de). U7 Eisenacher Strasse. **Open** 6pm-1am Mon-Sat. **€€€. Alsatian.** Map p117 B4 ⑩

One of our favourite places. The Alsatian food – soup and salad starters, a sauerkraut and choucroute platter, plus a daily selection of dishes from the place where German and French cuisines rub shoulders – is finely prepared and generously proportioned. House speciality is Alsatian tarte flambée: a crisp pastry base baked in a special oven and topped with either cheese, onion and bacon or (as dessert) with apple, cinnamon and flaming Calvados. Long wooden tables are shared by different parties.

Suzy's

NEW *Hohenstaufenstrasse 69 (0160 9147 8364). U1, U2, U3, U4 Nollendorfplatz.* **Open** 8pm-late Tue-Thur; 9pm-late Fri, Sat. No credit cards. **Bar.** Map p117 B3 ⑪

A friendly neighbourhood bar that often fills its two-room space with readings, DJs, performances and themed events, but is just as good for nursing a drink into the small hours at the counter, where the amiable owner holds court.

Tee Tea Thé

Goltzstrasse 2, Schöneberg (2175 2240). U7 Eisenacher Strasse. **Open** 9am-10pm Mon-Thur; 9am-midnight Fri; 9am-8pm Sat; 10am-8pm Sun. *Brunch* 10am-3pm Sat, Sun. No credit cards. **Café.** Map p117 B3 ⑫

See box p129.

Tim's Canadian Deli

Maassenstrasse 14 (2175 6960). U1, U2, U3, U4 Nollendorfplatz. **Open** 8am-1am Mon-Fri; 8am-late Sat; 9am-1am Sun. **Café.** Map p117 B2 ⑬

Against the odds, this place seems to have conquered the Winterfeldtplatz area, though there's not a café round here that's not full on a market day. Lots of bagels and muffins, egg breakfasts until 4pm and many light meal options.

Witty's

Wittenbergplatz (no phone). U1, U2, U3 Wittenbergplatz. **Open** 11am-1am daily. **€.** No credit cards. **German.** Map p117 A1 ⑭

There are *Imbiss* stands on every corner of Wittenbergplatz, but this one, on the north-west side over the road from KaDeWe, is one of the best in the city. It's a courteous operation, serves only Neuland organic meat, has stunning thick-cut chips with a variety of sauces to choose from, and usually has a queue of well-dressed folk eager to snack on a sausage that's as good as anything in the food hall over the road. Wash it down with an organic Asgard beer.

Zoulou Bar

Hauptstrasse 4 (7009 4737). U7 Kleistpark. **Open** 8pm-6am daily. No credit cards. **Bar.** Map p117 C3 ⑮

A small bar with a funky vibe and occasional DJs. It can get packed between 10pm and 2am; after that the crowd thins and the late hours provide the best time for a visit.

Shopping

Fingers

Nollendorfstrasse 35 (215 3441). U1, U2, U3, U4 Nollendorfplatz. **Open** 2.30pm-6.30pm Tue-Fri; 11am-2.30pm Sat. No credit cards. **Map** p117 B2 ⑯
Splendid finds from the 1940s, '50s and '60s, including lipstick-shaped cigarette lighters, vintage toasters, weird lighting and eccentric glassware.

Garage

Ahornstrasse 2, off Einemstrasse (211 2760/www.kleidermarkt.de). U1, U2, U3, U4 Nollendorfplatz. **Open** 11am-7pm Mon-Fri; 11am-6pm Sat. **Map** p117 B1 ⑰
Cheap second-hand clothing is priced by the kilo in this barn-like location. It's all well organised for rooting out cheap, last-minute party outfits.

KaDeWe

Tauentzienstrasse 21-4 (2121 2700/www.kadewe.de). U1, U2, U3 Wittenbergplatz. **Open** 10am-8pm Mon-Fri; 9.30am-8pm Sat. **Credit** AmEx, DC, MC, V. **Map** p117 A1 ⑱
The largest department store in continental Europe celebrates its 100th birthday in 2007. It carries name brands in all departments, though the merchandise is surprisingly hit and miss. KaDeWe is most famous for its lavish sixth-floor food hall, where among the food counters, gourmet bars offer everything from oysters and Champagne to beer and smoked sausage.

Mr Dead & Mrs Free

Bülowstrasse 5 (215 1449/www. deadandfree.com). U1, U2, U3, U4 Nollendorfplatz. **Open** 11am-7pm Mon-Fri; 11am-4pm Sat. **Map** p117 B2 ⑲
Long Berlin's leading address for independent and underground rock, Mr Dead & Mrs Free has bucket-loads of British, US and Australian imports, a large vinyl section, and staff who know and love their music. There's a small but choice selection of books and mags too.

Winterfeldt Markt

Winterfeldtplatz. U1, U2, U3, U4 Nollendorfplatz. **Open** 8am-2pm Wed, Sat. No credit cards. **Map** p117 B2 ⑳
Everybody shows up to buy their vegetables, cheese, wholegrain breads, wurst, meats, flowers, clothes, pet supplies and toys here; or simply to meet over a coffee, beer or falafel at one of the many cafés off the square. There is lots of mulled wine-drinking in winter.

BERLIN BY AREA

Mr Dead & Mrs Free

Bunker mentality

Old problem, new solutions.

Near the junction of Pallastrasse and Potsdamer Strasse, and across from a miserable housing development on the site of the former Sportpalast, stands a hulking concrete bunker. You might have seen it before. It's the location where Peter Falk was working on the film-within-a-film in Wim Wenders 1987 *Wings of Desire*. Although the movie offered a rare glimpse into the bunker's interior, what Wenders's cameras didn't show was the housing block (pictured) bridging Pallastrasse to rest on the bunker's roof.

The Nazis built dozens of such bunkers, air-raid shelters and flak towers, many connected by tunnels. The decision of post-war urban planners to incorporate the Pallastrasse bunker into their housing complex, even if only as a kind of giant concrete footrest, reflects the basic reality of such structures: that they are virtually impossible to destroy.

A variety of solutions has been adopted to deal with these oversized chunks of concrete. On the site of the old Anhalter Bahnhof in nearby Kreuzberg, a similar overground bunker now contains a chamber of horrors exhibit called the **Gruselkabinett** (p138) as well as an exhibition on the bunker itself. In the early 1990s, a bunker on Reinhardtstrasse in Mitte used to host a techno club called, appropriately enough, Bunker. It is currently being remodelled into an art centre.

In both Volkspark Friedrichshain and the Humboldthain park near Nordkreuz station, similar concrete hulks have been incorporated into the landscape by having earth piled around them to form artificial hills. At either location, you can walk to the top of the former bunker along wooded pathways, and enjoy a fine view from the summit. A local history group organises tours of the tunnels under the one at Humboldthain (www.berliner-unterwelten.de).

The most famous of them all, the Führer Bunker where Hitler played out the mad final moments of his regime, once lay under what is now the junction of An der Kolonnade and Gertrud-Kolmar-Strasse in Mitte, about 100 metres south of the documentation centre at the **Denkmal für die ermordeten Juden Europas** (p56). It was demolished by the East Germans in 1988 and there is nothing that marks the spot today.

BERLIN BY AREA

Nightlife

Ex 'n' Pop

Potsdamer Strasse 157 (2199 7470/
www.ex-n-pop.de). U2 Bülowstrasse.
Open 10pm-late daily. No credit cards.
Map p117 C2 ㉑
The last direct descendant of the 1980s
black-leather, speed-and-dope scene
that Nick Cave and Einstürzende
Neubauten once inhabited still rocks
through the night, most nights,
although not much happens before
3am. It's a dodgy dive full of rowdy
intellectuals, off-duty drag queens
and local bohos, with intense activity
around the Kicker table, a 50-seat cinema located in the back (with a mid
week programme of independent and
offbeat movies), occasional bands
performing on the small stage, and
an eclectic music policy that spreads
in all directions from a heartland of
left-field country and rock. At weekends the party carries on until the
following afternoon.

Hafen

Motzstrasse 19 (211 4118/www.
hafen-berlin.de). U1, U2, U3, U4
Nollendorfplatz. **Open** 8pm-late
daily. No credit cards. **Map** p117 B2 ㉒

A red, plush and vaguely psychedelic
bar in the centre of Schöneberg's gay
triangle. Popular with the fashion-
and body-aware, especially for the
Quizz-o-Rama, with questions in
English from 10pm on the first
Monday of the month.

Havanna Club

Hauptstrasse 30, Schöneberg
(784 8565/www.havanna-berlin.de).
U7 Eisenacher Strasse. **Open** 9pm-
late Wed; 10pm-late Fri, Sat.
Admission €2.50 Wed; €6.50 Fri; €7
Sat. No credit cards. **Map** p117 B4 ㉓
Made up of three dancefloors with
salsa, merengue and R&B music,
Havanna Club is a popular place with
expatriate South Americans and
Cubans. One hour before opening
there's a salsa class for €4, which is
reckoned to be a good place to meet people, as well as to learn a few steps.

Heile Welt

Motzstrasse 5 (2191 7507). U1,
U2, U3, U4 Nollendorfplatz. **Open**
6pm-4am daily. No credit cards.
Map p117 B2 ㉔
A stylish gay café, lounge and cocktail
bar for the fashion-conscious. The front
has a 1970s feel, the back lounge is all

Heile Welt

plush leather seating. A good place to practise chat-up lines and decide whether to go clubbing.

Kleine Nachtrevue

Kurfürstenstrasse 116, Schöneberg (218 8950/www.kleine-nachtrevue.de). U1, U2, U3 Wittenbergplatz. **Open** 7pm-3am Tue-Sat. *Performances* 10.45pm Tue-Sat.* **Map** p117 A1 ㉕
Used as a location for many a film, this is as close as you can get to real nostalgic German cabaret – intimate, dark, decadent but very friendly. Nightly shows consist of short song or dance numbers sprinkled with playful nudity and whimsical costumes. Special weekend shows at 9pm vary from erotic opera or a four-course meal to songs sung by the male reincarnation of Marlene Dietrich.

Neues Ufer

Hauptstrasse 157 (7895 7900/ www.neuesufer.de). U7 Kleistpark. **Open** 11am-2am daily. No credit cards. **Map** p117 C4 ㉖
Established in the early 1970s as Café Nemesis, and later renamed Anderes Ufer, this is the city's oldest extant gay café and was a favourite of David Bowie's when he lived two doors up the road.

Scheinbar

Monumentenstrasse 9 (784 5539/ www.scheinbar.de). U7 Kleistpark. **Open** *Performances* 8.30pm. No credit cards. **Map** p117 C4 ㉗
Experimental and fun-loving cabaret is performed in this tiny club exploding with fresh talent. If you like surprises and have a black sense of humour, try the open-stage nights, where great performers mix with terrible ones, creating a very surreal evening for all.

Tom's Bar

Motzstrasse 19 (213 4570/www. tomsbar.de). U1, U2, U3, U4 Nollendorfplatz. **Open** 10pm-6am daily. No credit cards. **Map** p117 B2 ㉘
The grandaddy of Schöneberg gay joints, Tom's is a cruising institution. The front bar is fairly chatty but the

Odeon Kino

closer you get to the darkroom the more intense things become. Popular with men of all ages and styles.

Arts & leisure

Odeon Kino

Hauptstrasse 116, Schöneberg (7870 4019/www.yorck.de). U4, S41, S42, S45, S46 Innsbrucker Platz or S1, S41, S42, S45, S46 Schöneberg. No credit cards. **Map** p117 B5 ㉙
Situated deep in the heart of Schöneberg, this is one of the last big, old, single-screen neighbourhood cinemas left in the city. It's worth a visit just for that. With an exclusively English-language programme, it provides a reasonably intelligent selection of Hollywood and UK fare.

Xenon

Kolonnenstrasse 5-6, Schöneberg (7800 1530/www.xenon-kino.de). U7 Kleistpark. No credit cards. **Map** p117 C4 ㉚
A snug little cinema dedicated exclusively to gay and lesbian programming. Most of this comes from the US and the UK, and so the films are predominantly in English.

BERLIN BY AREA

Deutsches Technikmuseum Berlin p137

Kreuzberg

Though it's now administratively joined to Friedrichstrasse across the river Spree, Kreuzberg has not only managed to maintain some of the independence of spirit that characterised its role as the centre of alternative politics and lifestyle during the Wall years, but it is also acquiring new life in the backwash from the last decade's drive to the east. Kreuzberg is fashionable once again. It's also the capital of Turkish Berlin, has a big gay community, and, in the northern area that borders Mitte, possesses a clump of important museums and landmarks.

Eastern Kreuzberg

The Oberbaumbrücke was once a border crossing for Berliners, mostly used by eastern pensioners.

Now, renovated by Santiago Calatrava in the 1990s, it's the only road connection to Friedrichshain. The area around its eastern foot, radiating out from Schlesisches Tor station and spilling eastwards over the border into Treptow, has been on the up for the last few years and is solidifying as a new centre for nightlife. A little to the west, Kottbusser Tor is the centre of Turkish Berlin and Oranienstrasse is the district's main drag. Though there's plenty of entertainment around here, there's little in the way of formal sightseeing.

Eating & drinking

Abendmahl
Muskauer Strasse 9 (612 5170/ www.abendmahl-berlin.de). U1 Görlitzer Bahnhof. **Open** 6pm-1am

Wed-Sun. €€€. No credit cards.
Vegetarian. Map p126 C1 ❶

The name means 'last supper' and, decked out in a little catholic kitsch, this is Berlin's temple of vegetarian gastronomy – although there is fish on the menu too. Dishes change with the seasons and their weird names are part of the offbeat charm: I Shot Andy Warhol for dessert, anyone? The soups are wonderful, great things are done with seitan, and creativity is at a high level throughout.

Anker-Klause

Kottbusser Brücke/corner of Maybachufer (693 5649/www. ankerklause.de). U8 Schönleinstrasse. **Open** 4pm-late Mon; 10am-late Tue-Sun. No credit cards. **Bar**. Map p126 A2 ❷

Although this place looks over the Landwehrkanal, the only thing nautical about this 'anchor den' is the midriff-tattooed, punk-meets-portside swank of the bar staff. A slamming jukebox, weathery terrace and good sandwich melts offer ample excuse to dock here.

Cake

Schlesische Strasse 32 (6162 4610/ www.cake-bar.de). U1 Schlesisches Tor. **Open** 4pm-late daily. No credit cards. **Bar/café**. Map p126 D2 ❸

A diverse crowd mills about in this lounge equipped with old easy chairs, sofas, art-bedecked walls and a dark red, musty interior. The vintage jukebox is equipped with a variety of oldies. DJs most weekends for free.

Careca

Falkenstein 42 (2501 1293). U1 Schlesisches Tor. **Open** 6pm-4am daily. No credit cards. **Bar/café**. Map p126 D2 ❹

This modern bar and café offers a comprehensive selection of cocktails, long drinks and wines, as well as tea and good coffee. Don't come for the desultory selection of snacks and beers. Women often dominate the scene, possibly because this is one place in the area that isn't dark and dingy. Sit at petite, well-lit tables in the front or lounge on couches in the side room. Sometimes there are DJs.

Hasir

Adalbertstrasse 10 (614 2373/www. hasir.de). U1, U8 Kottbusser Tor. **Open** 24hrs daily (often closes 2-3hrs early morning). €€. No credit cards. **Turkish**. Map p126 A1 ❺

You thought Turks had been chewing doner for centuries? Sorry, it was actually invented in Germany in 1971 by one Mehmet Aygun, who eventually opened this successful chain of Turkish restaurants. While you'll get one of the best doners in Berlin, the rest of the menu is great, too.

Henne

Leuschnerdamm 25 (614 7730/www. henne-berlin.de). U1, U8 Kottbusser Tor. **Open** 7pm-1am Tue-Sun. €. No credit cards. **German**. Map p126 A1 ❻

There's only one thing on the menu here – half a roast chicken – but Henne's birds are organically raised and milk-roasted. The only decisions are whether to have cabbage or potato salad, and which beer to wash it down with (try the Monchshof). Check out the letter from JFK over the bar, regretting that the President missed dinner here.

Markthalle p128

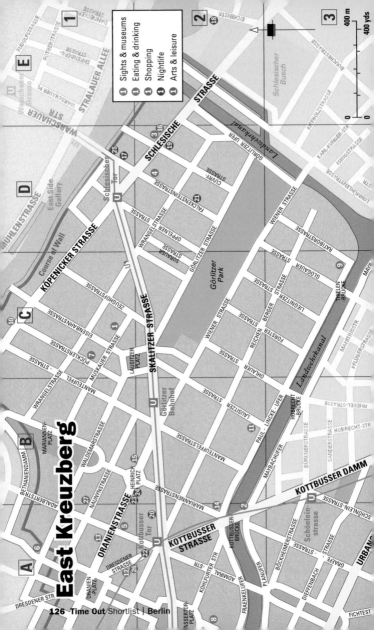

East Kreuzberg

1 Sights & museums
1 Eating & drinking
1 Shopping
1 Nightlife
1 Arts & leisure

400 m
400 yds

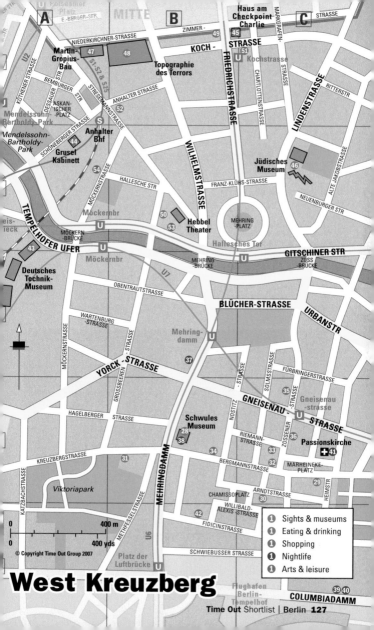

West Kreuzberg

Markthalle

Pücklerstrasse 34 (617 5502). U1 Görlitzer Bahnhof. **Open** 10am-2am daily. **€€**. **German**. Map p126 C1 ❼

This unpretentious schnitzel restaurant and bar, with chunky tables and wood-panelled walls, has become a Kreuzberg institution. Breakfast is served until 5pm, salads from noon and, in the evening, there's a selection of filling and reasonably priced meals. It's also fun just to sit at the long bar and sample the ample selection of grappas.

Old Emerald Isle

Erkelenzdamm 49 (615 6917/www. old-emerald-isle.de). U1, U8 Kottbusser Tor. **Open** noon-2am Mon-Thur, Sun; noon-4am Fri, Sat. No credit cards. **Bar**. Map p126 A2 ❽

Old Emerald Isle – Berlin's best Irish pub – offers draught Guinness, a selection of hearty meals, televisions for watching football and rugby, a pleasant beer garden on the quiet street outside and a cheerful atmosphere throughout.

Senti

Paul-Lincke-Ufer 4, (618 8606). U8 Schönleinstrasse. **Open** 10am-1am daily. No credit cards. **Spanish**. Map p126 C3 ❾

See box p129.

Spindler & Klatt

NEW *Köpenicker Strasse 16-17 (6956 6775/www.spindlerklatt.com). U1 Schlesisches Strasse.* **Open** 8pm-late daily. **€€€**. **Modern European**. Map p126 C1 ❿

This imaginatively repurposed industrial space has led the current fad for big beds to lounge around on. Here you can pick from the high-quality fusion menu either horizontally or at normal tables, and sometimes there are performances during dinner. On Saturdays, from midnight, they remove the tables and it becomes a club.

Svevo

Lausitzer Strasse 25 (6107 3216/ www.restaurant-svevo.de). U1 Görlitzer Bahnhof. **Open** 6pm-late Mon-Sat. **€€€€**. **Modern European**. Map p126 B2 ⓫

Old Emerald Isle

Brunching out is in

Senti

Given Berliners' enthusiasm for American popular culture on the one hand, and their taste for long, drawn-out breakfasts, traditionally served until late afternoon, on the other, it should be no surprise that elaborate brunch buffets are the latest café fad. The typical deal is that the brunch providers lay out a table of piled-up platters and brimming tureens, and you help yourself to as much as you want for a fixed, one-off sum. You don't even have to wait until Sunday to do it, as many places are offering brunch throughout the week.

The bank of Kreuzberg's Landwehrkanal, with willows weeping into the water and the metallic click of nearby games of boule, provides a soothing setting for the excellent brunch at **Senti** (p128). At other times of day, this canal-bank location is a tapas bar, so think of a meat-rich brunch menu with a Spanish accent. Paella is usually one of the items on offer for the €7.50 flat fee.

Up on Kastanienallee in Prenzlauer Berg, where the morning after is prone to last well into the following afternoon, brunch with an alternative flavour can be found at **Café Morgenrot** (p82). There ain't no such thing as a free brunch, but the deal at this former squatter hangout-turned-kitchen collective comes close. It serves up a big range of veggie and vegan fare in a colourful setting. Pay as much as you feel you can afford, between €3 and €7.

Not far away on Choriner Strasse, the best of the brunch in Mitte is at **Hazelwood** (p69). A new addition to the brunch scene, this is an American-style diner with a comfy dark wood interior. It offers a gourmet à la carte brunch with a main course costing up to €8.50.

So good they named it thrice, **Tee Tea Thé** (p119) in Schöneberg is quaint and always packed. The buffet (€8.50) often has regional variations or you can fork out a bit extra (€13.90) and sample a range of infusions from their boggling selection of teas. Booking is recommended.

Once this place was a well-kept secret, now you have to book days in advance. Chef Claudio Andretta successfully balances the best elements of European cuisine. Imagine mountain trout wrapped in bacon and chopped egg on a bed of peppery cress, or beef fillet poached in sour cream served on black salsify and potato gnocchi, and a pyramid of rich chocolate with cassis sauce for dessert. The interior is simple but gets cramped.

Würgeengel

Dresdener Strasse 122 (615 5560). U1, U8 Kottbusser Tor. **Open** 7pm-late daily. No credit cards. **Bar.** **Map** p126 A1 ⓬

Red walls and velvet upholstery convey an atmosphere aching for sin, while well-mixed cocktails and a fine wine list served by smart staff make this a place for the more discerning drinker. The glass-latticed ceiling and a 1920s chandelier elegantly belie the fairly priced drinks and tapas on offer.

Shopping

Cherrybomb

Oranienstrasse 32 (614 6151). U1 Görlitzer Bahnhof. **Open** 11am-8pm Mon-Fri; 11am-6pm Sat. **Map** p126 A1 ⓭

German labels including brands such as Blutsgeschwister, Boogaloo and Berlin's own Volksmarke, plus Holland's King Louis and Colcci from Brazil, rub shoulders in this lowlit storefront. Although Cherrybomb is popular with women, there's plenty of streetwear for men too.

Hard Wax

Paul-Lincke-Ufer 44a (6113 0111/www.hardwax.com). U8 Schönleinstrasse. **Open** noon-8pm Mon-Sat. **Map** p126 A2 ⓮

One of the world's leading dealers in electronic music and dance of all genres stocks a staggeringly good selection of vinyl releases, plus a few CDs too. It's owned by Mark Ernestus, half

of the duo behind Basic Channel and Rhythm & Sound. The shop is in the second courtyard.

IrieDaily

Depot 2, Oranienstrasse 9 (611 4655/www.iriedaily.de). U1 Görlitzer Bahnhof. **Open** 11am-8pm Mon-Fri; 11am-6pm Sat. **Map** p126 B1 ⓯

Eastern earthiness combined with a skater/hip hop aesthetic has made IrieDaily one of the most popular local streetware brands. Girls' tops and pants are flattering and edgy, the hoodies slinky and cosy; men's cargo pants are classy and velvety.

Killerbeast

Schlesische Strasse 31 (9926 0319/ www.killerbeast.de). U1 Schlesisches Tor. **Open** 3-7.30pm Mon; noon-7.30pm Tue-Fri; 11am-4pm Sat. No credit cards. **Map** p126 D2 ⓰

Old things are turned new again by designer Claudia Weiler who sits in the shop and sews solid and stylish jackets, shirts and skirts that sit nicely between office-suitable and street savvy. A children's line called Schnüllerbeast is her latest innovation.

Nightlife

103 Club

NEW *Falckensteinstrasse 47 (no phone/ www.103club.de). U1 Schlesisches Tor.* **Open** 11.30pm-late Fri, Sat. No credit cards. **Map** p126 D1 ⓱

This place is huge and weirdly proportioned, with a variety of rooms connected by a cramped hallway. Sometimes there are three different sets of DJs in the building, playing anything from Baile Funk to easy listening, though there is an emphasis on housier styles. Live acts such as Simian Mobile Disco or Schneider TM show up regularly, but the feel is down-to-earth and you can stretch out in the upstairs lounge.

Arena

Eichenstrasse 4, Treptow (533 2030/ www.arena-berlin.de). U1 Schlesisches Tor. **Open** varies. No credit cards. **Map** p126 E2 ⓲

Würgeengel

Just over the border into Treptow, this is a former bus garage and often sounds like it. But Arena hosts A-list concerts by acts such as Bob Dylan or Björk, and its moveable stage also allows for some smaller acts. The same complex includes the *Badeschiff*, a barge-turned-swimming-pool popular with the gay crowd, and the party boat MS *Hoppetosse*.

Barbie Deinhoff's

Schlesische Strasse 16 (no phone/www. bader-deinhoff.de). U1 Schlesisches Tor.

Open 6pm-2am Mon-Thur, Sun; 6pm-6am Fri, Sat. No credit cards.
Map p126 D2 ⑲

Run by the celebrity drag queen Lena Braun, this lively and unusual bar attracts both the more bourgeois members of Berlin's cross-dressing community, as well as the loucher denizens of Kreuzberg. The look is pitched somewhere between tacky kitsch and futuristic chic. Lectures and art events are often held at Barbie Deinhoff's before the debauchery kicks off later in the evening.

BERLIN BY AREA

Turkish Berlin

For many Berliners, a greasy kebab is the only way to finish a good night out. Turkish food is a Berlin staple, but not many realise that the doner kebab is no import from Turkey. It was actually invented in Kreuzberg, in 1971, by Mehmet Aygun, these days proprietor of the **Hasir** (p125) restaurant chain.

But Turkish culture stretches further than street food. In Kreuzberg, the mosques now attract more worshippers than the churches. Berlin has become home to the world's largest Turkish community outside Turkey. The hubs are in Kreuzberg and Neukölln, where today one in every three residents is of Turkish origin.

The meeting of cultures has had a difficult history. Immigration began in 1961 as a consequence of the Berlin Wall. With East German workers suddenly cut off from jobs in the West, the FDR government grasped about for another source of cheap labour. Thousands of Gastarbeiter (guest workers) were hurriedly recruited from Turkey, and crammed together in purpose-built blocks such as the shabby, hive-like structure at Kotbusser Tor. With German citizenship impossible until a 2001 change in the law, the Turkish community has remained quite isolated from mainstream society. A recent report found that up to 60 per cent of children in Kreuzberg kindergartens couldn't speak a word of German.

But in Kreuzberg there's also a genuine enthusiasm for multiculturalism. Turkish families, living side by side with punks and squatters, have developed into a uniquely indigenous community. The sound of Turkendeutsche – a hybrid language spoken by the immigrant population – fills the air around Oranienstrasse, while Turkish-German rappers like Cartel and Azziza-A spit lyrics on bar stereos. The Tuesday and Friday canalside Turkischer Markt on the Maybachufer (U1, U8 Kottbusser Tor) showcases the settlers' more traditional side, while regular Turkish gay nights at **SO36** (p133) reveal a corresponding cosmopolitanism. Turkish-born, Kreuzberg-bred comedian Kaya Yana is one of the biggest sensations on German TV – quoting his catchphrase, 'Was guckst du?' ('What are you looking at?'), has become an annoyingly regular national joke. And you can still buy that local invention, the doner kebab, any time of the day or night.

Festsaal Kreuzberg

Skalitzer Strasse 130, Kreuzberg (6165 6003/www.festsaal-kreuzberg.de). U1, U8 Kottbusser Tor. **Open** varies. No credit cards. **Map** p126 A2 ⓴

It looks an unlikely place to go raving, but, thanks to a westward-moving scene and an eclectic booking policy, this is a popular venue. Expect indie acts and DJs from Wolf Eyes to Miss Kittin and all over the map.

Konrad Tönz

Falckensteinstrasse 30 (612 3252/ www.konradtoenzbar.de). U1 Schlesisches Tor. **Open** 8.15pm-2am Tue-Sun. No credit cards. **Map** p126 D2 ㉑

This quirky lounge with small dance-floor embraces a retro, shaken-not-stirred aesthetic with patterned wallpaper and suave grooves from mono record players. DJs play from 9pm at weekends.

Möbel Olfe

End of Dresdener Strasse/Kottbusser Tor (6165 9612/www.moebel-olfe.de). U1, U8 Kottbusser Tor. **Open** 6pm-late Tue-Sun. No credit cards. **Map** p126 A2 ㉒

Odd location for a gay bar, wedged among Turkish businesses in a down-at-heel 1960s development, but this place has been packed since it opened. Unpretentious, crowded, mixed, fun and with regular DJ nights.

Roses

Oranienstrasse 187 (615 6570). U1, U8 Kottbusser Tor. **Open** 10pm-5am daily. No credit cards. **Map** p126 B1 ㉓

Whatever state you're in, you'll fit in fine at this boisterous gay den of glitter. Customers from across the sexual spectrum come to mingle and indulge in excessive drinking amid plush, kitsch decor. Roses is always full, and no place for uptights.

SO36

Oranienstrasse 190, Kreuzberg (6140 1306/www.so36.de). U1, U8 Kottbusser Tor. **Open** 9pm-late daily. No credit cards. **Map** p126 B2 ㉔

Berlin's legendary punk club continues to book the biggest names in DIY, from Bolt Thrower to Killing Joke, as well as edgy up-and-comers. It also hosts reggae nights and an assortment of popular gay and lesbian parties.

Watergate

Falckensteinstrasse 49 (6128 0396/ www.water-gate.de). U1 Schlesisches Tor. **Open** 11pm-late Wed, Fri, Sat. No credit cards. **Map** p126 D1 ㉕

This two-floor club has a slick feel, a panoramic view over the Spree and a better-than-average sound system. Both floors open up on weekends, usually hosting two different sets of acts. Music tends toward electro, house and minimal techno, though left-field acts appear from time to time.

Arts & leisure

Babylon Kreuzberg (A&B)

Dresdener Strasse 126 (6160 9693/ www.yorck.de). U1, U8 Kottbusser Tor. No credit cards. **Map** p126 A1 ㉖

This twin-screen cinema runs a varied programme of off-Hollywood, indie crossover and UK films. It's a cosy respite from all the multiplexes.

Ballhaus Naunynstrasse

Naunynstrasse 27 (347 459 844/ www.kunstamkreuzberg.de). U1, U8 Kottbusser Tor. **Open** varies. No credit cards. **Map** p126 B1 ㉗

A varied assortment of western and oriental music is on the menu at this Kreuzberg cultural centre, with drinks and snacks in the café out front. The long, rectangular hall, which seats 150, also plays host to the excellent Berliner Kammeroper, among others.

Western Kreuzberg

The neighbourhood around busy Bergmannstrasse – bustling with cafés, second-hand stores, fashion retailers, book and music shops – has long bucked the general trend for everything to drift eastwards and today is livelier

Viktoriapark

than ever. By day, anyway; there's not much of a scene by night. Some of Berlin's most beautiful streets are hereabouts – check the restored area around Chamissoplatz – and nearby **Viktoriapark**, its artificial hill and waterfall, is one of the city's most characteristic green spaces.

Sights & museums

Schwules Museum

Mehringdamm 61 (6959 9050/ www.schwulesmuseum.de). U6, U7 Mehringdamm. **Open** 2-6pm Mon, Wed-Sun. **Admission** €5; €3 reductions. No credit cards. **Map** p127 B4 ㉓

The Gay Museum opened in 1985 and is still one of the only such institutions anywhere. On the ground floor is the actual museum, housing permanent and temporary exhibitions. The third-floor library and archive houses around 8,000 books (500 or so in English) and 3,000 periodicals, plus photo collections, film and audio, all available for lending.

Eating & drinking

Austria

Bergmannstrasse 30, on Marheineke Platz (694 4440). U7 Gneisenaustrasse. **Open** 6pm-1am daily. €€€. **Austrian**. **Map** p127 C4 ㉙

With a collection of antlers, this place does its best to look like a hunting-lodge. The meat used here is organic, and there's a list of organic wines. Austria also offers Kapsreiter or Zipfer beer on tap, and a famously over-the-top schnitzel. Outdoor seating on a tree-lined square makes it a pleasant summer venue too.

Haifischbar

Arndtstrasse 25 (691 1352/www.haifischbar-berlin.de). U6, U7 Mehringdamm. **Open** 8pm-3am Mon-Thur, Sun; 8pm-5am Fri, Sat. No credit cards. **Bar**. **Map** p127 C4 ㉚

A well-run and friendly bar where the staff are expert cocktail-shakers, the music's hip and tasteful and the back room, equipped with a sushi bar, is a

good place to chill out at the end of an evening. Haifischbar is certainly the most happening place at night in the Bergmannstrasse area.

Osteria No.1

Kreuzbergstrasse 71 (786 9162). U6, U7 Mehringdamm. **Open** noon-2am daily. €€€. **Italian**. **Map** p127 B4 ㉛

Most of Berlin's best Italian chefs paid their dues at this well-worn 1977-founded establishment, learning their lessons from a family of restaurateurs who emigrated from Lecce. There's an excellent three-course lunch menu and, in summer, a lovely garden courtyard.

Pagoda

Bergmannstrasse 88 (691 2640). U7 Gneisenaustrasse. **Open** noon-midnight daily. €€. No credit cards. **Thai**. **Map** p127 C4 ㉜

You can watch the Thai ladies whipping up your meal behind the counter at Pagoda, which ensures that everything is fresh and authentic. Red and green curries here are sensational and the pad thai is heavenly. There are a few tables with stools on the ground floor plus extra seating in the basement. Or you can go next door to Sumo, an excellent sushi joint run by the same people.

Shopping

Another Country

Riemannstrasse 7 (6940 1150/ www.anothercountry.de). U7 Gneisenaustrasse. **Open** 11am-8pm Mon-Fri; noon-4pm Sat. No credit cards. **Map** p127 C4 ㉝

These spacious, welcoming premises house an ambitious bookshop and private library stocked with over 10,000 English-language titles – a large percentage of them science fiction. A small membership fee allows you to use the reading room downstairs and help yourself to tea and coffee, or borrow books for varying fees. Return them to recoup a deposit, or hang on to the book. Readings and other activities are also held here.

Colours

1st courtyard, Bergmannstrasse 102 (694 3348/www.kleidermarkt. de). U7 Gneisenaustrasse. **Open** 11am-7pm Mon-Fri; 11am-6pm Sat. **Map** p127 B4 ㉞

Rows of second-hand jeans, leather jackets and dresses, including party stunners and fetching Bavarian dirndls, plus the odd gem from the 1950s or '60s.

Knopf Paul

Zossener Strasse 10 (692 1212/www. paulknopf.de). U7 Gneisenaustrasse. **Open** 9am-6pm Tue, Fri; 2-6pm Wed, Thur. No credit cards. **Map** p127 C4 ㉟

A Kreuzberg institution that stocks thousands of buttons in every shape, colour and style. Whatever you're seeking, Paul Knopf ('button') will help you find it. His patient and amiable service is remarkable considering most transactions are for tiny sums.

Space Hall

Zossener Strasse 33 (694 7664/www. space-hall.de). U7 Gneisenaustrasse. **Open** 11am-8pm Mon-Fri; 10.30am-5pm Sat. **Map** p127 C4 ㊱

Space Hall offers a huge range of new and second-hand CDs and vinyl. Techno, house and electronica are the emphasis, but there's also a lot of hip hop, indie and rock music. There are several other music shops worth checking out in the vicinity.

Nightlife

BKA Theater

Mehringdamm 32-34 (2022 0044/ www.bka-luftschloss.de). U6, U7 Mehringdamm. **Open** *Performances* 8pm daily. **Map** p127 B3 ㊲

With a long tradition of taboo-breaking acts, BKA still features some of the weirdest and most progressive cabaret acts in town: intelligent drag stand-up, freaky chanteuses and power-packin' divas appear nightly.

Café Melitta Sundström/SchwuZ

Mehringdamm 61 (692 4414/www. schwuz.de). U6, U7 Mehringdamm. **Open** noon-late daily. No credit cards. **Map** p127 B4 ㊳

Schwules Museum p135

During the daytime this place serves as a cosy mixed café for students; in the evening it's full of gays too lazy to go to Schöneberg. Fridays and Saturdays from 11pm it becomes the entrance to SchwuZ, Berlin's longest-running gay dance institution, with two, sometimes three dancefloors, and much mingling between the three bars and the café out front.

Columbiaclub

Columbiadamm 9-11 (Trinity Ticketing 7809 9810/www.columbia club.de). U6 Platz der Luftbrücke. No credit cards. **Map** p127 C5 ③⑨
Despite being a place of entertainment since 1951, when this spot opened as a US Forces cinema, Columbiaclub can feel a little impersonal once you get past the old-fashioned box office. But the place showcases mid-size acts of every genre; John Cale, Lez Zeppelin, Grave Digger and Morgan Heritage have all performed here.

Columbiahalle

Columbiadamm 13-21 (tickets 6110 1313/www.columbiahalle.de). U6 Platz der Luftbrücke. **Open** 9am-7pm Mon-Fri; 10am-2pm Sat. No credit cards. **Map** p127 C5 ④⓪
Next door to Columbiaclub, this unappealing, roomy venue with great sound hosts larger acts that haven't made it to stadium status, with past acts including Moby, the Killers, the White Stripes, Snow Patrol and Goldfrapp. Drinks cost too much, but it's a good place to see superstar hip hop acts, such as Jay-Z and Eminem, that would be playing amphitheatres in other cities.

Passionskirche

Marheinekeplatz 1-2, Kreuzberg (tickets 6959 3624/6940 1241/ www.akanthus.de). U7 Gneisenaustrasse. No credit cards. **Map** p127 C4 ④①
The likes of Beck, Ryan Adams and Marc Almond have graced the stage of this deconsecrated church. But get there early, as Passionskirche is the only church in Berlin whose pews regularly overflow, and where you can drink more than wine.

Arts & leisure

F40

NEW *Fidicinstrasse 40, Kreuzberg (box office 691 1211/information 693 5692/www.fidicin40.de). U6 Platz der Luftbrücke.* No credit cards. **Map** p127 B5 ④②
Berlin's English-language theatre – formerly Friends of Italian Opera, now English Theatre Berlin – has moved to a new, larger, posher space on the same premises. It is continuing with the same high-quality mixture of international guest shows, co-productions and staged readings.

Northern Kreuzberg

The area between the Landwehr Canal and the border with Mitte suffered greatly in World War II and today is a disjointed part of town with wastelands punctuating patches of new buildings. Some of the city's major cultural institutions and historical memorials are scattered around here though, especially along the line of the former Wall and in the area left blank by the disappearance of Anhalter Bahnhof, once the city's biggest station.

Sights & museums

Deutsches Technikmuseum Berlin

Trebbiner Strasse 9 (902 540/ www.dtmb.de). U1, U7 Möckernbrücke. **Open** 9am-5.30pm Tue-Fri; 10am-6pm Sat, Sun. **Admission** €4.50; €2.50 reductions. **Map** p127 A2 ④③
In the former goods depot of Anhalter Bahnhof, the German Museum of Technology is a large and eclectic collection. The station sheds naturally provide an ideal setting for the rail exhibits. There are also exhibitions about the Industrial Revolution, seafaring, computer technology, aviation and space travel, and printing. Behind the main complex lies an open-air section consisting of two windmills and

a smithy. The Spectrum annexe at Möckernstrasse 26 houses over 200 interactive devices and experiments.

Gruselkabinett

Schöneberger Strasse 23A (2655 5546/ www.gruselkabinett-berlin.de). S1, S2, S25 Anhalter Bahnhof. **Open** 10am-3pm Mon; 10am-7pm Tue, Thur, Sun; 10am-8pm Fri; noon-8pm Sat. **Admission** €7; €5 reductions. No credit cards. **Map** p127 A2 ⓐ

This chamber of horrors is housed in one of the city's only visitable World War II air-raid shelters. Built in 1943, the five-level concrete bunker also includes an exhibit on itself. The 'horrors' include an exhibit on medieval medicine, a simulated cemetery, strange cloaked figures and lots of canned screaming.

Haus am Checkpoint Charlie

Friedrichstrasse 43-5 (253 7250/ www.mauermuseum.de). U6 Kochstrasse. **Open** 9am-10pm daily. **Admission** €9.50; €5.50 reductions. No credit cards. **Map** p127 C1 ⓑ

A little tacky, but essential for anyone interested in the Cold War. This private museum opened not long after the GDR erected the Berlin Wall to document what was taking place. The exhibition charts the history of the Wall, detailing the ingenious and hair-raising ways people escaped from the GDR, and exhibits some of the actual contraptions used.

Jüdisches Museum

Lindenstrasse 9-14 (2599 3300/ guided tours 2599 3305/www. juedisches-museum-berlin.de). U1, U6 Hallesches Tor. **Open** 10am-8pm Mon; 10am-10pm Tue-Sun. **Admission** €5; €2.50 reductions. No credit cards. **Map** p127 C2 ⓒ

Daniel Libeskind's building, completed in 1998, is partly based on an exploded Star of David, and partly on lines drawn between the site and former addresses of figures in Berlin's Jewish history. The entrance is via a tunnel from the Kollegienhaus next door into an underground geometry startlingly independent of the above-ground building. One passage leads to the exhibition halls, two others intersect en route to the Holocaust Tower and the ETA Hoffmann Garden, a grid of 49 columns, tilted to disorientate. Throughout, diagonals and parallels carve out surprising spaces, while windows slash through the structure and its zinc cladding like the knife-wounds of history. Then there are the 'voids', negative spaces that stand for the emptiness left by the destruction of German Jewish culture. The permanent exhibition struggles in places with such powerful surroundings. It tells the stories of prominent Jews, what they contributed to their community and to the life of Berlin and Germany, before documenting their fate in the Holocaust.

Martin-Gropius-Bau

Niederkirchnerstrasse 7 (254 860/ www.gropiusbau.de). S1, S2, S25 Anhalter Bahnhof. **Open** 10am-8pm Mon; 10am-8pm Wed-Sun. **Admission** varies. **Map** p127 A1 ⓓ

Cosying up to where the Wall once ran (there is still a short, pitted stretch running along the south side of Niederkirchnerstrasse), the Martin-Gropius-Bau is named after its architect, uncle of the more famous Walter. Built in 1881, it has been renovated and serves as a venue for an assortment of art exhibitions and touring shows. 'Im Zeichen der Goldenen Greifen' runs from 6 July to 1 Oct 2007. There's no permanent exhibition, but there is a decent bookshop.

Topographie des Terrors

Niederkirchnerstrasse 8 (2548 6703/ www.topographie.de). S1, S2, S25 Anhalter Bahnhof. **Open** Oct-Apr 10am-dusk daily. *May-Sept* 10am-8pm daily. **Admission** free. **Map** p127 B1 ⓔ

Essentially a piece of waste ground where the Gestapo headquarters and offices of the Reich SS once stood. This was the centre of the Nazi police state apparatus and it was from here that the

Jüdisches Museum

Holocaust was directed. Not much here now except an open-air exhibition about the site's baleful history and a temporary building where you can buy the excellent catalogue and pick up a free audio guide. Work on a permanent documentation centre should be completed in 2010. A surviving segment of the Berlin Wall runs along the site's northern boundary.

Eating & drinking

Café Adler

Friedrichstrasse 206 (251 8965). U6 Kochstrasse. **Open** 10am-midnight Mon-Sat; 10am-7pm Sun. **Café. Map** p127 B1 ④⑨

You once could have watched history in the making from your table in this elegant corner café next to what used to be Checkpoint Charlie. Today it's a bustling and business-like corner, with Café Adler an oasis of calm, coffee and decent light meals.

Grossbeerenkeller

Grossbeerenstrasse 90 (251 3064). U1, U7 Möckernbrücke. **Open** 4pm-1am Mon-Fri; 6pm-1am Sat. **€€**. No credit cards. **German. Map** p127 B2 ⑤⓪

In business for nearly a century and a half, Grossbeerenkeller serves good home cooking of a solid *Berlinisch* bent. This is the place to come if you want to sample indigenous eats in their natural habitat. The Hoppel-Poppel breakfast is legendary.

Sale e Tabacchi

Kochstrasse 18 (252 1155). U6 Kochstrasse. **Open** 9am-2am Mon-Fri; 10am-2am Sat, Sun. **€€€. Italian. Map** p127 C1 ⑤①

Classy Italian well known for fish dishes, pretty courgette flowers filled with ricotta and mint, and an impressive selection of Italian wines. The interior is meant to reflect a time when salt (*sale*) and tobacco (*tabacchi*) were sold exclusively by the state. In summer, enjoy dining in the garden under lemon, orange and pomegranate trees.

Solar

NEW *Stresemannstrasse 76 (0163 765 7200/www.solar-berlin.com). S1, S2, S25 Anhalter Bahnhof.* **Open** 6pm-2am Mon-Thur, Sun; 6pm-5am. **Bar. Map** p127 B1 ⑤②

A stunning view is the main attraction at this smart two-floor cocktail lounge, perched at the top of a tower block. There are also – sometimes – decent chill-out DJs and plenty of sofas for lying about. Don't come just for the indifferent food, but there's an international menu if you do get hungry. Almost worth it, though, just for the ride up in the glass elevator on the side of the building.

Arts & leisure

HAU

Main office, HAU2, Hallesches Ufer 32, Kreuzberg (box office 2590 0427/ information 259 0040/www.hebbel-am-ufer.de). U1, U7 Möckernbrücke or U1, U6 Hallesches Tor. **Map** p127 B2 ⑤③

The 2003 amalgamation of the former Hebbel Theater (HAU1), Theater am Halleschen Ufer (HAU2) and Theater am Ufer (HAU3) created a cultural powerhouse that can develop, rehearse and present internationally renowned guest ensembles, innovative theatre projects and dance productions – all at the same time. Within its first year of operation, HAU was voted Theatre of the Year by German critics. **Other locations:** HAU1, Stresemannstrasse 29, Kreuzberg; HAU3, Tempelhofer Ufer 10, Kreuzberg.

Tempodrom

Möckernstrasse 10 (5200 0060/www. tempodrom.de). U1 Möckernbrücke. **Map** p127 A2 ⑤④

The descendant of a tent venue that was once pitched in various parts of west Berlin – with tent-like architecture nodding to that nomadic past – this is a modern all-purpose performance and event space on the site of the old Anhalter Bahnhof. What's on could be anything from Chris Rea to the Chinese National Circus, from the Dubliners to Holiday on Ice.

East Side Gallery

Friedrichshain

Stretching eastwards from Mitte along the Stalinist spine of Karl-Marx-Allee, and taking in a post-industrial area by the river, Friedrichshain is the inner-Berlin district that most clearly recalls the old East. **Karl-Marx-Allee** is a grand avenue built in Soviet style – it was the builders working on its construction who started the 1953 East Berlin uprising. Most of the district's life is centred around **Simon-Dach-Strasse**, the hub for a young, anarchic community of bohos and students, while the slowly disappearing former factories near the river have been hosting nightclubs for a decade or so. There's no sightseeing to speak of, save for the **East Side Gallery** – a stretch of former Wall situated east of the Oberbaumbrücke on Mühlenstrasse, which is bedecked with paintings from international artists.

Eating & drinking

Café 100Wasser

Simon-Dach-Strasse 39 (2900 1356).
U5 Frankfurter Tor or U1, S3, S5,
S7, S9, S75 Warschauer Strasse.
Open 9am-late daily. No credit cards.
Café. Map p143 C2 ❶
The all-you-can-eat brunch buffet (€8.90, 9.30am-3pm daily) has a cult following among students and other late risers. Take your time over the food and don't panic as the buffet gets plundered: just when the food seems to be finished, out comes loads of new stuff.

Conmux

Simon-Dach-Strasse 35 (291 3863).
U5 Frankfurter Tor or U1, S3, S5,

S7, S9, S75 Warschauer Strasse.
Open 10am-late daily. No credit cards. **Café**. **Map** p143 C2 **②**

For those into sitting outside, there are pavement tables here even in winter, when the waiters will light big gas heaters to keep you warm. Inside there are sewing-machine tables and pieces of scrap-metal art. The menu offers well-crafted light meals. Service is at best monosyllabic, at worst totally indifferent.

Ehrenburg

Karl-Marx-Allee 103A (4210 5810). U5 Weberwiese. **Open** 10am-2am daily. No credit cards. **Café**. **Map** p143 B1 **③**

Named after Russian-Jewish novelist Ilja Ehrenburg, a dedicated socialist, this café and espresso bar, with its sober, geometric decoration, is one of the few stylish places to be found around Weberwiese U-Bahn station. Although the library looks like it's part of the decorative style, you're free to pick up a book and study the works of Ehrenburg, Lenin, Stalin, Engels or Marx as you enjoy your latte macchiato and other capitalist achievements.

Frittiersalon

Boxhagener Strasse 104 (2593 3906/ www.frittiersalon.de). U5 Frankfurter Tor. **Open** 6pm-midnight Mon; noon-midnight Tue-Fri; 1pm-midnight Sat, Sun. **€**. No credit cards. **German/American**. **Map** p143 C1 **④**

Organic burgers, bratwurst and fries are served with home-made ketchup, sauces and dips in this 'multikulti' gourmet chip shop. There are some curious clashes of culture – a Middle East-influenced 'halloumi burger', for example, where fried cheese is embellished with a yoghurt sauce, sesame dip and salad.

Intimes

Boxhagener Strasse 107 (2966 6457). U5 Samariterstrasse. **Open** 10am-late daily. No credit cards. **Café**. **Map** p143 C1 **⑤**

Next to the cinema of the same name, decorated with painted tiles and offering a good variety of Turkish and vegetarian food as well as breakfast at reasonable prices. Pleasures can be as simple as fried potatoes with garlic sausage; best deal is the Wednesday special. Decent selection of beers, friendly service.

Kingston Pizzerei & Cocktail Bar

Simon-Dach-Strasse 12 (2904 4433). U1, S3, S5, S7, S9, S75 Warschauer Strasse or U5 Samariterstrasse. **Open** 4pm-10pm daily. **€**. **Italian**. No credit cards. **Map** p143 C2 **⑥**

There are only five dishes on the menu and two of them are pizza, which comes in mini (€1.50) and biggie (€3) sizes. The ultra-thin, crispy crust is a welcome change for this district, and you can pile on as many of the 18 toppings as you like for no extra charge. Tables are limited, but in summer there's plenty of outdoor seating.

Küntsliche BEATmung

Simon-Dach-Strasse 20 (0176 2334 8125). U1, S3, S5, S7, S9, S75 Warschauer Strasse. **Open** 7.30pm-late daily. No credit cards. **Bar**. **Map** p143 C2 **⑦**

The low-domed ceiling, plastic furniture and coloured neon can make this trendy cocktail bar feel like the inside of a space capsule – and slightly weird before the crowds arrive. Around midnight, though, the beautiful young things start dribbling in and any oddness is soon swallowed in the crush. The elaborate drinks menu provides hundreds of lurid opportunities for experimental boozing.

Meyman

Krossener Strasse 11A (no phone). U1, S3, S5, S7, S9, S75 Warschauer Strasse or U5 Samariterstrasse. **Open** 11am-2am Mon-Thur, Sun; 11am-4am Fri, Sat. **€€**. No credit cards. **North African**. **Map** p143 C2 **⑧**

Moroccan, North African and Arabic specialities plus fresh fruit shakes and

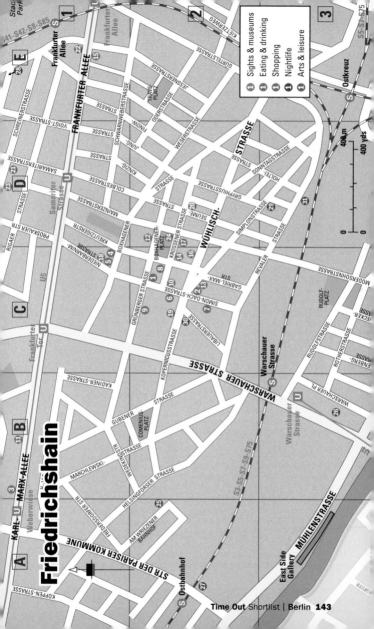

Friedrichshain

Legend
- Sights & museums
- Eating & drinking
- Shopping
- Nightlife
- Arts & leisure

400 m
400 yds

East Side Gallery

All white now

Berlin's new self-conscious colour scheme.

Schneeweiss

Tucking into a chanterelle ragoût at **Schneeweiss** (p145), and looking at that restaurant's snowy 'Alpine' decor, one might reflect not only on the quality of the Spätzle, but also that white is most definitely *the* colour in the city these days.

Back when Iggy Pop, in his Berlin days, sang of 'nightclubbing, bright white clubbing', the city's favourite colour was actually black. Black clubs with dark, black corners full of people in black leather. These days all the new restaurants and clubs, all the fresh-faced discos and multi-purpose event locations, seem to come in gleaming white.

White walls do make it easier to see and be seen in a bar such as **Perlweiss** (p70). White everything (all that cleaning!) impresses a sense of slightly decadent luxury in a designer hotel such as **Lux 11** (p166). And white certainly sets off the food presentation in a fashionable new restaurant such as **Shiro i Shiro** (p71), **Spindler & Klatt** (p128) or **Bangaluu** (p64). But there's more to it than that.

Back when black was the colour, West Berlin was a kind of sanctuary, a place to hide from history. Black allows you to fade into the corners, to see without being seen, to relax in comfy anonymity.

New Berlin is different, spruced-up and polished, nothing to hide, everything to prove. White is clean, a *tabula rasa*, ready for anything. But anything placed against it stands out, any mark shows right up. There's no way to relax in anonymity when your surroundings shine like a sun-bleached skull. People will notice those scuffed-up shoes. Make an effort!

But maybe white is already on the out. The biggest, whitest club of all was Goya on Nollendorfplatz. In 2006, the vast, gloomy recesses of the old Metropol disco were transformed into a stunning alabaster atrium. Outfits could easily be envied or scorned, sexual opportunities quickly surveyed. No hiding place in *that* place. But it only lasted for a few months; nobody wanted to go there – and the building is once again dark.

pizza are served in this warm and comfortable *Imbiss*, where there are usually plenty of tables. It's a bit pricier than comparable places, but fresh ingredients and a wide variety of dishes keep them coming – and few others are open this late.

Nil

Grünberger Strasse 52 (2904 7713).
U1, S3, S5, S7, S9, S75 Warschauer
Strasse or U5 Frankfurter Tor.
Open 11am-midnight daily. **€**.
No credit cards. **North African**.
Map p143 C2 ❾

Nil is a friendly Sudanese *Imbiss* offering good-value lamb and chicken dishes and an excellent vegetarian selection that includes falafel, halloumi and aubergine salad. Hot peanut sauces are the tasty but sloppy speciality. Grab an extra napkin.

Paule's Metal Eck

Krossener Strasse 15 (291 1624).
U5 Frankfurter Tor or U1, S3, S5,
S7, S9, S75 Warschauer Strasse.
Open *Winter* 7pm-late daily. *Summer*
5pm-late daily. No credit cards.
Bar. **Map** p143 C2 ❿

Neither a typical heavy metal bar, nor remotely typical for this area, the Egyptian-themed *Eck* attracts a young crowd with relentless metal videos, a decent selection of beers, and both pool and table football. Inoperative disco balls, mummy overhead lamps and formidable dragon busts deck an interior that is half designed like a mausoleum, and half in gloomy medieval style. A small menu changes weekly and there's live Bundesliga football at weekends.

Prager Hopfenstube

Karl-Marx-Allee 127 (426 7367).
U5 Weberwiese. **Open** 11am-midnight daily. **€€**. **Czech**. **Map** p143 B1 ⓫

Get all the favourites from your last Prague holiday: *svickova* (roast beef), *veprova pecene* (roast pork), *knedliky* (dumplings) and the lone vegetarian prospect, *smazeny syr* (breaded and deep-fried hermelin cheese served with remoulade and fries). Sluice

down this heavy fare with mugs of Staropramen beer; afterwards, a Becherovka herbal digestif might help stave off indigestion. The fast and friendly service is a pleasingly inauthentic touch.

RotWild

Grünberger Strasse 77 (2900 5719/
www.rotwild.tv). *U5 Frankfurter Tor or*
U1, S3, S5, S7, S9, S75 Warschauer
Strasse. **Open** 5pm-late Mon-Fri; 10am-late Sat, Sun. No credit cards. **Café**.
Map p143 D2 ⓬

Any place with a happy hour and a 'hungry hour' can't be bad. From 6pm to 8pm every day you can buy cheap drinks but also get a hearty meal for €3. There's an ample Sunday brunch buffet from 10am to 4pm, the pool table and amiable waitstaff should keep you entertained, and the kitchen is open until midnight.

Schneeweiss

NEW *Simplonstrasse 16 (2904 9704/*
www.schneeweiss-berlin.de). *U1, S3,*
S5, S7, S9, S75 Warschauer Strasse.
Open 10am-1pm daily. **€€€**. **Modern European**. **Map** p143 C2 ⓭

This smart and understated establishment in fashionably minimalist white offers modern European dishes they describe as 'Alpine' – essentially a well-presented fusion of Italian, Austrian and south German ideas. There are daily lunch and dinner menus, plus a breakfast selection and snacks, shakes and schnitzels throughout the day. Although upmarket for the area, it's great quality for the price and deservedly popular, so best to book.

Shisha

Krossener Strasse 19 (2977 1995).
U1, S3, S5, S7, S9, S75 Warschauer
Strasse or U5 Samariterstrasse.
Open 10am-late daily. **€€**. No credit cards. **Middle Eastern**.
Map p143 C2 ⓮

An Arabic restaurant/bar that serves both exotic vegetarian and meat dishes from Lebanon, Syria and Iraq. Hookahs are the real attraction for the twentysomething crowd: take advantage of

RotWild p145

the ten flavoured tobaccos and huge elevated couch to settle down and smoke yourself silly.

Supamolly

Jessnerstrasse 41 (2900 7294). U5, S4, S8, S85 Frankfurter Allee. **Open** 8pm-late Tue-Sun. No credit cards. **Bar. Map** p143 E1 ⑮

Having opened in the early 1990s as a semi-legal bolthole fronting a lively squat, Supamolly is a miracle of survival. Frequent live punk and ska shows in the club behind the bar dictate only some of the clientele; a healthy mix of young and ageing punks, unemployed activists and music lovers of all types gather in this dim, mural-smeared, candlelit watering hole until the early morning. DJs at weekends.

Tagung

Wühlischstrasse 29 (2977 3788). U5 Samariterstrasse. **Open** 7pm-4am Mon-Fri; 7pm-5am Sat, Sun. No credit cards. **Bar. Map** p143 C2 ⑯

Tagung is a small bar decked out in GDR memorabilia and still serving things like Club Cola – the old Eastern brand. The patrons are twenty- and thirtysomethings and the place seems to provide good laughs and drunken nights for all who frequent it. The small club downstairs is likewise 'ostalgically' decorated and offers mainstream dance music as well as occasional one-off events.

Volkswirtschaft

Krossener Strasse 17 (2900 4604). U1, S3, S5, S7, S9, S75 Warschauer Strasse or U5 Samariterstrasse. **Open** 6pm-midnight Mon-Wed; 1pm-midnight Thur-Sat; 11am-late Sun. **€€**. No credit cards. **Vegetarian. Map** p143 D2 ⑰

There's a little of everything here: occasional live music, movie nights, book readings, vegetarian and vegan Sunday brunches and Pinkus – a seldom-found organic beer. As a restaurant, Volkswirtschaft prides itself on healthy, hearty dishes and has an extensive menu that changes daily.

Power after hours

Berghain is currently the big club on the block.

In contrast to deliberately semi-derelict techno clubs of old, **Berghain/Panorama Bar** (p148) represents a major investment in a former power station to give hedonists a happening home. Though concrete remains the appropriate decor for this three-floor post-industrial palace, everything here is polished and finished – like the city itself these days – rather than left ragged around the edges.

Big, brash Berghain on the first floor fills with shirtless, mainly gay men, dancing to techno from international DJs. Panorama Bar upstairs booms to a more minimal beat for happy heteros who delight in daylight dancing when the huge blinds open to reveal a new dawn. The soundsystem is peerless and there's no shortage of bars, chill-out areas and darkrooms. Shameless pleasure-seeking might explain the strict no-cameras policy.

It's really an after-hours place, albeit a very big one, and doesn't get going until after 4am. Clubbers queue way into the morning after lesser haunts close their doors. In summer the outside bar opens around 11am, but the year-round closing time is late afternoon. Judging by the numbers, repaying the initial outlay is well under way. But competition looms as the people from much-missed Tresor embark on the renovation of yet another former power station over the river on Köpenicker Strasse.

Every day of the week has a culinary theme: Friday's fish and Tuesday's creative home cooking are especially successful.

Shopping

Anziehend

Niederbarnimstrasse 16 (2936 7829). U5 Frankfurter Tor. **Open** 11am-7pm Mon-Fri; 11am-4pm Sat. No credit cards. **Map** p143 C1 ⑱

This sweet second-hand store buys and sells well-maintained clothes and accessories, most of them with a modern tinge. There are lots of elegant and playful scarves and neckwear, plus vintage stuff from H&M.

Big Brobot

Kopernikusstrasse 19 (7407 8388/ www.bigbrobot.com). U5 Frankfurter Tor. **Open** 11am-8pm Mon-Fri; 11am-6pm Sat. **Credit** MC, V. **Map** p143 C2 ⑲

This is the first German home for British streetwear label Fenchurch. Big Brobot also stocks Boxfresh and Motel, and US classics Stüssy and X-Large. There are all sorts of cultish accessories, as well as comics and small-edition publications. Staff are friendly and know their urban brands.

Das Blaue Wunder

Seumestrasse 12, Friedrichshain (2576 8900). U5 Samariterstrasse. **Open** 4-8pm Mon-Fri; 10am-4pm Sat. No credit cards. **Map** p143 D2 ⑳

This neighbourhood treasure stocks organic wines from all over Germany – and beyond. Owner Klaus loves to sit you down for a chat and some tasting.

East of Eden

Schreinerstrasse 10, Friedrichshain (423 9362/www.east-of-eden.de). U5 Samariterstrasse. **Open** noon-7pm Mon-Sat. No credit cards. **Map** p143 D1 ㉑

The owners of this old-school second-hand bookshop shuttle to London in search of paperback staples and rare editions. Books are also available to borrow at a small fee. Readings and concerts too.

F95

NEW *Frankfurter Allee 95-97 (4208 3358/www.f95store.com). U5, S8, S41, S42, S85 Frankfurter Allee.* **Open** noon-8pm Mon-Fri; 11am-6pm Sat. **Map** p143 E1 ㉒

Style-conscious Slovenian store manager Slavko Felkar selects his favourite designs from Berlin's Premium fashion fair to sell at F95, the trade show's store on Frankfurter Allee. Scandinavian designers have the edge in this open-plan emporium, but the collection is international. Accessories, books, fragrances and chocolate are displayed on freight pallets adding a down-to-earth touch to designer prices, ranging from €29 to €1,800.

Mondos Arts

Schreinerstrasse 6, Friedrichshain (4201 0778/www.mondosarts.de). U5 Samariterstrasse. **Open** 10am-7pm Mon-Fri; 11am-4pm Sat. **Map** p143 D1 ㉓

The best of what's left of the East: Mondos stocks every type of 'ostalgic' GDR memorabilia, including flags, posters, clocks, border signs and various products embossed with the no longer endangered *Ampelmännchen* – the characterful East German green and red traffic-light men.

Trödelmarkt Boxhagener Platz

Boxhagener Platz, Friedrichshain (0177 827 9352). U1, S3, S5, S7, S9 Warschauer Strasse. **Open** 10am-6pm Sun. **Map** p143 D2 ㉔

A lot of local young artists and T-shirt designers set up stalls at this overflowing market, while punky types and bohemian mothers shop for vintage sunglasses and unusual crockery.

Nightlife

Berghain/Panorama

NEW *Am Wriezener Bahnhof (no phone/www.berghain.de). S3, S5, S7, S9, S75 Ostbahnhof.* **Open** Berghain midnight-late Sat; *Panorama Bar* 11pm-late Fri, Sat. No credit cards. **Map** p143 A2 ㉕

See box p147.

Das Haus B

NEW *Warschauer Platz 18, under the S-Bahnbogen (296 0800/www. dashausb.de). U1, S3, S5, S7, S9, S75 Warschauer Strasse.* **Open** 10pm-7am Fri, Sat. No credit cards. **Map** p143 B3 26

An East German relic, until recently known as Die Busche, this is east Berlin's oldest gay disco in a new location. Loud, tacky, resolutely mixed and always packed with stylish lesbians, gay teens and their girlfriends. It's a must for kitsch addicts and Abba fans; a no-go area for guys who like a masculine atmosphere.

Fritzclub im Postbahnhof

NEW *Strasse der Pariser Kommune 3-10, Friedrichshain (tickets 6110 1313/698 1280/www.fritzclub.com). S3, S5, S7, S9, S75 Ostbahnhof.* **Open** 9am-7pm Mon-Fri; 10am-2pm Sat. No credit cards. **Map** p143 A2 27

Housed in a restored industrial building, Fritzclub is a newcomer as a rock venue, but its association with RadioFritz is the clout to book on-their-way indie acts such as Arcade Fire and Maximo Park, mid-level names such as Luka Bloom, the Kooks, Clap Your Hands Say Yeah and Fun Lovin' Criminals and even some old-school near-legends, the likes of Sonic Youth.

K17

Pettenkofer Strasse 17 (4208 9300/ www.k17.de). U5, S8, S9, S41, S42, S85 Frankfurter Allee. **Open** 10pm-late Tue-Fri. No credit cards. **Map** p143 E1 28

Goth, EBM, industrial and metal are undead and well in this three-floor club and venue. Parties held here have names such as House of Pain and Schwarzer Donnerstag and the midweek Jailbreak concert series features live earaches from hardcore, nü-metal and crossover bands.

lovelite

Simplonstrasse 38/40 (no phone/ www.lovelite.de). U1, S3, S5, S7, S9, S75 Warschauer Strasse. **Open** from 11pm daily. No credit cards. **Map** p143 D3 29

A low-key and unfinished-looking late-night space that offers an eclectic selection of bands and DJs. They're usually of a local bent for a local crowd, but interesting smaller acts do sometimes arrive at lovelite from the outside world, such as Rogers Sisters and the Poets of Rhythm. The funk nights are always a good bet. Weekends feature a GDR-era truck outside selling tasty waffles.

Raumklang

Libauer Strasse 1, corner Kopernikusstrasse (2930 9802/ www.raum-klang.de). U1, S3, S5, S7, S9, S75 Warschauer Strasse. **Open** 11pm-late daily. No credit cards. **Map** p143 C2 30

Simple, 1970s chic and drenched in multicoloured light, this club resembles its neighbour lovelite (see above) following a shower and a shave. Boasting a sophisticated, ear-saving sound system suspended over the crowd, the DJs tend towards techno perhaps a bit better suited for a larger spot, emphasising locals such as Suzi Wong and Kotai. But there are also ragga nights and live acts from all over the map.

Rosi's

Revaler Strasse 29 (no phone/ www.rosis-berlin.de). S3, S5, S7, S8, S9, S41, S42, S75, S85 Ostkreuz. **Open** 9pm-late Thur; 11pm-late Fri, Sat. No credit cards. **Map** p143 D3 31

The sort of place eastern Berlin seemed to be full of in the early to mid 1990s: a rambling former industrial space decorated with flea-market furniture and graffiti, with a comfortable, unpretentious vibe. Music is provided by live acts and DJs, and runs the gamut from indie, punk and electro to drum 'n' bass, reggae/dancehall and even wacky Norwegian country-cabaret. The beer garden is a popular neighbourhood hangout in the summer.

BERLIN BY AREA

Schloss Charlottenburg p155

Other Districts

North of Mitte, the working-class industrial district of Wedding, formerly on the western side of the Wall, is now politically part of Mitte. The main thing to see here is on the border – the **Gedenkstätte Berliner Mauer**, a memorial incorporating one of the last stretches of the Wall.

Much of the eastern part of the city remains a depressing wasteland of decaying communist blocks, but there are a few things to see and do in Lichtenberg and Treptow, including the latter's Treptower Park, with its giant Sowjetisches Ehrenmal (Soviet War Memorial) built over a mass grave of Russian soldiers who perished in the 1945 assault on Berlin.

Further out east, the charming town of Köpenick, older than Berlin proper, has retained much of its

18th-century character. Schloss Köpenick, with its medieval drawbridge, Renaissance gateway and baroque chapel, stands on an island at the confluence of the rivers Spree and Dahme.

South of Kreuzberg, the district of Tempelhof is known principally for the giant Nazi-era airport of the same name (p178). To the south-west, the smart residential district of Dahlem contains the Freie Universität and a clutch of important museums. Deeper into affluent suburbia, Zehlendorf shades into the Grunewald and a district of forest and lakes.

West of central Charlottenburg, that district stretches a long way into more well-heeled residential suburbia, with a bunch of sights and museums around Schloss Charlottenburg, the enormous

Messe-Gelände trade fair grounds near the Funkturm, and the recently renovated **Olympia-Stadion**.

Still further west is the town of Spandau which, like Köpenick to the east, is older than the rest of the city. The Juliusturm in the **Zitadelle** is Berlin's oldest secular structure and there's a well-preserved Altstadt.

Sights & museums

Alliierten Museum

Clayallee 135, corner of Huttenweg, Zehlendorf (818 1990/www.alliierten museum.de). U3 Oskar-Helene-Heim. **Open** 10am-6pm Mon, Tue, Thur-Sun. **Admission** free.

The Allies arrived as conquerors, kept West Berlin alive during the 1948 Airlift, and finally went home in 1994. In what used to be a United States Forces cinema, this museum is mostly about the Blockade and Airlift, documented with photos, vehicles, planes, weapons and military uniforms. Outside stands the building that was once the stop-and-search centrepiece of Checkpoint Charlie.

Botanischer Garten

Königin-Luise-Strasse 6-8, Dahlem (8385 0100/www.bgbm.fu-berlin.de). S1 Botanischer Garten. **Open** *Garden* 9am-dusk daily. *Museum* Nov-Jan 9am-4pm daily; Feb-Oct 9am-dusk daily. **Admission** *Combined* €5; €2.50 reductions. *Museum only* €2; €1 reductions. No credit cards.

The Botanical Garden was landscaped at the beginning of the 20th century. Home to 18,000 plant species, 16 greenhouses and a museum, the gardens make a pleasant stroll. The museum is a bit dilapidated and there's no information in English, but it's the place to come for advice on whether those mushrooms you found in the forest are delectable or deadly. The S-Bahn is 15 minutes' walk.

Brücke Museum

Bussardsteig 9, Zehlendorf (831 2029/www.bruecke-museum.de). U3 Oskar-Helene-Heim, then bus 115 to Pücklerstrasse. **Open** 11am-5pm Mon, Wed-Sun. **Admission** €4; €2 reductions. No credit cards.

This small but satisfying museum is dedicated to the Berlin-based group of Expressionist painters known as Die Brücke ('The Bridge'). Oils, watercolours,

Alliierten Museum

drawings and sculptures from the authoritative collection of works by the main members (Schmidt-Rottluff, Heckel, Kirchner, Mueller and Pechstein) are rotated in temporary exhibitions.

Ethnologisches Museum

Lansstrasse 8, Dahlem (830 1438/ www.smb.spk-berlin.de). U3 Dahlem-Dorf. **Open** 10am-6pm Tue-Fri; 11am-6pm Sat, Sun. **Admission** €6; €3 reductions. No credit cards.
Extensive, authoritative, beautifully laid out, the Ethnological Museum encompasses cultures from around the world. Highlights include the Südsee (South Sea) room with New Guinean masks and effigies and a remarkable collection of canoes and boats, and the African rooms with superb carvings from Benin and the Congo, and beaded artefacts from Cameroon. There are three other museums in the same building: the Museum für Indische Kunst (Museum of Indian Art) representing more than 3,000 years of Indian culture; the Museum für Ostasiatische Kunst (East Asian Art) with archaeological objects and fine art from Japan, China and Korea; and the Museum Europäischer Kulturen (European Cultures) with exhibits about European everyday culture since the 18th century.

Forschungs- & Gedenkstätte Normannenstrasse (Stasi Museum)

Ruschestrasse 103, Lichtenberg (553 6854/www.stasimuseum.de). U5, S41, S42, S8, S85 Frankfurter Allee or U5 Magdalenenstrasse. **Open** 11am-6pm Mon-Fri; 2-6pm Sat, Sun. **Admission** €3.50; €2.50 reductions. No credit cards.
In what used to be the headquarters of the Ministerium für Staatssicherheit (the Stasi), you can look round the old offices of secret police chief Erich Mielke and see bugging devices and spy cameras concealed in books, plant pots and Trabant car doors. There's also a lot of communist kitsch, including banners and busts of Lenin.

Funkturm

Messedamm, Charlottenburg (3038 2900/www.capital-catering.de). U2 Theodor-Heuss-Platz or Kaiserdamm. **Open** 10am-11pm Tue-Sun. **Admission** €4; €2 reductions. No credit cards.
The 138m-high (453ft) Radio Tower was built in 1926 and looks a bit like a smaller Eiffel Tower. The observation deck stands at 126m (413ft); vertigo sufferers should seek solace in the restaurant, only 55m (180ft) from the ground. You get a free snack with your admission price.

Gedenkstätte Berliner Mauer

Bernauer Strasse 111, Wedding (464 1030/www.berliner-mauer-dokumentationszentrum.de). U8 Bernauer Strasse or S1, S2, S25 Nordbahnhof. **Open** *Documentation centre* Nov-Mar 10am-5pm Wed-Sun; Apr-Oct 10am-6pm Wed-Sun. **Admission** free.
This impeccably restored stretch of the Wall is as sterile a monument as any in Berlin. The documentation centre, featuring displays on the Wall and a

Funkturm

database of escapees, is across the street and from its roof you can view the Wall and the Kapelle der Versöhnung (Chapel of Reconciliation) – built on the site of a church destroyed by the East Germans.

Gedenkstätte Haus der Wannsee-Konferenz

Am Grossen Wannsee 56-8, Zehlendorf (805 0010/www.ghwk.de). S1, S7 Wannsee, then bus 114. **Open** 10am-6pm daily. **Admission** free.
Here, on 20 January 1942, a meeting of prominent Nazis, chaired by Heydrich, drew up plans for the Final Solution, making jokes and sipping brandy as they sorted out the practicalities of genocide. Today this infamous villa has been converted into the Wannsee Conference Memorial House, a place of remembrance, with a photo exhibition on the conference and its consequences.

Gedenkstätte Plötzensee

Hüttigpfad, Charlottenburg (344 3226/ www.gedenkstaette-ploetzensee.de). Bus 123. **Open** *Mar-Oct* 9am-5pm daily. *Nov-Feb* 9am-4pm daily. **Admission** free.
This memorial stands where the Nazis executed over 2,500 (largely political) prisoners. On one night in 1943, 186 people were hanged. In 1952 it was declared a memorial to the victims of fascism. There is little to see, apart from the execution area with its meat hooks from which victims were hanged, and a small room with an exhibition. The stone urn near the entrance is filled with earth from concentration camps.

Museum Berlin-Karlshorst

Zwieseler Strasse 4, corner of Rheinsteinstrasse, Lichtenberg (5015 0810/www.museum-karlshorst.de). S3 Karlshorst. **Open** 10am-6pm Tue-Sun. **Admission** free.
After the Soviets took Berlin, they commandeered this former German officers' club and it was here, on the night of 8-9 May 1945, that German commanders signed the unconditional surrender. The museum looks at the German-Soviet relationship over 70 years. Divided into 16 rooms including

the one where the Nazis surrendered, it takes you through two world wars and one cold one, plus assorted pacts, victories and capitulations.

Museum für Vor- & Frühgeschichte

Langhansbau, Schloss Charlottenburg, Charlottenburg (3267 4840/ www.smb. spk-berlin.de). U2 Sophie-Charlotte-Platz or U7 Richard-Wagner-Platz. **Open** 9am-5pm Tue-Fri; 10am-5pm Sat, Sun. **Admission** €3; €1.50 reductions. No credit cards.
The Primeval and Early History Museum – which is spread over six different galleries – traces the evolution of Homo sapiens from 1,000,000 BC to the Bronze Age. The highlights are the replicas (and some originals) of Heinrich Schliemann's famous treasure of ancient Troy, including weapons and works of ceramics and gold. Keep an eye out also for the sixth- century BC grave of a girl buried with a gold coin in her mouth.

Museumsdorf Düppel

Clauertstrasse 11, Zehlendorf (802 6671/www.dueppel.de). S1 Mexikoplatz, then bus 211, 629. **Open** *early Apr-late Oct* 3-7pm Thur; 10am-5pm Sun (last entry 4pm). **Admission** €2; €1 reductions. No credit cards.
At this 14th-century village, reconstructed around archaeological excavations, workers demonstrate handicrafts, medieval technology and farming techniques. There are ox-cart rides for kids, and a small snack bar.

Olympia-Stadion

Olympischer Platz 3, Charlottenburg (2500 2322/www.olympiastadion-berlin.de). U2 Olympia-Stadion or S5, S75 Olympiastadion. No credit cards.
Designed by Werner March for the 1936 Olympic Games, the 74,000-seat stadium underwent a major refitting for the 2006 FIFA World Cup, including better seats and a roof over the whole stadium. Home of Hertha BSC (see p156), it also hosts the German Cup Final, plus other sporting events, as well as major concerts. See also box p154.

BERLIN BY AREA

Olympia-Stadion

From Jesse medals to Zidane's head-butt.

The refusal of history to lie down and be ignored is perhaps the thing that most marks Berlin as different from comparable big cities. How to leave the past behind without simply brushing it under the carpet? The process of post-Wall reconstruction has been marked by debate at every level from the renaming of streets to ways in which the city's connection to some of the most appalling events of the 20th century should be memorialised, or not, in the disposition of major landmarks.

The **Olympia-Stadion** is one such. It was built in the early years of the Nazi regime for the 1936 Olympics. With its neo-classical monumentalism, heroic statuary and alignment among a complex of other symbolic structures, the stadium, designed by Werner March, was Nazi ideology written in stone. Of course, history had a joker to play. The Games are remembered more for the four gold medals won by African-American athlete Jesse Owens than for any success of the Nazis.

Unlike most of Berlin, the stadium was barely damaged in World War II and remained in continuous use – for major sporting events, as home ground for Hertha BSC, as venue for U2 or the Rolling Stones. But since 1966 it's also been a listed building, memorial as well as event location.

It was only when Berlin began considering its failed bid for the 2000 Olympics that debates began about the significance of the site. Many thought it should be demolished. Instead, as the 2006 World Cup hove into view, it was decided to renovate. The main feature of the new design, completed in 2004, is a delicate ring roof that appears to hover over the seating area, leaving much of the original architecture intact.

Of course, history had another joker to play. The 2006 World Cup Final will be remembered as much for Zidane's head-butt as for any achievement of the Germans.

Sammlung Berggruen: Picasso & seine Zeit

Westlicher Stülerbau, Schlossstrasse 1, Charlottenburg (3269 5815/www.smb. spk-berlin.de). U2 Sophie-Charlotte-Platz or U7 Richard-Wagner-Platz. **Open** 10am-5pm Tue-Sun. **Admission** €6; €3 reductions. No credit cards.

Heinz Berggruen was an early Picasso dealer in Paris, and the subtitle of this museum, 'Picasso and His Time', sums up the satisfying collection. Over a digestible three circular floors, Picasso's prolific and diverse output is well represented. There are also works by Braque, Giacometti, Cézanne and Matisse, while most of the second floor is given over to paintings by Paul Klee.

Schloss Charlottenburg

Luisenplatz & Spandauer Damm, Charlottenburg (320 911/www.spsg. de). U2 Sophie-Charlotte-Platz or U7 Richard-Wagner-Platz. **Open** *Old Palace* 9am-5pm Tue-Sun. *New Wing* Apr-Oct 10am-5pm Tue-Sun; Nov-Mar 11am-5pm Tue-Sun. *New Pavilion* 10am-5pm Tue-Sun. *Mausoleum* Apr-Oct 10am-noon, 1-5pm Tue-Sun. *Belvedere* Apr-Oct 10am-5pm Tue-Sun; Nov-Mar noon-4pm Tue-Sun. **Admission** *Combination tickets* €8; €5 reductions. No credit cards.

Queen Sophie Charlotte was the impetus behind this sprawling palace and garden complex (and gave her name to both building and district) – her husband Friedrich III (later King Friedrich I) built it in 1695-9 as a summer home for his queen. Later kings also summered here, tinkering with and adding to the buildings. It was severely damaged during World War II, but has now been restored, and stands as the largest surviving Hohenzollern palace. There are various parts to which the public are admitted; easiest option is to go for the combination ticket that allows entrance to nearly all of them. The one must-see is the Neue Flügel (New Wing), containing the State Apartments of Frederick the Great. The Neue Pavillon (New Pavilion) was built by Schinkel in 1824 for Friedrich Wilhelm III, who liked it so much that he chose to live here in preference to the main palace. It's currently closed for renovations. Within the huge gardens is the 18th-century Belvedere, containing a collection of Berlin porcelain, and the sombre Mausoleum, with the tombs of Friedrich Wilhelm III, his wife Queen Luise, Kaiser Wilhelm I and his wife.

Museum Berlin-Karlshorst p153

BERLIN BY AREA

Tierpark Berlin-Friedrichsfelde

Am Tierpark 125, Friedrichsfelde (515 310/www.tierpark-berlin.de). U5 Tierpark. **Open** *Jan, Feb, Oct-Dec* 9am-4pm daily. *Mar, Sept* 9am-5pm daily. *Apr-Aug* 9am-6pm daily. **Admission** €10; €7 reductions; €16.50-€26.50 family. No credit cards.

Spread over 1.6sq km (0.6sq miles), this is one of Europe's largest zoos, with plenty of roaming space for herd animals, though some others are still kept in distressingly small cages. Resident beasts include bears, elephants, big cats penguins and snakes. In the northwest corner is Schloss Friedrichsfelde.

Zitadelle

Am Juliusturm, Spandau (354 944 200/tours 334 6270/www.zitadelle-spandau.de). U7 Zitadelle. **Open** 9am-5pm Tue-Fri; 10am-5pm Sat, Sun. **Admission** €2.50; €1.50 reductions. No credit cards.

The oldest structure inside the citadel (and the oldest secular building in Berlin) is the Juliusturm, dating back to about 1160. The bulk of the Zitadelle was designed in 1560-94, in the style of an Italian fort, to dominate the confluence of the Spree and Havel rivers. There are two museums. One tells the story of the citadel; the other is about local history.

Nightlife

Insel

Alt-Treptow 6, Treptow (2091 4990/www.insel-berlin.net). S8, S9, S41, S42, S85 Treptower Park. **Open** 7pm-1am Wed; 10pm-late Fri, Sat. No credit cards.

Out of the way, but a brilliant club and venue – like a miniature castle on a tiny Spree island, with several levels and a top-floor balcony. Once a communist youth club, it now has lots of neon and ultra-violet, crusties and hippies, techno and hip hop, punk and metal.

KitKatClub

Bessemer Strasse 4, Tempelhof (no phone/www.kitkatclub.de). Bus 204. **Open** 11pm-late Fri, Sat; 8pm-late Sun. No credit cards.

Berlin's best-known straight sex club is no place for the narrow-minded, with half the crowd in fetish gear, the other half in no gear at all, and every kind of sexual activity taking place in full view. Actually, it's relaxing. No one has anything to prove and everyone knows why they're there – and will almost certainly get it. If you're not dressed up (or down) enough, you probably won't get in.

Arts & leisure

Berlin Thunder

Friesenhof 1, Hanns-Braun-Strasse, Charlottenburg (3006 4400/www.berlin-thunder.de). U2 Olympia-Stadion or S5, S75 Olympiastadion. **Tickets** €8-€31.50.

The NFL Europe has grown in stature and popularity since it started in the early 1990s. Initially viewed as a last-chance saloon for players who couldn't make it in the NFL, it has earned a reputation as something of a finishing school. Berlin Thunder won the World Bowl in 2001, 2002 and 2004 and went to the final in 2005. They now play at the Olympia-Stadion (p153 and box p154) drawing crowds of around 20,000.

EHC Eisbären Berlin

Wellblechpalast, Steffenstrasse, Hohenschönhausen (971 8400/tickets 9718 4040/www.eisbaeren.de). S8, S41, S42, S85 Landsberger Allee, then tram M5 Simon-Bolivar-Strasse. No credit cards.

East Berlin's hockey team survived both communism and the transition to capitalism, as well as the loss of their big city rivals. In 2008 they move from their current 'corrugated-iron palace' a little way down the same street into the new Sportforum Berlin.

Hertha BSC

0180 518 9200/www.herthabsc.de.

Repeatedly touted as title contenders, Berlin's only major football club so far hasn't found the strength in depth to claim any significant silverware and in 2006-07 got knocked out of the UEFA Cup at the first hurdle. Its home ground is the Olympia-Stadion (see p153), where the team attracts a big crowd.

Schloss Cecilienhof p159

Day Trips

Potsdam & Babelsberg

Just south-west of the city limits, Potsdam is Berlin's Versailles. Tourists cram into the town in summer, attracted by its parks, palaces and baroque architecture, so make a day trip of it and avoid peak times if possible.

Potsdam was the summer residence of the Hohenzollerns and, despite the damage wrought during World War II and by East Germany's socialist planners, much remains of the legacy of these Prussian kings. In 1990 Potsdam was assigned UNESCO world heritage status and some 80 per cent of its historic buildings have since been restored. The best-known landmark is **Sanssouci**, the huge landscaped park created by Frederick the Great.

Cross over the bridge from the station to reach the Old Town, starting at the **Nikolaikirche** and the **Altes Rathaus**. The Stadtschloss marks the centre of the town. The baroque quarter is bounded by Schopenhauerstrasse, Hegelallee, Hebbelstrasse and Charlottenstrasse. Some of the most impressive houses can be found in Gutenbergstrasse and on Brandenburger Strasse, Potsdam's pedestrianised shopping drag. Three baroque town gates – the Nauener Tor, Jäger Tor and Brandenburger Tor – stand on the northern and the western edges of the quarter. North-east of the Nikolaikirche is the Holländisches Viertel (the Dutch quarter).

The vast Park Sanssouci stretches away on the west side of town. North-east of the centre lies another large park complex, the **Neuer Garten**, with the Schloss Cecilienhof at its northern end. Potsdam's third royal park, **Park Babelsberg**, to the east, also makes for a good walk. The nearby town of Babelsberg is home to Babelsberg film studio; its Filmpark is the only part open to the public.

Potsdam is too spread out to do everything on foot. A Potsdam Card from the tourist office (p159) costs €9.80 and provides free public transport plus discounted entry to most attractions.

Sights & museums

Altes Rathaus
Am Alten Markt (0331 289 6336/ www.altesrathauspotsdam.de). Tram X98, 90, 92, 93, 96 Alten Markt. **Open** 10am-6pm Tue-Sun. **Admission** €3; €2 reductions. No credit cards.

Sanssouci

Potsdam's former town hall is a mid 18th-century baroque building with Corinthian columns and a stepped dome. Badly damaged in the war, it was rebuilt in the 1960s and is now used for exhibitions and lectures.

Filmpark Babelsberg
August-Bebel-Strasse 26-53, entrance on Grossbeerenstrasse (0331 721 2717/ www.filmpark.de). S1 Babelsberg, bus 601, 602, 618, 619, 690 to Filmpark. **Open** Apr-Oct 10am-6pm daily. **Admission** €17; €15.50 reductions. No credit cards.
In the 1920s the Babelsberg film studio was the largest in the world outside Hollywood and it was here that Josef von Sternberg's *The Blue Angel* and Fritz Lang's *Metropolis* were produced. These days there are state-of-the-art facilities for film and TV production. The Filmpark is the only part open to the public; there's an assortment of largely tawdry attractions, ranging from themed restaurants and rides to set tours and stunt displays.

Gedenkstätte Lindenstrasse
Lindenstrasse 54 (0331 289 6136/www. potsdam.de). Tram 94, 96 Dortusstrasse. **Open** 10am-6pm Tue, Thur, Sat. **Admission** €1.50. No credit cards.
Built in 1737, this former palace was used by the Nazis and then by the Stasi to hold and interrogate people. There's a warrenous complex of cells; the place is now a memorial against political violence.

Haus der Brandenburgisch-Preussischen Geschichte
Kutschstall, Am Neuen Markt (0331 620 8549/www.hbpg.de). Tram X98, 90, 92, 93, 96 Alter Markt. **Open** 10am-6pm Tue, Thur-Sun; 10am-8pm Wed. **Admission** €5; €4 reductions. No credit cards.
The permanent exhibition here charts 900 years of Prussian history from the middle ages to the modern day.

Nikolaikirche
Am Alten Markt (0331 291 682/www. nikolaipotsdam.de). Tram X98, 90, 92, 93, 96 Alter Markt. **Open** 2pm-5pm Mon; 10am-5pm Tue-Sun. **Admission** free.

Filmpark Babelsberg

This 19th-century church, with its huge dome, was inspired by St Paul's in London and is one of the most dominant buildings in Potsdam. It was the last work by Berlin's most famous architect, Karl Friedrich Schinkel.

Sanssouci

Potsdam (0331 969 4202/www. spsg.de). Bus X15, 695. **Open** *Palace Apr-Oct 9am-5pm Tue-Sun; Nov-Mar 9am-4pm daily. Park 9am-dusk daily.* **Admission** *Palace €8; €5 reductions. Park free.* No credit cards.

An elegant legacy of Frederick the Great, this is Potsdam's biggest tourist magnet. Atop terraced vineyards, Sanssouci ('without worries') is the result of the king's desire for an exquisite sanctuary to pursue philosophical, musical and literary interests. You could spend a whole day wandering around the park; the Drachenhaus (Dragon House), a pagoda-style café, and the Chinesisches Teehaus (Chinese Tea House), with its collection of porcelain, are two of the attractions.

Schloss Cecilienhof

Im Neuen Garten (0331 969 4244/ www.spsg.de). Bus 692. **Open** *Apr-Oct 9am-5pm Tue-Sun. Nov-Mar 9am-4pm Tue-Sun.* **Admission** €5; €4 reductions. No credit cards.

Built from 1913 to 1917, this mock-Tudor mansion was spared wartime damage and, in summer 1945, hosted the Potsdam Conference where Stalin, Truman and Churchill (and later Clement Attlee) met to discuss the future of Germany.

Getting there

By train

There are frequent S-Bahn and Regionalbahn trains to Potsdam. Regionalbahn trains take about 25 minutes from Hauptbahnhof, S-Bahn trains (S1) about 40 minutes. From some parts of Berlin it's easier to take the S7 to Wannsee and change to the S1 there. There is also a direct, hourly Regionalbahn train to Babelsberg that takes just 20 mins from Mitte.

Tourist information

Potsdam Tourismus Service

Brandenburger Strasse 3 (0331 275 580/www.potsdam-tourism.com). Tram 94, 96/Bus X15, 695 Luisenplatz. **Open** *Apr-Oct 9.30am-6pm Mon-Fri; 9.30am-4pm Sat, Sun. Nov-Mar 10am-6pm Mon-Fri; 9.30am-2pm Sat.*

BERLIN BY AREA

Sachsenhausen

Many Nazi concentration camps have been preserved and opened to the public as memorials and museums. **Sachsenhausen**, named after a district of the town of Oranienburg, on the banks of the Havel river, is the one nearest to Berlin.

Immediately upon coming to power, Hitler set about rounding up and interning his opponents. From 1933 to 1935 an old brewery on this site was used to hold them. The present camp received its first load of prisoners in July 1936. It was designated with cynical euphemism as a *Schutzhaftlager* ('Protective Custody Camp'). The first *Schutzhaftlagern* here were political opponents of Hitler's government: communists, social democrats, trade unionists. Soon, the variety of prisoners widened to include anyone guilty of 'anti-social' behaviour, gays and Jews.

About 6,000 Jews were forcibly brought here after Kristallnacht alone. It was here that some of the first experiments in organised mass murder were made: thousands of POWs from the Eastern Front were killed at Station Z.

The SS evacuated the camp in 1945 and began marching 33,000 inmates towards the Baltic Sea, where they were to be packed into boats and sunk in the water. Some 6,000 died during the march before the survivors were rescued by the Allies. Another 3,000 prisoners were found in the camp's hospital when it was finally captured on 22 April 1945.

The horror did not end here. After the German capitulation, the Russian secret police, the MVD, reopened Sachsenhausen as Camp 7 for the detention of war criminals; in fact, it was filled with anyone suspected of opposition. Following the fall of the GDR, the remains of some 10,000 prisoners were found in mass graves.

On 23 April 1961 the partially restored camp was opened to the public as a national monument and memorial. The inscription over the entrance, *Arbeit Macht Frei* ('Work Sets You Free'), could be found over the gates of all concentration camps.

The parade ground, where morning roll-call was taken and from where inmates were required to witness executions on the gallows, stands before the two remaining barrack blocks. One is now a museum and the other a memorial hall and cinema, where a film about the history of the camp is shown. Next door stands the prison block.

There are another couple of small exhibitions in buildings in the centre of the camp (no English labelling), but perhaps the grimmest site here is the subsiding remains of Station Z, the surprisingly small extermination block.

A map traces the path that the condemned would follow, depending upon whether they were to be shot (the bullets were retrieved and reused) or gassed. All ended up in the neighbouring ovens. Note: it's a good idea to hire an audio guide (available in English) at the gate.

KZ Sachsenhausen

Strasse der Nationen 22, Oranienburg (0330 120 00/www.gedenkstaette-sachsenhausen.de). **Open** *15 Mar-14 Oct* 8.30am-6pm Tue-Sun. *15 Oct-14 Mar* 8.30am-4.30pm Tue-Sun. **Admission** free.

Getting there

By train

Oranienburg is at the northern end of the S1 S-Bahn line (40mins from Mitte). From the station follow signs to 'Gedenkstätte Sachsenhausen'. It's a 20min walk.

Essentials

Hotel Concorde p175

Hotels

The number of hotel beds in Berlin has mushroomed in recent years, though the expansion has been top-heavy, primarily in the four- and five-star categories. Of course, there are also openings at the other end of the market, and there's always room for a few more art and design hotels in the city.

Their distribution is far from uniform. The most fashionable area to land in is Mitte. But despite all the new openings in that district, it still hasn't really caught up with Charlottenburg, Berlin's west end. The area around Zoo and Savignyplatz is equipped with the kind of characterful old pensions that disappeared in the east under communism, and has its own new establishments too (see box p173). Some districts, such as Friedrichshain, Prenzlauer Berg or Schöneberg, have hardly any hotels at all.

Berliner Tourismus Marketing (p186), the city's privatised tourist information service, can also sort out hotel reservations. It provides a free listings booklet of over 400 hotels – but note that these have all paid to be included.

Money matters

Whatever your budget, the good news is that the average price of a Berlin hotel room remains much lower than in comparable European cities such as Rome, Paris or London. Many hotels will offer special deals, particularly for weekends, so it's worth checking their websites in advance. But you won't find many bargains when the city fills up for major cultural events, such as February's Berlin International Film Festival (p36) or July's Love Parade. In general, the best bargains are to be found in the Charlottenburg area.

Mitte

Alexander Plaza Berlin

*Rosenstrasse 1 (240 010/www.hotel-
alexander-plaza.de). S5, S7, S9, S75
Hackescher Markt.* €€€.

Handily located, this handsome building has been renovated as a comfortable modern establishment. Despite
its proximity to one of the liveliest
parts of Mitte, the hotel stands in an
oasis of quiet, close to the river. Staff
are polite and the decor isn't bad.
There are 92 rooms, each with wireless internet; also a fitness centre and
'wellness landscape'.

Art'otel Berlin Mitte

*Wallstrasse 70-73 (240 620/
www.artotels.de). U2 Märkisches
Museum.* €€€.

This delightful fusion of old and new
houses both immaculately restored
rococo reception rooms and ultra-
modern bedrooms designed by archi-
tects Nalbach & Nalbach. The hotel
showcases the works of artist Georg
Baselitz: rooms and corridors contain
originals of his paintings. Every detail
of the decor has been meticulously
attended to, from Philippe Starck
bathrooms to the Marcel Breuer chairs
in the conference rooms.

Circus Hostel

*Weinbergsweg 1A (2839 1433/
www.circus-berlin.de). U8 Rosenthaler
Platz.* No credit cards. €.

The Circus Hostel has two locations
(the other is situated on nearby Rosa-
Luxemburg-Strasse). They are friendly
hostels with clean and bright rooms
– something of a rarity for backpacker
places. The owners are young travellers themselves and work hard to
offer value for money. For longer stays,
the apartments on the top floor are well
priced and have fine views.
Other locations: Rosa-Luxemburg-
Strasse 39, Mitte (2839 1433).

CityStay Hostel

*Rosenstrasse 16 (2362 4031/
www.citystay.de). S5, S7, S9,
S75 Hackescher Markt.* €.

ESSENTIALS

This place is perfect for the price range. It's sparkling clean. The location is central, but on a quiet, pedestrianised street. Rooms are spacious and there are large showers with lockable doors on every floor. Security's high for a hostel; you need an access card to get into the building. The breakfast buffet has fresh organic bread and the kitchen staff will make your eggs however you want.

Dietrich-Bonhoeffer-Haus

Ziegelstrasse 30 (284 670/www. hotel-dbh.de). U6, S1, S2, S5, S7, S9, S75 Friedrichstrasse or S1, S2 Oranienburger Strasse. **€€€.**
Built in 1987 as a meeting place for Christians from East and West, this friendly hotel is named after a theologian who was executed by the Nazis. The building is on a quiet side street near the Museumsinsel; rooms are enormous, there's a friendly atmosphere and the breakfast is good.

Dorint Sofitel D

Charlottenstrasse 50-52 (203 750/ www.sofitel.com). U2, U6 Stadtmitte. **€€€€.**

Honigmond Garden Hotel

It's not easy to get a room here and for good reason: it really is a very lovely hotel. A great deal of attention has been paid to detail, from the calming colour scheme to the excellent lighting. The atmosphere is intimate and each room is beautifully styled, with perhaps the best-looking bathrooms in Berlin.

Helter Skelter Hostel

Kalkscheunenstrasse 4 (2804 4997/ www.helterskelterhostel.com). U6, S1, S2, S5, S7, S9, S25, S75 Friedrichstrasse. No credit cards. **€.**
The feel is relaxed and the location is central, above a historic building and cultural centre. Rooms are curiously decorated with everything from an upside-down ceiling pool table to a sort of Legoland-ish map carpet. The international staff are amiable and speak English. No smoking except in the communal room, where there are also kitchen facilities.

Honigmond Restaurant-Hotel

Tieckstrasse 12 (284 4550/ www.honigmond-berlin.de). U6 Oranienburger Tor. **€€.**
The 40 rooms in this 1899 building are attractive and spacious. This is probably the best and prettiest mid-price hotel east of the Zoo. The beautiful new reception area has comfy chairs around a gas fireplace, and breakfast is served in the Honigmond restaurant (see p69). In their sister hotel up the road, the Honigmond Garden Hotel, choose between big rooms facing the busy street or smaller cabin-like ones facing the Tuscan-style garden.
Other locations: Honigmond Garden Hotel, Invalidenstrasse 122 (2844 5577).

Hotel Adlon

Unter den Linden 77 (226 10/ www.hotel-adlon.de). S1, S2 Unter den Linden. **€€€€.**
The original Adlon, renowned for its luxurious interiors and discreet atmosphere, burned down after World War II. The new Adlon, rebuilt by the Kempinski group on the original site, opened in 1997. Next to the

Lux 11

Brandenburg Gate and handy for the diplomatic quarter, this is the first choice for movie stars and heads of state – there are three bulletproof presidential suites. The other 409 rooms are decorated in a sort of international executive style.

Hotel de Rome

NEW *Behrenstrasse 37, off Bebelplatz (460 6090/www.roccofortehotels.com). U6 Französische Strasse.* €€€€.
The former East German central bank has undergone a €70 million transformation, becoming Sir Rocco Forte's 11th European hotel. It makes great use of the original bank features. The vault, for example, has been transformed into an atmospheric wellness suite and pool area. It's in a prime historical location in Bebelplatz and the terrace offers a panoramic view of the city.

Hotel Hackescher Markt

Grosse Präsidentenstrasse 8 (280 030/ www.loock-hotels.com). S5, S7, S9, S75 Hackescher Markt. €€€.
An elegant hotel in a nicely renovated townhouse that solves the noise problem at its Hackescher Markt location by having many rooms facing inwards on to a tranquil green courtyard. Some

rooms have balconies, all have their own bath with heated floor and suites are spacious and comfortable.

Künstlerheim Luise

Luisenstrasse 19 (284 480/www. kuenstlerheim-luise.de). U6, S1, S2, S5, S7, S9, S75 Friedrichstrasse. €€.
This 'artist home' deserves its reputation as one of the city's most imaginative small hotels, with 50 rooms each decorated by a different artist. These range from Dieter Mammel's room containing an invitingly larger-than-life bed to Angela Dwyer's 'Room Like Any Other', whose surfaces are covered in stream-of-consciousness scrawlings. Some rooms get a little noise from the S-Bahn trains, but this is a great place.

Lux 11

NEW *Rosa-Luxemburg-Strasse 9-13 (936 2800/www.lux-eleven.de). U2 Rosa-Luxemburg-Platz.* €€€.
The no-nonsense hotel-apartments here are stylish, comfortable and well located. Each one has a queen- or king-sized bed, a sitting area, a kitchen and a raised shower up a couple of steps. Minty-white walls create a cool but clean atmosphere and the longer you

ESSENTIALS

stay, the cheaper it gets. There's an in-house Aveda salon and the Shiro i Shiro (p71) restaurant is downstairs.

mitArt Pension

Linienstrasse 139-40 (2839 0430/ www.mitart.de). U6 Oranienburger Tor. €€.

This elegant pension in a beautifully restored printing-house is a good base for gallery-hopping: Auguststrasse is around the corner and the owner knows the art scene. Warm and bright rooms get their character from an ever-changing gallery of sculpture and paintings, but have no phones or TVs. Breakfast, included in the price, is served in the organic café on the ground floor.

Mitte's Backpacker Hostel

Chausseestrasse 102 (2839 0965/ www.backpacker.de). U6 Zinnowitzer Strasse. €.

Here since 1994, this is the oldest backpacker hostel in Mitte. It has a cosy atmosphere and rooms decorated by artistically minded former guests. The

East Side Hotel p169

'Berlin Room' has light fittings in the shape of the Fernsehturm; the 'Green Poem Room' has walls covered in lengthy verses. There's a kitchen, bike rental and a video room.

Radisson SAS Berlin

Karl-Liebknecht-Strasse 5 (238 280/ www.berlin.radissonsas.com). S5, S7, S9, S75 Hackescher Markt. €€€.

The world's largest free-standing aquarium is in the middle of the atrium and many bedrooms have a 'sea view' on to the breathtaking 25m-high (82ft) tank, which houses 2,500 varieties of fish in a million litres of water. German-born designer Yasmine Mahmoudieh (she also did the new Airbus A380 interiors) has worked wonders with the 427 rooms, which are fresh, uncluttered and free of the blandness so typical of big chain hotels.

Prenzlauer Berg

Ackselhaus & Bluehome

Belforter Strasse 21 (4433 7633/www. ackselhaus.de). U2 Senefelderplatz. No credit cards. €€€.

There are two buildings, doors apart – Bluehome is at No.24. What ties them together is their 'modernised colonial style' and shared reception at the above address. In Ackselhaus each apartment has a bedroom, sitting-room, bathroom and kitchenette, with old wooden floorboards, white walls, antique furniture and a Mediterranean feel. The pricier Bluehome has balconies overlooking Belforter Strasse.

Hotel Garni Transit Loft

Immanuelkirchstrasse 14a (4849 3773/www.transit-loft.de). Tram M4 Hufelandstrasse. €.

In an old, renovated factory, this newish loft hotel caters for backpackers and groups of young travellers. The rooms all have en suite bathrooms and in the same building are a sauna, gym and billiard salon, which all offer special rates to guests of the hotel. There's good wheelchair access, an all-night bar and a cinema at street level.

ESSENTIALS

Hotel Greifswald

Greifswalder Strasse 211 (442 7888/
www.hotel-greifswald.de). Tram M4
Hufelandstrasse. €€.

This clean, friendly, no-nonsense hotel
has cheerful rooms with colourful curtains, good-sized beds and staff that
are bright and helpful. In the foyer
you'll find an interesting collection of
signed photographs from the many
bands and musicians who've stayed
here – the hotel is handy for the clubs
Knaack and Magnet (p91). Breakfast is
taken in the courtyard in summer.

Lette'm Sleep Hostel

Lettestrasse 7, 10437 (4473 3623/
www.backpackers.de). U2 Eberswalder
Strasse. €.

This small hostel is just off the
Helmholtzplatz, which means greenery
and cafés. Breakfast is not provided,
but you can make your own in the
kitchen. The bathrooms and floors in
the rooms have recently been renovated, as has the biergarten in the back.
Three new apartments can sleep up to
ten people each.

Myer's Hotel

Metzer Strasse 26 (440 140/www.
myershotel.de). U2 Senefelderplatz. €€.

This renovated 19th-century townhouse is on a very quiet street.
There's a garden, a glass-ceilinged
gallery and big leather furniture in
the smoking-room. But as far as the
rooms go, it seems a little overpriced.
The lovely Kollwitzplatz is around the
corner and the hotel is within walking
distance of Mitte.

Friedrichshain

East Side Hotel

Mühlenstrasse 6 (293 833/www.
eastsidehotel.de). U1, S3, S5, S7,
S9, S75 Warschauer Strasse. €€.

The East Side Hotel is a modest, simply decorated hotel, but with a great
view of one of the last remaining
stretches of the Berlin Wall. Get a
room at the back if you want peace
and quiet, but then you'll miss the
sunset across the old red-brick factory
buildings and the Oberbaumbrücke.
Each double room comes with a large
bathroom and bath.

Eastern Comfort

NEW *Mühlenstrasse 73-7 (6676*
3806/www.eastern-comfort.com).
U1, S3, S5, S7, S9, S75 Warschauer
Strasse. €.

Berlin's only 'hostel boat' is moored on
the Spree. The rooms are clean and
pretty spacious considering it's a boat,
and all have their own shower and toi-
let. There are two common rooms, one
lounge and three terraces offering
beautiful river views.

Odyssee Globetrotter Hostel

Grünberger Strasse 23 (2900 0081/
www.hostel-berlin.de). U5 Frankfurter
Tor. No credit cards. €.

Follow a long, dark corridor to the
back yard, turn right, go up the stairs
and you'll find the dimly lit reception,
complete with billiards and table football. The hostel is clean and the showers have good water pressure, but if
you're not into metal and tattoos, the
common area may not suit you.

Hotel Riehmers Hofgarten p170

Hotel Angleterre

NEW *Friedrichstrasse 31 (2021 3700/ www.gold-inn.de). U6 Kochstrasse.* €€€.
The Berlin hotel group Gold Inn has cleared the graffiti on this former squatted building and the original 1871 façade now fronts a warmly furnished mid-range hotel offering a touch of Englishness near Checkpoint Charlie. There's a Speakers' Corner restaurant and the Commonwealth Bar serves Newcastle Brown Ale and Fosters.

Hotel Riehmers Hofgarten

Yorckstrasse 83 (7809 8800/www. hotel-riehmers-hofgarten.de). U6, U7 Mehringdamm. €€€.
In a historic building with 22 rooms and a lovely courtyard, this place is wonderful. The styling is exquisite, the staff charming, the rooms airy and well furnished and the prices are reasonable. The location is a little off the beaten track, but Viktoriapark and the shops and cafés of Bergmannstrasse are nearby.

Hotel Transit

Hagelberger Strasse 53-4 (789 0470/www.hotel-transit.de). U6, U7 Mehringdamm. €.

This converted factory hostel is bright and airy, and located in one of the most beautiful parts of Kreuzberg. The 49 rooms are basic but clean and the dormitory is pretty good value. All rooms have showers and toilets, staff speak good English and there's a 24-hour bar.

Pension Kreuzberg

Grossbeerenstrasse 64 (251 1362/ www.pension-kreuzberg.de). U6, U7 Mehringdamm. No credit cards. €.
A small, friendly 12-room pension in a typical old Berlin building. It's not for the lazy or infirm, as there are four steep flights of stairs up to reception. Only half the rooms have their own bathrooms (there's a communal one on each floor), although they all have washbasins. The vibe is cheap and cheerful.

Berlin Marriott Hotel

Inge-Beisheim-Platz 1 (220 000/ www.marriott.de/BERMC). U2, S1, S2, S25 Potsdamer Platz. €€€€.
Opened in 2004 and more modest and moderately priced than the neighbouring Ritz-Carlton (p171), the Berlin Marriott also has five stars. The cool white interior of the enormous atrium is impressive and the rotating globe fountain is mesmerising, but the rooms are a bit bland.

Grand Hotel Esplanade

Lützowufer 15 (254 780/www. esplanade.de). U1, U2, U3, U4 Nollendorfplatz. €€€€.
One of Berlin's better luxury hotels, next to the Landwehr Canal and close to the Tiergarten. The lobby is spacious and beautifully decorated. The rooms are tasteful and gratifyingly free of frilly decor; three floors have been set aside for non-smokers. There's a fitness centre and a triangular swimming pool, while Harry's New York Bar is on the ground floor, underlining the distinctly American feel of the place.

Ritz-Carlton

ESSENTIALS

Grand Hyatt

Marlene-Dietrich-Platz 2 (2553 1234/ www.berlin.grand.hyatt.com). U2, S1, S2, S9, S26 Potsdamer Platz. €€€€.
The lobby – all matte black surfaces and wood panelling with the odd minimalist art touch – sets the classy tone. Rooms are spacious and elegant. The rooftop spa and gym has a splendid pool with views across the city. And the lobby restaurant – the Tizian Lounge – is truly excellent, with a menu of international classics and a good wine list.

Hotel Alt Berlin

Potsdamer Strasse 67 (260 670/ www.altberlin-hotel.de). U1 Kurfürstenstrasse. €€.
This 'turn-of-the-century-Berlin' hotel actually opened just a few years ago – the furnishings only look retro. The restaurant is like a cluttered museum and serves hearty, traditional Berlin food. The hotel is within walking distance of Potsdamer Platz, the Nationalgalerie and the Philharmonie. If you need wireless internet, ask to be put on the first or second floor.

Hotel Intercontinental

Budapester Strasse 2 (260 20/www. interconti.com). U2, U9, S5, S7, S9, S75 Zoologischer Garten/bus 200. €€€€.
Overlooking the Zoo and on the western edge of the new diplomatic quarter, the plush and spacious 'Interconti' exudes luxury. The rooms are large, tastefully decorated and graced with elegant bathrooms. Thomas Kammeier of the hotel restaurant Hugo's (p102) has been voted Berlin Masterchef.

Ritz-Carlton

Potsdamer Platz 3 (337 777/www. ritzcarlton.com). U2, S1, S2, S26 Potsdamer Platz. €€€€.
It's flashy, it's trashy, it's Vegas-meets-Versailles – so chock-a-block with black marble, gold taps and taffeta curtains that the rooms seem stuffy, small and cramped. The oyster and lobster restaurant is deliciously decadent, and the service throughout fantastic. Bring a fat wallet, and get ready to be pampered.

Hotel Art Nouveau p172

Charlottenburg

Askanischer Hof

Kurfürstendamm 53 (881 8033/www. askanischer-hof.de). U7 Adenauerplatz or S5, S7, S9, S75 Savignyplatz. €€.
This friendly place has hosted visiting actors and literary types since long before World War II. The breakfast room doesn't seem to have changed since 1910 and each room spans a century of European interiors: 1970s chrome standard lamps teamed with overstuffed leather chesterfields, heavy Prussian desks and 1940s wallpaper. Full of atmosphere and in dodgy taste, this is vintage Berlin.

Hecker's Hotel

Grolmanstrasse 35 (889 00/www. heckers-hotel.com). U1 Uhlandstrasse or S5, S7, S9, S75 Savignyplatz. €€€.
A smart, high-quality hotel with a roof terrace, a stylish lobby and an air of privacy. The rooms are both spacious and comfortable – especially the suites, which come with air-conditioning and Bang & Olufsen DVD TVs. Bathrooms are clean and well lit, with marble tiling.

ESSENTIALS

Hotel Art Nouveau

*Leibnitzstrasse 59 (327 7440/www.
hotelartnouveau.de). U7 Adenauerplatz
or S5, S7, S9, S75 Savignyplatz.* €€€.
One of the loveliest small hotels in Berlin.
The rooms are decorated with flair in
a mix of Conran-modern and antique
furniture. The en suite bathrooms are
well integrated into the rooms without
disrupting the elegant townhouse
architecture. Even the TVs are stylish.

Hotel Bleibtreu

*Bleibtreustrasse 31 (884 740/www.
bleibtreu.com). U1 Uhlandstrasse or
S5, S7, S9, S75 Savignyplatz.* €€€.
This cosy and smart establishment is
popular with media and fashion visitors. Renovated in 2005, the rooms are
a little on the small side but they're all
individually and lovingly decorated with
environmentally friendly materials. The
restaurant features speciality low-fat
foods prepared without sugar, sugar-
free bread, fresh fruit and veggie juices.

Hotel Bogota

*Schlüterstrasse 45 (881 5001/www.
hotelbogota.de). S5, S7, S9, S75
Savignyplatz.* €€.

The stylish and attractive foyer of
this characterful two-star belies
rooms more functional than fancy.
That said, this place is terrific value
with a great atmosphere, friendly
staff and interesting history. The
1930s fashion photographer Else
Simon, who worked under the name
Yva and taught Helmut Newton his
craft, had her atelier in this building.
Some of her photos are displayed in her
former studio, now a fourth-floor hallway. See box p109.

Hotel Brandenburger Hof

*Eislebener Strasse 14 (214 050/
www.brandenburger-hof.com).
U3 Augsburger Strasse.* €€€€.
Privately owned, Brandenburger Hof
is a discreet jewel that's tucked in a
quiet side street behind the department store KaDeWe (p120). Staff are
friendly and not at all aloof. The 72
rooms are spacious and decorated in a
warmed-up Bauhaus style, and eight
new suites are located in the quietest
section of the hotel. There's a pretty
winter garden and the Quadriga
restaurant is Michelin-starred.

Hotel-Pension Funk p175

Go West

Q!

For obvious reasons, most of Berlin's new hotels have opened on the eastern side of town, where the unifying city has raced to develop the tourist infrastructure mostly lacking under communism. Mitte is now first choice for most visitors. In the past it would have been Charlottenburg. But those west end hotels didn't all disappear in the last decade's *Drang nach Osten*. While almost everything in Mitte is either new or refurbished, along the Kurfürstendamm and in the streets around Savignyplatz there are small hotels such as the **Askanischer Hof** (p171) or characterful pensions such as the **Hotel-Pension Funk** (p175) and **Hotel-Pension Dittberner** (p175), that have a real sense of history.

But the west end isn't without new arrivals. The current glossy mag favourite is **Q!** (p176) on Knesebeckstrasse. It's not hard to see why. The curvaceous reception desk, red lino flooring in the bar sweeping sexily up to the ceiling, and bathtubs built into the sleeping area set the standards in modern hotel design. The fabulous spa facilities alone would be enough

to put this place on anyone's recommended list. After 6pm the bar is for the exclusive use of guests and there is a camera ban, which probably explains why assorted pop stars feel free to whoop it up there, while Brad Pitt and Angelina Jolie call Q! their Berlin home.

The new French-owned **Hotel Concorde** (p175) is an innovation of a different kind. Just off the Ku'damm and designed by Berlin architect Jan Kleihues, it's a grandly proportioned hotel with a refreshingly minimalist and contemporary approach. From the outside, the building resembles the prow of a ship. Inside there are 311 rooms and 44 individually designed suites with views of the west of the city. The Concorde is aiming for a professional/artistic clientele and last year was the partner hotel of the Christopher Street Day gay pride event.

And there's one more reason why the west still might be best. As the area strives to compete with Mitte for the visitor's attention, there are plenty of bargains to be found.

Hotel Concorde

NEW *Augsburger Strasse 41 (800 9990/www.hotelconcordeberlin.com). U1, U9 Kurfürstendamm.* €€€€.

This new five-star is a world away from traditional top-end French hotels – not a fleur-de-lys in sight. Designed by Jan Kleihues, the decor here is minimal and modern with warm colour tones. Shaped like the bow of an ocean liner in a prime location just off the Ku'damm, it attracts a professional, creative crowd. See box p173.

Hotel-Pension Dittberner

Wielandstrasse 26, 10707 (884 6950/www.hotel-ditterberner.de). U7 Adenauerplatz or S5, S7, S9, S75 Savignyplatz. €€.

Stylish, eclectic and grand, this wonderful pension is furnished with enormous crystal chandeliers and has comfortable rooms – some of which could be described as palatial – decorated with love and care. There's a delightful breakfast room.

Hotel-Pension Funk

Fasanenstrasse 69 (882 7193/www.hotel-pensionfunk.de). U1 Uhlandstrasse. €.

This pension is extremely good value for the fancy address. It's the former apartment of Danish movie star Asta Nielsen and the current proprietor does his best to maintain the ambience of a graceful pre-war flat. The 14 large and comfortable rooms are furnished to cosy effect with elegant pieces from the 1920s and 1930s.

Kempinski Hotel

Kurfürstendamm 27 (884 340/www.kempinskiberlin.de). U1, U9 Kurfürstendamm. €€€€.

Probably Berlin's most famous hotel, this is the well-aged mother of all Kempinskis. The rooms aren't as plush as one might expect at the price, but the original Berlin artwork, wonderful pool and saunas make up for it. It's well situated and the staff are helpful and nice.

Pension-Gästezimmer Gudrun

Bleibtreustrasse 17 (881 6462/www.pension-gudrun-berlin.de). S5, S7, S9, S75 Savignyplatz. No credit cards. €.

This tiny pension has huge rooms and friendly, helpful owners who speak English, French, Arabic and German. The rooms are decorated with lovely turn-of-the-century Berlin furniture and, for families or small groups travelling together, are really good value.

Propeller Island City Lodge p176

Pension Kettler

*Bleibtreustrasse 19 (883 4949/www.
brunnenfee.de). U1 Uhlandstrasse
or S5, S7, S9, S75 Savignyplatz.*
No credit cards. **€**.

Owner Isolde Josipovici can tell you
some captivating stories about Berlin
and has imbued this small hotel with
her own distinctive style over the past
33 years. The four rooms are furnished with a cosy blend of art deco
and *Gründerzeit*, with a touch of hip-
pie. Corridor walls are festooned with
mixed-media art, including a chunk of
the Berlin Wall.

Propeller Island
City Lodge

*Albrecht Achilles Strasse 58 (891
9016/fax 892 8721/www.propeller-
island.com). U7 Adenauerplatz.* **€€**.

This is a guesthouse out of *Alice in
Wonderland*. Designed by owner Lars
Stroschen, the 30 rooms are a collection of jaw-dropping theatre sets. The
Upside Down Room, for example, has
all its furniture on the ceiling. The
Flying Room has tilted walls and floor,
and a double bed seemingly suspended in thin air. There are few of the

Dorint Sofitel D p165

usual accoutrements, such as room
service or telephones. View the rooms
on the website, then choose your three
favourites. Bookings only by fax or
through the website.

Q!

*Knesebeckstrasse 67 (810 0660/www.
loock-hotels.com). U1 Uhlandstrasse or
S5, S7, S9, S75 Savignyplatz.* **€€€**.

It's almost worth staying here just for
the beautiful spa, complete with a
Japanese washing room, two saunas,
a sand lounge and optional massage.
Rooms are wonderfully crafted; both
bed and bath are part of the same
wooden unit, meaning you are literally able to roll into bed after a com-
forting soak. The floor, ceiling and
walls of the bar are red, the furniture
blue-grey and organically shaped.
Despite winning the *Travel & Leisure*
Design Award 2005, Q! is no stiff
magazine feature – the vibe here is
young and friendly.

Savoy Hotel Berlin

*Fasanenstrasse 9-10 (311 030/www.
hotel-savoy.com). U2, U9, S3, S5, S7,
S9, S75 Zoologischer Garten.* **€€€**.

This smart, stylish hotel was erected
in 1929 and continues to impress. The
rooms have recently been renovated;
there's a new Greta Garbo suite in
white and a Henry Miller suite in
black marble. The beautiful Weinrot
restaurant serves South American cuisine. Best of all is the fabulous Times
Bar, with its own library and excellent
collection of Cuban cigars.

Swissôtel Berlin

*Augsburger Strasse 44 (220 100/
www.swissotel.com). U2, U9, S3, S5,
S7, S9, S75 Zoologischer Garten or
U1, U9 Kurfürstendamm.* **€€€€**.

The styling at Swissôtel is elegant and
the second-floor foyer – situated away
from the frantic Ku'damm – is an
expression of architectural genius.
Rooms overlook the inner courtyard or
the Ku'damm; choose the latter, on a
high floor, for a great sunset view. The
Restaurant 44 (see p109) is one of
Berlin's top gourmet spots.

Getting Around

Arriving & leaving

By air

Until the new **Berlin-Brandenburg International Airport** is ready in 2011, Berlin is served by three airports: **Tegel**, **Schönefeld** and **Tempelhof**. Information in English on all of them (including departure and arrival times) can be found at www.berlin-airport.de.

Tegel Airport

Airport information: 0180 500 0186/ www.berlin-airport.de. **Open** 4am-midnight daily.
Most scheduled flights use the compact Tegel Airport, just 8km (5 miles) north-west of Mitte. The airport contains tourist information, exchange facilities, restaurants, bars, shops and car rental desks. A cab can drop you right by the check-in desk and departure gate.

Buses 109 and X9 (the express version) run via Luisenplatz and the Kurfürstendamm to Zoologischer Garten (also known as Zoo Station, Bahnhof Zoo or just Zoo) in western Berlin. Tickets cost €2.10 (and can also be used on U-Bahn and S-Bahn services). Buses run every five to 15 minutes, and take 30-40 minutes to reach Zoo. From there, you can connect to anywhere in the city (same tickets are valid). You can also take bus 109 to Jakob-Kaiser-Platz U-Bahn (U7), or bus 128 to Kurt-Schumacher-Platz U-Bahn (U6), and proceed on the underground from there.

The JetExpressBus TXL is the direct link to the new Berlin Hauptbahnhof and Mitte. This runs from Tegel to Alexanderplatz with useful stops at Beusselstrasse S-Bahn (connects with the Ringbahn), Berlin Hauptbahnhof (regional and intercity trains, as well as the S-Bahn), Unter den Linden S-Bahn (north and south trains on the S1 and S2 lines). It costs €2.10, runs every 15 or 20 minutes between 6am-11pm, and takes 30-40 minutes.

A taxi to anywhere central will cost around €20-€25, and takes 20-30 minutes, depending on traffic and precise destination.

Schönefeld Airport

Airport information: 0180 500 0186/www.berlin-airport.de. **Open** 24hrs daily.
The former airport of East Berlin is 18km (11 miles) south-east of the city centre. It's small but is used by UK budget airlines. The usual foreign exchange, shops, snack bars and car hire facilities are found here.

Train is the best way into the city. S-Bahn Flughafen Schönefeld is a five-minute walk from the terminal (a free shuttle bus runs every ten minutes between 6am-10pm; at other times, bus 171 also runs to the station). From here, the Airport Express train runs to Mitte (25 minutes to Alexanderplatz), Berlin Hauptbahnhof (30 minutes) and Zoo (35 minutes) every half hour from 5am-11.30pm. Be warned that the final destination of the trains varies, so check the timetable for your stop. You can also take S-Bahn line S9, which runs into the centre every 20 minutes (40 minutes to Alexanderplatz, 50 minutes to Zoo) stopping along the way. The S45 line from Schönefeld connects with the Ringbahn, also running every 20 minutes. Bus 171 from the airport takes you to Rudow U-Bahn (U7), from where you can connect with the underground.

ESSENTIALS

Tickets from the airport to the city cost €2.10, and can be used on any combination of bus, U-Bahn, S-Bahn and tram. There are ticket machines at the airport and at the station. A taxi to Zoo or Mitte is expensive (€30-€35) and takes 45-60 minutes.

Tempelhof Airport

Airport information: 0180 500 0186/www.berlin-airport.de. Flight information: 6951 2288. **Open** 5am-11pm daily.

Berlin's third airport, Tempelhof is just 4km (2.5 miles) south of Mitte, but the runways are too short for most modern passenger aircraft and only a few airlines use it. It is scheduled to close in October 2007.

Platz der Luftbrücke U-Bahn station (U6 – direct to Mitte in around ten minutes) is a short walk from the terminal building.

Tickets to the centre from Tempelhof cost €2.10, and can be used on any combination of bus, U- and S-Bahn.

A taxi to Mitte or Zoo costs €12-€18, and takes about 15 minutes and 20 minutes respectively.

By bus

Zentraler Omnibus Bahnhof (ZOB)

Masurenallee 4-6, Charlottenburg (information 301 0380). **Open** 6am-9pm Mon-Fri; 6am-3pm Sat, Sun.

Buses arrive at the Central Bus Station, opposite the Funkturm and the ICC (International Congress Centrum) in Charlottenburg. From the nearby Kaiserdamm station, U-Bahn line U2 runs east to the centre. There's also a left luggage office.

By train

Berlin Hauptbahnhof

118 61/www.hbf-berlin.de.
Since June 2006 the new Berlin Hauptbahnhof has been the central

point of arrival for all long-distance trains, with the exceptions of night trains from Moscow, Warsaw and Kiev, which start and end at Berlin Lichtenberg (U5, S5, S7, S75).

Hauptbahnhof is inconveniently located in a no-man's land over the river Spree just north of the government quarter, and is linked to the rest of the city by S-Bahn (S5, S7, S9, S75), but not yet by U-Bahn. The line U55, which will run two stops to the Brandenburger Tor, is set to open in late 2007. Eventually, the line will extend to connect to the U5 at Alexanderplatz, but work on the second stage may not commence until 2010; this short stretch of line will not connect to the rest of the U-Bahn network until after that.

Hauptbahnhof is the largest railway interchange in Europe, and equipped with a whole mall's worth of shops, restaurants and services, as well as banks, rail and tourist information offices, left-luggage facilities, and car-rental agencies.

On their way in and out of town, intercity and international trains also stop at Nordkreuz (formerly Gesundbrunnen), Südkreuz (formerly Papestrasse) and Spandau, depending on destinations.

In Town

The city is served by an efficient and comprehensive network of buses, trains, trams and ferries, which all interlink. Services are usually regular and frequent, timetables can be trusted and one ticket can be used for two hours on all legs of a journey and all forms of transport. The Berlin transport authority, the BVG, operates the bus, U-Bahn and tram networks, and a few ferry services. The S-Bahn (overground railway) is run by its own authority, but services are totally integrated within the same tariff system.

The BVG website (www.bvg.de) has a wealth of information in English. The S-Bahn has its own website at www.s-bahn-berlin.de.

The **Liniennetz**, a map of U-Bahn, S-Bahn, bus and tram routes for Berlin and Potsdam, is available free from info centres and ticket offices. It includes a city centre map. A map of the U- and S-Bahn can also be picked up free at ticket offices or from the grey-uniformed *Zugabfertiger* – passenger assistance personnel – who can be found wandering about the larger U-Bahn and S-Bahn stations.

Fares & tickets

The bus, tram, U-Bahn, S-Bahn and ferry services operate on an integrated three-zone system. Zone A covers central Berlin, zone B extends out to the edge of the suburbs and zone C stretches into Brandenburg.

The basic single ticket is the €2.10 (€1.40 for 6-14s) *Normaltarif* (zones A and B). Unless going to Potsdam, few visitors are likely to travel beyond zone B, making this, in effect, a flat-fare system. For €1.20 (€1) you can buy a short-journey ticket, called a *Kurzstrecke*, which is valid for three U- or S-Bahn stops, or six stops on the bus or tram, without any changes. A *Tageskarte* (day ticket) for zones A and B costs €5.80 (€4.20) and can be used until 3am the day after validating.

Tickets can be bought from the yellow or orange machines at U- or S-Bahn stations, and by some bus stops. The machines take coins and sometimes notes, give change and have a limited explanation of the ticket system in English. There are also ticket offices in some stations. Once you've purchased your ticket, validate it in the small red or yellow box next to the machine. Tickets bought from the drivers on buses are usually already validated. Many trams have ticket machines.

If an inspector catches you without a valid ticket, you will be fined €40 on the spot. Ticket inspections are frequent, particularly at weekends and at the beginning of the month.

U-Bahn

The first stretch of Berlin's U-Bahn consists of nine lines and 170 stations. The first trains run shortly after 4am; the last between midnight and 1am, except on Fridays and Saturdays when trains run all night on lines U1, U2, U5, U6, U7, U8 and U9. The direction of travel is indicated by the name of the last stop on the line.

S-Bahn

Especially useful in eastern Berlin, the S-Bahn covers long distances faster than the U-Bahn and is a more efficient means of getting to outlying areas. The 2002 completion of the Ringbahn, which circles central Berlin in around an hour, was the final piece of the S-Bahn system to be renovated.

Buses

Berlin has a dense network of 150 bus routes, of which 54 run in the early hours. The day lines run from 4.30am to about 1am the next morning. Enter at the front of the bus and exit in the middle. The driver sells only individual tickets, but all tickets from machines on the U- or S-Bahn are valid.

Trams

There are 21 tram lines (five of which run all night), mainly in the east, though one or two have now been extended a few kilometres

ESSENTIALS

into the western city. **Hackescher Markt** is the main tram terminus. Tickets are available from machines on the trams, at the termini and in U-Bahn stations.

Travelling at night

Berlin has a comprehensive *Nachtliniennetz* ('night-line network') that covers all parts of town via 59 bus and tram routes running every 30 minutes between 12.30am and 4.30am. Before and after these times the regular timetable for bus and tram routes applies.

Night-line network maps and timetables are available from BVG information kiosks at stations, and large maps of the night services are usually found next to the normal BVG map on station platforms. Ticket prices are the same as during the day. Buses and trams that run at night are distinguished by an 'N' in front of the number.

Truncated versions of U-Bahn lines U1, U2, U5, U6, U7, U8 and U9 run all night Fri and Sat, every 15mins. The S-Bahn also runs on weekend nights,with S1, S2, S3, S5, S7, S8, S9, S25, S26, S41, S42, S46, S47 and S75 in service.

Boat trips

Getting about by water is more of a leisure activity than a practical means of getting around the city, but the BVG network does include a handful of boat services on Berlin's lakes. There are also several private companies offering water tours.

Reederei Heinz Riedel

Planufer 78, Kreuzberg (693 4646). U8 Schönleinstrasse. **Open** *Mar-Sept* 6am-9pm Mon-Fri; 8am-6pm Sat; 10am-3pm Sun. *Oct* 8am-5pm Mon-Fri; 8am-6pm Sat; 10am-3pm Sun. *Nov-Feb* 8am-4pm Mon-Fri.
This company operates excursions that start in the city and pass through

industrial suburbs into rural Berlin. A tour through the city's network of rivers and canals costs €7-€16.

Stern & Kreisschiffahrt

Puschkinallee 15, Treptow (536 3600/ www.sternundkreis.de). S8, S9, S41, S42, S85 Treptower Park. **Open** 9am-4pm Mon-Thur; 9am-2pm Fri.
Offers around 25 different cruises along the Spree and lakes in the Berlin area. Departure points and times vary. A 3hr 30min tour costs €16.

Taxis

Berlin taxis are pricey, efficient and plentiful. The starting fee is €2.50 and thereafter the fare is €1.53 per kilometre (about €3 per mile). The rate remains the same at night. For short journeys ask for a *Kurzstrecke* – up to two kilometres for €3 and very useful for hopping about. These are only available when you've hailed a moving cab rather than taken one from a rank. There are numerous taxi stands in the city, especially in central areas near stations and at major intersections.

You can phone for a cab 24 hours daily on 261 026. Most taxi firms can transport people with disabilities, but require advance notice. Cabs accept all credit cards except Diners Club, subject to a €0.50 charge.

Most cabs are Mercedes. If you want an estate car (station wagon), ask for a *Combi*. As well as normal taxis, Funk TaxiBerlin (261 026) operates vans capable of transporting up to seven people (ask for a *Berliner Taxi*) and has two vehicles for people with disabilities.

Driving

Despite some congestion, driving in Berlin, with its wide, straight roads, presents few problems. It's probably the only capital city in Europe that's adequately equipped to deal with

21st-century traffic. Visitors from the UK and US should bear in mind that, in the absence of signals, drivers must yield to traffic from the right, except at crossings marked by a diamond-shaped yellow sign. Trams always have right of way. An *Einbahnstrasse* is a one-way street. Watch out for cyclists.

Parking

Parking is free in Berlin side streets, but spaces are hard to find. On busier streets you may have to buy a ticket (€1 per hour) from a nearby machine. Without a ticket, or if you park illegally, you risk getting your car clamped or towed.

There are long-term car parks at Schönefeld and Tegel airports (p177). Otherwise, there are various *Parkgaragen* and *Parkhäuser* (multi-storey and underground car parks) around the city, open 24 hours, that charge around €2 an hour.

Vehicle hire

Car hire in Germany isn't expensive and all major companies are have offices in Berlin. There are car hire desks at Hauptbahnhof and all three of the city's airports. Look under 'Autovermietung' in the *Gelbe Seiten* (*Yellow Pages*).

Or you could try Niki Lauda's car rental service, LaudaMotion (0900 124 0120/www.laudamotion.com), which provides smart cars to rent for just €1 per day. The only catch is that you have drive a minimum of 30 kilometres (19 miles) within the city limits – the cars are plastered with advertising.

Cycling

Berlin is great for cycling, especially on the western side – flat, with lots of cycle paths, parks to scoot through and canals to cruise beside. East Berlin has fewer cycle paths and

more cobblestones and tram lines. But throughout the city, cyclists are fully integrated into the transport network with cycle routes, cycle-specific lanes and lights at many junctions – and drivers are used to looking out for them.

Cycles can be taken on the U-Bahn, up to a limit of two at the end of carriages that have a bicycle sign on them. Bikes may not be taken on the U-Bahn during rush hour (6-9am and 2-5pm). More may be taken on to S-Bahn carriages, and at any time of day. In each case an extra ticket (€2.60) must be bought for each bike. The *ADFC Fahrradstadtplan*, available in bike shops (€6.50), is a good guide to cycle routes.

DB (Deutsche Bahn) operates a fleet of '**CallBikes**'. There are 4,200 of them scattered about, chained to posts or railings near major intersections. They're a silvery colour with a distinctive curving metal child seat bearing the red DB logo. To rent one, you need a mobile phone and a credit card number. Register by calling 0700 0522 5522 (they speak English). You will be billed at a rate of €0.07 a minute up to a maximum of €15 for 24 hours.

For more conventional bike hire, try the companies below or see 'Fahrradverleih' in the *Yellow Pages*.

Fahrradstation

Dorotheenstrasse 30, Mitte (2045 4500/www.fahrradstation.de). U6, S1, S2, S5, S7, S9, S75 Friedrichstrasse. **Open** *Summer* 8am-8pm daily. *Winter* 10am-7pm Mon-Sat. **Rates** from €15/day; €30/3 days.
Other locations: Bergmannstrasse 9, Kreuzberg (215 1566); Hackesche Höfe, Mitte (2838 4848).

Pedalpower

Grossbeerenstrasse 53, Kreuzberg (5515 3270/www.pedalpower.de). U1, U7 Möckernbrücke. **Open** 10am-6.30pm Mon-Fri; 11am-2pm Sat. **Rates** from €10/day.
No credit cards.

Resources A-Z

Accident & emergency

For the **police** dial 110; for an **ambulance** or the **fire brigade** it's 112. If you need a doctor rather than an ambulance call the **Medizinische Notdienst** (Medical Emergency Service) on 310 031. The **poison helpline** is at 192 40. To find the nearest **pharmacist** that's open at night or on Sundays or holidays go to www.apotheken.de and type in your district or postcode.

Hospitals are in the *Gelbe Seiten* (*Yellow Pages*) under 'Krankenhäuser/Kliniken'. These are the most central:

Charité
Schumann Strasse 20-21, Mitte (450 50/www.charite.de). U6, S1, S2, S5, S7, S9, S75 Friedrichstrasse/ bus 147.

Klinikum Am Urban
Dieffenbachstrasse 1, Kreuzberg (6970). U7 Südstern.

St Hedwig Krankenhaus
Grosse Hamburger Strasse 5, Mitte (231 10). S5, S7, S9, S75 Hackescher Markt or S1, S2 Oranienburger Strasse.

Age restrictions

The legal age for drinking alcohol is 16; for smoking it is 16; for driving it is 18; and the age of consent for heterosexual and homosexual sex is 16.

Credit card loss

If you've lost a credit card, or had one stolen, phone one of the 24-hour emergency numbers listed below.

American Express
0180 523 2377.

Diners Club
069 6616 6123.

MasterCard/Visa
0697 933 1910.

Customs

EU nationals over 17 years of age can import limitless goods for personal use, if bought tax-paid. For non-EU citizens and duty-free goods, the limits are:

- 200 cigarettes or 50 cigars or 250 grams of tobacco
- 1 litre of spirits (over 22% alcohol), or 2 litres of fortified wine (under 22%), or 2 litres of wine
- 50 grams of perfume
- 500 grams of coffee
- Other goods to the value of €175 for non-commercial use
- The import of meat, meat products, fruit, plants, flowers and protected animals is restricted

Non-EU citizens can claim back German VAT (*Mehrwertsteuer* or *MwSt*) on goods purchased in the country (it's only worth the hassle on sizeable purchases). Ask to be issued with a Tax-Free Shopping Cheque for the amount of the refund and present this, with the receipt, at the airport's refund office before checking in bags.

Dental emergency

Dr Andreas Bothe
Kurfürstendamm 210, Charlottenburg (882 6767). U1 Uhlandstrasse.
Open 8am-2pm Mon, Wed, Fri; 2-8pm Tue, Thur.

Mr Pankaj Mehta

*Schlangenbader Strasse 25, Wilmersdorf
(823 3010). U1 Rüdesheimer Platz.*
Open 9am-noon, 2-6pm Mon, Tue,
Thur; 8am-1pm Wed, Fri.

Klinikum im Friedrichshain

*Landsberger Allee 49, Friedrichshain
(4221 1437/www.kvz-berlin.de).
Tram M5, M6, M8 Klinikum am
Friedrichshain.* **Open** 8pm-2am.

Klinik für Zahn-, Mund- und Kieferheilkunde

*Assmannshauser Strasse 4-6,
Wilmersdorf (8445 6379). U3,
S41, S42, S46 Heidelberger Strasse.*
Open 8pm-2am.

Disabled travellers

Only some U- and S-Bahn stations
have wheelchair facilities; the map
of the transport network (look
for the blue wheelchair symbol)
indicates which ones.

   Berlin Tourismus Marketing
(p186) can tell you which hotels
have disabled access, but if you
require more specific information,
try the **Beschäftigungswerk
des BBV** or **Touristik Union
International**.

Beschäftigungswerk des BBV

*Bizetstrasse 51-5, Weissensee (924
0050). S8, S41, S42, S85 Greifswalder
Strasse.* **Open** 8am-4.30pm Mon-Fri.
The Berlin Centre for the Disabled
provides legal and social advice,
together with a transport service
and travel information.

Touristik Union International (TUI)

*Unter den Linden 17, Mitte (2005
8550/www.tui.com). S1, S2 Unter
den Linden.* **Open** (by appointment)
9am-9pm Mon-Fri; 10am-6pm Sat.
This service provides information
on accommodation and travel in
Germany for disabled people.

Drugs

Berlin is relatively liberal in its
attitude towards drugs. In recent
years, possession of hash or grass
has been decriminalised. Anyone
caught with under ten grams is
liable to have the stuff confiscated,
but nothing more. Joint smoking
is tolerated in some of Berlin's
younger bars and cafés. It's usually
easy to tell whether you're in one.
Anyone caught with small amounts
of hard drugs will net a fine, but is
unlikely to be incarcerated.

Electricity

Electricity in Germany runs on
220V. Change the plug or use an
adaptor for British appliances
(240V); US appliances (110V)
need a converter.

Embassies & consulates

Australian Embassy

*Wallstrasse 76-9, Mitte (880 0880).
U2 Märkisches Museum.* **Open** 8.30am-
5pm Mon-Thur; 8.30am-4.15pm Fri.

British Embassy

*Wilhelmstrasse 70, Mitte (204 570).
S1, S2 Unter den Linden.* **Open**
9-11am, noon-4pm Mon-Fri.

Irish Consulate

*Friedrichstrasse 200, Mitte (220 720).
U2, U6 Stadtmitte.* **Open** 9.30am-
12.30pm, 2.30-4.45pm Mon-Fri.

US Consulate

*Clayallee 170, Zehlendorf (832 9233/
visa enquiries 0190 850 055). U3
Oskar-Helene-Heim.* **Open** *Consular
enquiries* 8.30am-noon Mon-Fri. *Visa
enquiries* 8.30-11.30am Mon-Fri.

US Embassy

*Neustädtische Kirchstrasse 4, Mitte
(830 50). S1, S2 Unter den Linden.*
Open 24hrs daily.

ESSENTIALS

Internet

There's a free wireless network in the Sony Center at Potsdamer Platz and at Barcomi's (p67). For an ISP, try www.snafu.de or www.gmx.de.

British Council

Hackescher Markt 1, Mitte (311 0990/ www.britishcouncil.de). S5, S7, S9, S75 Hackescher Markt. **Open** 9am-6pm Mon-Fri.

Half an hour of internet access is free at the terminals to the left of reception.

easyInternetCafé

Dunkin' Donuts, Sony Center, Tiergarten (www.easyinternetcafe. com). U2, S1, S2, S26 Potsdamer Platz. **Open** 7am-11pm Mon-Thur, Sun; 7am-midnight Fri, Sat.

Dozens of computers, no staff, mechanised system to buy time online, and plenty of doughnuts. Other branches are similarly lodged with Dunkin' Donuts. **Other locations**: Hardenbergplatz 2, Charlottenburg; Kurfürstendamm 224, Charlottenburg; Rathaus Passagen, Rathausstrasse 5, Mitte; Karl-Marx-Strasse 78, Neukölln; Schlossstrasse 102, Steglitz.

Internet Café Alpha

Dunckerstrasse 72, Prenzlauer Berg (447 9067/www.alpha-internetcafe.de). U2 Eberswalder Strasse. **Open** noon-1am Mon-Fri; 2pm-1am Sat, Sun.

Opening hours

Most banks are open from 9am to noon Monday to Friday, and 1pm to 3pm or 2pm to 6pm on varied weekdays.

Shops can stay open until 8pm on weekdays, and 6pm on Saturdays, although many places close earlier. Most big stores open their doors at 9am, newsagents a little earlier, while the majority of smaller or independent shops open at around 10am or later.

An increasing number of all-purpose neighbourhood shops (*Spätkauf*) open around 5pm and close around midnight. Many Turkish shops open on Saturday afternoons and on Sundays from 1pm to 5pm. Many bakers open to sell cakes on Sundays from 2pm to 4pm. Most 24-hour fuel stations also sell basic groceries.

Opening times of bars vary, but many are open during the day, and most stay open until at least 1am, if not through until morning.

Police stations

You are unlikely to come into contact with the *Polizei*, unless you commit a crime or are the victim of one. There are few pedestrian patrols or traffic checks.

The **central police HQ** is at Platz der Luftbrücke 6, Tempelhof (466 40), and there are local stations at: Jägerstrasse 48, Mitte (466433 2700); Bismarckstrasse 111, Charlottenburg (466 422 7700); Friesenstrasse 16, Kreuzberg (466 455 2700); Hauptstrasse 44, Schöneberg (466 444 2700); Eberswalder Strasse 6-9 (466 411 5700). Police will be dispatched from the appropriate office if you just dial 466 40.

Postal services

Most post offices (simply *Post* in German) are open from 8am to 6pm Monday to Friday, and 8am to 1pm Saturday.

For non-local mail, use the *Andere Richtungen* ('other destinations') slot in post-boxes. Letters of up to 20 grams (7oz) to anywhere in Germany and the EU need 70¢ in postage. Postcards require 65¢. For anywhere outside the EU, a 20-gram airmail letter is €1.70, a postcard €1.

You can search for the nearest post office at www.deutschepost.de.

Postamt Friedrichstrasse

Georgenstrasse 12, Mitte. U6, S1, S2, S5, S7, S9, S75 Friedrichstrasse.
Open 8am-10pm daily.
Berlin has no main post office. This branch, actually inside Friedrichstrasse station, has the longest opening hours.

Smoking

Many Berliners smoke and, though the habit is in decline, there is far less stigma attached than in the UK or US. Smoking is banned on public transport, in theatres and many public institutions, but is tolerated almost everywhere else. No-smoking sections in restaurants are rare but on the increase.

Telephones

All telephone numbers listed in this guide are local Berlin numbers (other than in the **Day Trips** chapter), but note that numbers beginning with 0180 have higher tariffs. To call from outside the city, see below.

Dialling & codes

To phone Berlin from abroad, dial the international access code (00 from the UK, 011 from the US, 0011 from Australia), then 49 (for Germany) and 30 (for Berlin), followed by the local number.

To phone abroad from Germany dial 00, then add the appropriate country-code:

Australia 61
Canada 1
Ireland 353
New Zealand 64
United Kingdom 44
United States 1

And then the local area code (minus the initial zero) and the local number.

To call Berlin from elsewhere in Germany, dial 030 and then the local number.

Making a call

Calls within Berlin from 9am-6pm cost 10¢ per minute. Numbers prefixed 0180 are charged at 12¢ per minute.

A call from Berlin to the UK and Ireland costs 60¢ per minute, to the US and Canada 90¢ per minute and to Australia €2.60 per minute.

Both local and international calls can be a lot cheaper if you simply dial a prefix before the international code. There are various numbers and they change from time to time. Look in local newspapers or visit www.tariftip.de.

Public phones

At post offices you'll find both coin- and card-operated phones, but most pavement phone boxes are card-only.

You can sometimes find a coin-operated phone in a bar or café. Phonecards can be bought in newsagents and at post offices for various sums from €5 to €50, and you'll find phonecard machines in Alexanderplatz and Zoo stations.

To make international calls, look for phone boxes marked 'international' and with a ringing-bell symbol – you can be called back on them.

Operator services

For online directory enquiries (available in English), go to www.teleauskunft.de.
Alarm calls/Weckruf 0180 114 1033 (automated, in German)
International directory enquiries 118 34
Operator assistance/German directory enquiries 118 33 (118 37, English-speaking only)

ESSENTIALS

**Phone repairs/
Störungsannahme** 080 0330 2000
Telegram/Telegrammaufnahme
0180 512 1210

Mobile phones

German mobile phone networks
operate at 900MHz, so all UK and
Australian mobiles should work
in Berlin (if roaming is activated).
US and Canadian cellphone users
(whose phones operate at 1900MHz)
should check whether their phones
can switch to 900MHz. If they
can't, you can rent a 'Handy'
(as the Germans call them) at
www.edicom-online.com. They'll
deliver to your hotel, and pick
the phone back up from there up
when you're gone.

Time

Germany is on Central European
Time – making it one hour ahead
of Greenwich Mean Time – and
uses a 24-hour system. 8am is '8
Uhr' (usually written 8h); noon is
'12 Uhr Mittags' or just '12 Uhr';
5pm is '17 Uhr' and midnight is
'12 Uhr Mitternachts' or just
'Mitternacht'; 8.15 is '8 Uhr 15'
or 'Viertel nach 8'; 8.30 is '8 Uhr
30' or 'halb 9'; and 8.45 is '8 Uhr
45' or 'Viertel vor 9'.

Tipping

A 17 per cent service charge will
already be part of your restaurant
bill, but it's common to leave a
small tip too. In a taxi round up
the bill to the nearest euro.

Tourist information

Berlin Tourismus
Marketing (BTM)

*Hauptbahnhof (250 025/www.btm.
de). S5, S7, S9, S75 Hauptbahnhof.*
Open 8am-10pm daily.

Berlin's official (though private)
tourist organisation. There are
other offices at the Brandenburg
Gate (p53), the Reichstag (p99),
the Fernsehturm (p79), the
Neues Kranzler Eck Passage
at Kurfürstendamm 21, and the
Europa-Center, Budapester
Strasse 45, near the Zoo.

EurAide

*Main hall, Bahnhof Zoologischer
Garten, Charlottenburg (www.
euraide.de). U2, U9, S5, S7, S9,
S75 Zoologischer Garten.* **Open**
June-Oct 8am-noon, 1-6pm Mon-
Fri. *Nov-May* 8am-noon, 1-4.45pm
Mon-Fri.
Behind the Reisezentrum in
Bahnhof Zoo, this excellent office
offers info in English. Staff can
advise on sights, hostels, tours
and local transport, and can sell
you rail tickets.

Visas & immigration

A passport valid for three months
beyond the length of stay is all
EU, US, Canadian and Australian
citizens need for a stay in Germany
of up to three months. EU citizens
with valid national ID cards need
only show their ID cards.

Citizens of other countries
should check with their local
German Embassy or consulate,
or look on www.germanyinfo.com.

What's on in Berlin

Berlin has two comprehensive
fortnightly listings magazines,
tip and *Zitty*, which come out on
alternate weeks. The monthly
Exberliner is a lively but rather
self-absorbed English-language
alternative. The city is also awash
with listings freebies which can
normally be picked up in bars and
cafés: *[030]* (music and nightlife),
Sergei and *Siegessäule* (both gay)
are the best.

ESSENTIALS

Vocabulary

Pronunciation

z – pronounced **ts**
w – like English **v**
v – like English **f**
s – like English **z**, but softer
r – like a throaty French **r**
a – as in f**a**ther
e – sometimes as in b**e**d,
sometimes as in d**a**y
i – as in s**ee**k
o – as in n**o**te
u – as in l**oo**t
ch – as in Scottish lo**ch**
ä – combination of a and e,
sometimes as in p**ai**d and
sometimes as in s**e**t
ö – combination of o and e, as
in French **eu**
ü – combination of u and e, like tr**u**e
ai – like p**ie**
au – like h**ou**se
ie – like fr**ee**
ee – like h**ey**
ei – like f**i**ne
eu – like c**oi**l

Useful phrases

hello/good day *guten Tag;*
goodbye *auf Wiedersehen;*
goodbye (informal) *tschüss;* **good
morning** *guten Morgen;* **good
evening** *guten Abend;* **good night**
gute Nacht; **yes** *– ja;* (emphatic)
jawohl; **no** *nein, nee;* **maybe**
vielleicht; **please** *bitte;* **thank you**
danke; **thank you very much**
danke schön; **no thanks** *nein
danke;* **excuse me** *entschuldigen
Sie mir bitte;* **sorry!** *Verzeihung!*
**I'm sorry, I don't speak
German** *entschuldigung, ich
spreche kein Deutsch;* **do you
speak English?** *sprechen Sie
Englisch?* **can you please speak
more slowly?** *können Sie bitte
langsamer sprechen?* **my name**

is... *ich heisse...* **open/closed**
geöffnet/geschlossen; **with/
without** *mit/ohne;* **cheap/
expensive** *billig/teuer;* **big/small**
gross/klein; **entrance/exit** *Eingang/
Ausgang;* **push/pull** *drücken/
ziehen;* **how much is...** *wieviel
kostet...?* **I would like...** *ich
möchte...* **a table for four** *ein
Tisch für vier;* **can I/can we pay
please?** *kann ich/können wir bitte
bezahlen?* **could I have a receipt?**
darf ich bitte eine Quittung haben?
how do I get to...? *wie komme
ich nach...?* **how far is it to...?**
wie weit ist es nach...? **where is...
?** *wo ist...?* **airport** *der Flughafen;*
railway station *der Bahnhof;*
train/platform *Zug/Gleis;* **petrol**
das Benzin; **lead-free** *bleifrei;*
please leave me in peace! *lass
mir bitte im Rühe!* **can you call
me a cab?** *können Sie bitte mir
ein Taxi rufen?* **no problem!** *kein
Problem!* **left** *links;* **right** *rechts;*
straight ahead *gerade aus;* **far**
weit; **near** *nah;* **street** *die Strasse;*
square *der Platz;* **help!** *Hilfe!* **I
feel ill** *ich bin krank;* **doctor** *der
Arzt;* **pharmacy** *die Apotheke;*
hospital *das Krankenhaus*

Numbers

0 *null;* 1 *eins;* 2 *zwei;* 3 *drei;* 4 *vier;*
5 *fünf;* 6 *sechs;* 7 *sieben;* 8 *acht;*
9 *neun;* 10 *zehn;* 11 *elf;* 12 *zwölf;*
13 *dreizehn;* 14 *vierzehn;* 15
fünfzehn; 16 *sechszehn;* 17 *siebzehn;*
18 *achtzehn;* 19 *neunzehn;*
20 *zwanzig;* 21 *einundzwanzig;*
22 *zweiundzwanzig;* 30 *dreissig;*
40 *vierzig;* 50 *fünfzig;* 60 *sechszig;*
70 *siebzig;* 80 *achtzig;* 90 *neunzig;*
100 *hundert;* 101 *hunderteins;*
110 *hundertzehn;* 200 *zweihundert;*
201 *zweihunderteins;* 1,000
tausend; 2,000 *zweitausend*

Menu Glossary

Useful phrases

I'd like to reserve a table for... people *Ich möchte einen Tisch für... Personen reservieren;* Are these places free? *Sind diese Plätze frei?* The menu, please *Die Speisekarte, bitte;* I am a vegetarian *Ich bin Vegetarier;* I am a diabetic *Ich bin Diabetiker;* I am allergic to... *Ich habe eine Allergie gegen...* What is that? *Was ist das?;* We'd/I'd like to order *Wir möchten/Ich möchte bestellen;* We'd/I'd like to pay *Bezahlen, bitte*

Berlin specialities

Berliner jam doughnut; *Berliner Weisse mit Schuss weak* wheat beer with a 'shot' of either Himbeer (raspberry) syrup or Waldmeister (artificial woodruff-flavoured syrup), served in a goblet and often drunk through a straw; *Boulette* meat pattie that's Berlin's version of the hamburger; *Currywurst* pork sausage sliced and doused in warm ketchup and curry powder; *Eisbein* fatty pork knuckle usually served with pea puree; *Hoppel-Poppel* omelette-like breakfast dish made with eggs, smoked pork, potatoes and onions; *Königsberger Klöpse* veal meatballs; *Senfeier* boiled eggs in a mustard sauce; *Strammer Max* bread fried in butter and topped with ham and fried egg; *Strammer Otto* same as *Strammer Max* only topped with roast beef

Basics

Frühstück breakfast; *Mittagessen* lunch; *Abendessen* dinner; *Imbiss* snack; *Vorspeise* appetiser/starter; *Hauptgericht* main course; *Nachspeise* dessert; *Belegtes Brot* open sandwich; *Brot/Brötchen* bread/rolls; *Butter* butter; *Ei/Eier* egg/eggs; *Essig* vinegar; *Honig* honey; *Käse* cheese; *Nudeln/Teigwaren* noodles/pasta; *Pfeffer* pepper; *Reis* rice; *Rühreier* scrambled eggs; *Senf* mustard; *Sosse* sauce; *Salz* salt; *Spiegeleier* fried eggs; *Zucker* sugar; *gekocht* boiled; *gebraten* fried/roasted; *gedunstet* steamed; *paniert* breaded/battered; *Gabel* fork; *Glas* glass; *Löffel* spoon; *Messer* knife; *Tasse* cup; *Teller* plate

Soups (Suppen)

Bohnensuppe bean soup; *Brühe* broth; *Erbsensuppe* pea soup; *Hühnersuppe* chicken soup; *klare Brühe mit Leberknödeln* clear broth with liver dumplings; *Kraftbrühe* clear meat broth; *Linsensuppe* lentil soup

Meat & poultry (Fleisch & geflügel)

Ente duck; *Gans* goose; *Hackfleisch* ground meat/mince; *Hirsch* venison; *Huhn/Hühnerfleisch* chicken; *Hähnchen* chicken (when served in one piece); *Kaninchen* rabbit; *Kohlrouladen* cabbage-rolls stuffed with pork; *Kotelett* chop; *Lamm* lamb; *Leber* liver; *Nieren* kidneys; *Rindfleisch* beef; *Rindwurst* beef sausage; *Sauerbraten* marinated roast beef; *Schinken* ham; *Schnitzel*

ESSENTIALS

thinly pounded piece of meat; usually breaded and sautéed; *Schweinebraten* roast pork; *Schweinefleisch* pork; *Speck* bacon; *Truthahn* turkey; *Wildschwein* wild boar; *Wachteln* quail; *Wurst* sausage

Fish (Fisch)

Aal eel; *Forelle* trout; *Garnelen* prawns; *Hummer* lobster; *Kabeljau* cod; *Karpfen* carp; *Krabbe* crab or shrimp; *Lachs* salmon; *Makrele* mackerel; *Matjes/Hering* raw herring; *Miesmuscheln* mussels; *Schellfisch* haddock; *Scholle* plaice; *Seezunge* sole; *Thunfisch* tuna; *Tintenfisch* squid; *Venusmuscheln* clams; *Zander* pike-perch

Pasta (Nudeln)

Maultaschen big pasta pockets (like giant ravioli) filled with meat or spinach; *Nudelauflauf* pasta bake; *Spätzle* Swabian noodles, often served with cheese (*Käsespätzle*)

Herbs & spices (Kräuter & gewurze)

Basilikum basil; *Kümmel* caraway; *Mohn* poppyseed; *Nelken* cloves; *Origanum* oregano; *Petersilie* parsley; *Thymian* thyme; *Zimt* cinnamon

Vegetables (Gemüse)

Austernpilze oyster mushrooms; *Blumenkohl* cauliflower; *Bohnen* beans; *Bratkartoffeln* fried potatoes; *Brechbohnen* green beans; *Champignons/Pilze* mushrooms; *Erbsen* green peas; *Erdnüsse* peanuts; *grüne Zwiebel* spring onion; *Gurke* cucumber; *Kartoffeln* potatoes; *Knoblauch* garlic; *Kichererbsen* chick peas; *Knödel* dumpling; *Kohl* cabbage; *Kürbis* pumpkin; *Linsen* lentils *Möhren* carrots; *Paprika* peppers; *Pfifferlinge* chanterelles; *Pommes* chips/fries; *Rosenkohl* Brussels sprouts; *Rösti* roast grated potatoes; *rote Bete* beetroot; *Rotkohl* red cabbage; *Salat* lettuce; *Salzkartoffeln* boiled potatoes; *Sauerkraut* shredded white cabbage; *Spargel* asparagus; *Tomaten* tomatoes; *Zucchini* courgettes; *Zwiebeln* onions

Fruit (Obst)

Ananas pineapple; *Apfel* apple; *Apfelsine* orange; *Banane* banana; *Birne* pear; *Erdbeeren* strawberries; *Heidelbeeren* blueberries; *Himbeeren* raspberries; *Kirsch* cherry; *Limette* lime; *Pfirsich* peach; *Trauben* grapes; *Zitrone* lemon

Drinks (Getränke)

Apfelsaft apple juice; *Alsterwasser* shandy; *Bier* beer (*dunkles/helles* dark/lager); *Glühwein* mulled wine; *Kaffee* coffee; *Kaffee mit Milch* coffee with milk; *Mineralwasser* mineral water (*mit Gas* sparkling, *ohne Gas* still); *Orangensaft* orange juice; *Rotwein* red wine; *Schnapps* any kind of spirit or short; *Saft* juice; *Tee* tea; *Tomatensaft* tomato juice; *Trinkschokolade* drinking chocolate; *Wein* wine; *Weinbrand* brandy; *Weisswein* white wine; *Weizenbier* wheat beer (*hefe/kristall* yeasty/clear)

ESSENTIALS

Index

ESSENTIALS

ESSENTIALS

THE KENNEDYS

MUSEUM POWERED BY CAMERA WORK

WWW.THE-KENNEDYS.DE

PARISER PLATZ 4A 10117 BERLIN

OPEN DAILY 10 A.M. – 6 P.M.

TEL. +49 30 20653570